Workshop Proceedings:

Debating Multiculturalism 1

The Dialogue Society is a registered charity, established in London in 1999, with the aim of advancing social cohesion by connecting communities through dialogue. It operates nation-wide with regional branches across the UK. Through localised community projects, discussion forums, teaching programmes and capacity building publications it enable people to venture across boundaries of religion, culture and social class. It provides a platform where people can meet to share narratives and perspectives, discover the values they have in common and be at ease with their differences.

www.DialogueSociety.org

info@dialoguesociety.org

Tel: +44 (0)20 7619 0361

Dialogue Society

402 Holloway Road
London N7 6PZ

**DIALOGUE
SOCIETY**
LONDON 1999

Registered Charity No: 1117039

Workshop Proceedings: Debating Multiculturalism 1

First published in Great Britain 2012

For citation please refer to this publication as *Unedited Workshop Proceedings: Debating Multiculturalism 1*

© Dialogue Society 2012

ISBN 978-0-9569304-4-6

About the Workshop Editors

Max Farrar

Professor Max Farrar, a cultural sociologist, is an Emeritus Professor at Leeds Metropolitan University, where until 2010 he was the Head of Community Partnerships and Volunteering and Professor for Community Engagement. An adviser to several boards and organisations on the issue of race, Professor Farrar has previously lectured in sociology and written research papers on the subject. He is the author of a book about Chapeltown in Leeds, The Struggle for 'Community' in a British Multi-Ethnic Inner-City Area (Edwin Mellen Press, 2002). He is also co-author of Teaching Race in the Social Sciences.

He has worked in adult and community education, at a community Law Centre, for a 'race' think-tank and as a freelance writer and photographer. His life-long interest, both as a scholar and as an activist, is in the movements for social justice emanating from the multi-cultural inner cities of the UK. His current research focuses on the rise of Islamism.

Simon Robinson

Simon Robinson is Professor of Applied and Professional Ethics at Leeds Metropolitan University, Associate Director of the Ethics Centre of Excellence, and Visiting Fellow in Theology at the University of Leeds. Educated at Oxford and Edinburgh universities, Professor Robinson entered psychiatric social work before ordination in the Church of England in 1978. He served in university chaplaincy at Heriot-Watt and Leeds universities, developing research in areas of applied ethics and practical theology.

His ongoing research interests are as follows: religious ethics and care; interfaith pastoral care; professional ethics; ethics in higher education; spirituality and professional practice; corporate social responsibility; and ethics in global perspective. Among his publications are: Moral Meaning and Pastoral Counselling; (ed. with Chris Megone) Case Histories in Business Ethics; Living Wills; (with Kevin Kendrick and Alan Brown) Spirituality and Healthcare; Ministry Amongst Students; (ed. with Clement Katulushi) Values in Higher Education; (with Ross Dixon, Chris Preece and Kris Moodley) Engineering, Business and Professional Ethics.

Omer Sener

Omer Sener is a graduate of Kadir Has University, Istanbul, and holds a BA in American Literature. He studied at Frankfurt University for a semester as part of the ERASMUS student exchange programme. Omer is currently an associate staff at Leeds Metropolitan University, and he is in the final phases of his PhD research in Cultural Studies and Literary Criticism. His research interests include representation, linguistics, comparative literature, ethnicity, Asian American literature, and cultural narratives. As an active volunteer he contributes to the work of the Dialogue Society through project management, arranging seminars and organising events.

Contents

Preface

The Dialogue Society is organising two academic workshops on the theme of 'Debating Multiculturalism' to take place in April and May 2012. This publication comprises the papers accepted for 'Debating Multiculturalism 1', to take place in Konya, Turkey, in April.

The Dialogue Society is organising this first workshop through its Leeds Branch in partnership with Leeds Metropolitan University and Mevlana University. It is very grateful for the support of its two partners and to Mevlana University for hosting the event. The second workshop, to be held in Istanbul, is being organised by the Dialogue Society's Birmingham Branch in partnership with Keele University and Fatih University, Istanbul, which will be hosting the event. While the second workshop looks at multiculturalism across Europe as well as in the UK, the first workshop focuses primarily on the UK context. Each workshop balances the perspectives of academics with those of practitioners concerned with intercultural relations.

The acute contemporary relevance of the topic of these workshops hardly requires introduction. Since the Second World War, European societies have increasingly experienced 'multiculturalism' in the sense of people of diverse cultural backgrounds living side by side. The 'state multiculturalism' publicly criticised last year in David Cameron's Munich Speech was a UK example of European government policies embodying a concern to ensure acceptance and respect for the cultural and religious identities of minorities. Cameron is one of a number of prominent voices in the European political mainstream, including also German Chancellor Angela Merkel and French President Nicolas Sarkozy, who claim that multiculturalism has failed to counteract fragmentation and extremism. Meanwhile, proponents of multiculturalism continue to stress its achievements in terms of reduced discrimination and progress towards inclusive, sustainable national identities. They urge that to abandon multiculturalism would be to abandon an achievable future of genuine equality, mutual respect and creative intercultural symbiosis. Whether multiculturalism should be jettisoned as a failure or defended as the path to a flourishing diversity is a crucial and pressing question for our time.

While the geographical focus of the first workshop's papers is the UK, Konya provides a fitting backdrop for debates concerning multiculturalism. It was the home of the Sufi poet Rumi, who lived at a time when the Konya region was significantly more diverse in terms of community and confession than it is today. Rumi's profound spiritual insights and his conception and practice of the religious life encouraged peaceful coexistence on the basis of respect for different traditions and engagement in shared social and cultural activities.

Naturally the views expressed in the papers are those of the authors and do not necessarily reflect the position and views of the Dialogue Society. The papers presented here are unedited papers submitted and printed in advance of the workshop. A further volume of selected papers taken from the two workshops will be published in due course.

The Dialogue Society extends heartfelt thanks to the organising committee and especially our editors for the first workshop, Professor Max Farrar, Professor Simon Robinson and Mr Omer Sener.

Part I
MULTICULTURALISM IN THEORY AND PRACTICE

Multiculturalism, Compassion, and the Law

Michael Connolly [1]

Introduction – a Specific Issue for Multiculturalism

The most visible and heavily reported problems of different cultures living together, unsurprisingly perhaps, centre on housing and accommodation. The principal areas of tension appear to be two-fold. First, recent immigrants being housed in already-deprived areas.[2] Second, Romany Travellers, with their own form of desperation, trying to settle en masse against the wishes of locals and often in breach of planning laws. This problem has grown in recent times as their nomadic lifestyle has been increasingly outlawed, beginning most notably in recent times with section 39 of the Public Order Act 1986, expressed to prevent New Age Travellers from converging on or around festival sites, such as Stonehenge, but used from day one against Romany Travellers on the waysides of England.[3]

---

1   Michael Connolly is a Lecturer in Law, at the School of Law, University of Surrey, Guildford, Surrey. His qualifications include, LL.M, (by research) University of Warwick (2002); Barrister, Inns of Court School of Law, Gary's Inn, London (1995); LL.B, (Class 2.1 Hons, 2 prizes) Ealing College, London (1990); and Fellow of the Higher Education Academy (2001). He has teaching experience in Discrimination Law, Employment Law, Contract Law, Sale of Goods, Agency, Legal Skills (Wigmorean analysis of evidence). He was also a contributor to the Discrimination Law Association Response to the Single Equality Act Green Paper (2008). His recent book publications include Discrimination Law, (2nd ed, 2011) London: Sweet and Maxwell, and Townshend-Smith on Discrimination Law: Text, Cases and Materials, (2nd edn), 2004 London: Cavendish. His research interests include Discrimination and Equality Law, Comparative Discrimination Law, Legal Education, Police Powers, Public Order Law, Commercial/Consumer law, Evidence and the Wigmorian Analysis.

2   See e.g. problems encountered in Depford, a poor area of South East London, where Vietnamese 'boat people' were housed: 'Problem estate is 'picking on' its boat people'. The Times 12 Mar. 1982, p 5. Other episodes are detailed below.

3   Civil Liberty Briefing No 5, Liberty, London, June 1987.

These facts alone are enough to explain the tensions between different cultures. But a slightly deeper look reveals a rather more contradictory picture. It involves the politicians, who pass equality laws to protect such people, yet with their public comments, provoke animosity towards the same people. The matter is aggravated by some more subtle, but equally populist, judicial comments.

These comments, alongside some of saddest events in recent British social history, are considered below. It is suggested that Britain's equality laws cannot achieve their potential to facilitate multiculturalism whilst being undermined by the lawmakers.

Words and Events

In the late 1990's, Tony Blair's government operated a 'dispersal' policy for asylum seekers. The thinking behind this was to avoid spreading refugees too thinly and leaving them without community support, and at the same time avoid ghettos and disproportionate burdens on the local authorities, such as those at the port of Dover or Heathrow airport.[4]

Accordingly, Glasgow City Council contracted with central Government to house refugees over 5 years for £110m.[5] The council placed them in its most deprived district, Sighthill. Many locals – whose area had been deprived of council spending – watched blocks of flats being refurbished and occupied by foreigners. The resentment grew. There were warnings that the council were not doing enough to educate the population about the plight of the refugees, and some of the terrible stories behind their arrival in Britain.[6] In April 2001, Glasgow police reported a steady increase in crime, including assaults, against refugees housed in the Sighthill district of Glasgow.[7] Local human rights lawyer, Aamer Anwar, observed that: 'The council has failed to produce even one leaflet explaining to people in Sighthill who these asylum seekers are, where they have come from and why they are here.'[8] This vacuum was filled with racist leafleting by ring-wing groups.[9]

And so, in the Spring of 2001, a time when political leaders should have been defusing the tensions, the Conservative Party (opposition) leader, William Hague, made a pre-election speech at the party's Harrogate conference, culminating with

---

4   See e.g. The Independent, November 25, 1998, p 7 (Queen's Speech), and April 5 1999, p 2 (Home Office comment).

5   The Sunday Herald August 12, 2001, p 1; The Herald August 7, 2001, p 1.

6   See e.g. the considered appraisal in The Sunday Herald, August 12, 2001, p 8, and an undercover report, The Daily Record June 12, 2001 pp 14-15.

7   Sunday Mail April 22, 2001, pp 6, 7.

8   Daily Record (Scotland), August 6, 2001, pp 4, 5.

9   Ibid.

heavily trailed (and subsequently spun) line: 'Let me take you to a foreign land - Britain after a second term of Tony Blair'. This section of the speech actually focussed on EU monetary policy threatening Britain's economic independence. But the subtext was clear. The speech railed at Labour's asylum policy, promising to establish refugee camps and to 'lock up' all asylum seekers until their claims were processed, thus assimilating refugees with 'bogus asylum seekers' and 'criminals'.[10] That year, The Daily Mail featured the phrase 'bogus asylum seeker' in 66 articles.[11] The message was that asylum seekers – bogus or otherwise - are a 'problem', a threat to Britain as we know it, and one likely to be associated with crime.

None of this was directed at the cumulating problems in Sighthill, but of course, the best that can be said is that it did nothing to defuse the tensions there. In the early hours of August 5th, a 22 year old Kurd refugee, Firsat Dag, was stabbed to death. Even then, a tabloid newspaper proclaimed (incorrectly) on its front page that the victim had 'conned' his way into Britain as a bogus asylum seeker.[12] The attacks continued.[13]

Was Hague's speech a one-off? It seems not. A year later, the Home Secretary (David Blunket) - the minster responsible for asylum policy and a prominent member of the Labour Government - asserted that the children of asylum seekers were 'swamping' some schools.[14]

More recently, one of his successors was at it again. Here are some extracts from Teresa May's speech to the Conservative Party conference in October 2011.[15] She stated: 'When a terrorist cannot be deported on human rights grounds, all our rights are threatened.'

From this apparently isolated statement she goes on to say, in the next sentence, 'And

---

10 Sunday Times March 4, 2001; The Guardian March 5, 2001, p 1; The Daily Telegraph, March 5, p 10.

11 This includes The Mail on Sunday.

12 The Daily Record, August 8, 2001, p 1. In fact, he changed his name and story to protect his politically persecuted family: The Sunday Herald August 12, 2001, p 8. See also, The Independent August 14, 2001, Tuesday, p 8. The murder trial is reported: The Scotsman, December 2, 2002, p 4.

13 'The cases were among more than 107 recorded incidents - 56 of those assault - involving asylum seekers since the beginning of the year. The Scotsman August 6, 2001, p 5; Evening Times August 7, 2001. See also, Gezer v Secretary of State for the Home Department [2004] EWHC Civ 1730.

14 The Times April 25, 2002.

15 October 4, 2011. http://www.conservatives.com/News/Speeches/2011/10/May_Conservative_values_to_fight_crime_and_cut_immigration.aspx (accessed 23.12.11).

as Conservatives, we understand too the need to reduce and control immigration', thus suggesting that terrorism is an 'immigration problem'. She then spent three minutes listing 'problems' of immigration (on housing, public services, and infrastructure), concluding with this inevitable attack on the Human Rights Act:

> ...we need to make sure that we're not constrained from removing foreign nationals who, in all sanity, should have no right to be here.

We all know the stories about the Human Rights Act. The violent drug dealer who cannot be sent home because his daughter - for whom he pays no maintenance - lives here. The robber who cannot be removed because he has a girlfriend. The illegal immigrant who cannot be deported because - and I am not making this up - he had a pet cat.'

Within a space of four minutes, she put it in the air that the Human Rights Act prevents the deportation of terrorists and serious criminals, solely because they had acquired a pet.

Of course, the 'pet cat' story *was* made up.[16] The case in question involved a Bolivian student who had committed no crimes, and who was discovered living with his partner two years after his visa had expired.[17] He won his appeal against deportation because the Home Office had not followed its own rules on deporting persons with family ties in Britain. The cat was mentioned by the judge as part of the picture of the man's family life in Britain.[18] It was not decisive. Nevertheless, for Theresa May, this is why 'the Human Rights Act needs to go'. And so, a benign immigration case involving someone *not* a criminal was associated with terrorism.

This man's story has been aired now and again since the tribunal ruling, which actually was given back in 2008.[19] The story appeared under headlines such as: *The 'Rights' I Would Give These Scum,*[20] *Rights That Make a Mockery of Justice,*[21] *Fugitive*

---

16 But not be her. The speech was lifted from an even more extravagant misrepresentation of the case ('Peruvian convicted of manslaughter') by the leader of UKIP, Nigel Farange. The Guardian, October 8, 2011, p 5. His speech was recorded and covered in more detail by a local newspaper, the Eastleigh News October 4, 2011, http://www.eastleighnews.org.uk/news/2011/10/04/farage-cat-tale-snares-may/ (accessed 23.12.11).

17 He was arrested, but not charged, for shoplifting. The arrest brought him to the attention of the authorities. The Sunday Telegraph, October 9, 2011, p 13.

18 The Times, October 5, 2011, pp 14-15.

19 Sunday Telegraph, October 9, 2011, p 13.

20 Sunday Express, June 19, 2011, p 23.

21 Daily Mail, June 20, 2011: 'In one instance, a Bolivian criminal was allowed to stay because he and his girlfriend owned a British cat.'

Foreign Killers Use Your Money to Avoid Being Deported,[22] *The Secret of Our Imported Crime Wave is Finally Out,*[23] *102 Foreign Offenders We Can't Deport,*[24] *Killer and rapist use 'right to family life' to stay in Britain.*[25]

The year 2011 also saw all politicians rounding on a group of Romany Travellers, sited at Dale Farm, in Essex, England. This lawful but overcrowded site expanded into an adjacent disused scrapyard, where many Romany Travellers settled without planning permission. After a ten year legal battle, they were due for eviction. When asked in Parliament to support the eviction, the Prime Minister, David Cameron stated:

> What I would say is that it is a basic issue of fairness: everyone in this country
> has to obey the law, including the law about planning permission and about
> building on green belt land. Where this has been done without permission it
> is an illegal development and so those people should move away.[26]

This typified the inflammatory language being poured over the issue. The Prime Minister made three misleading points that have been repeated ad infinitum by politicians and the media. First, the reference to an 'illegal development' suggests that the travellers were criminals from day one. In fact, the only criminal wrongdoing here was the resisting of the enforcement notice.[27] Establishing homes on the land (much of which was owned by the travellers) was not a crime, it was a breach of planning law, a civil matter. Anyone else, say, resisting a planning order (or indeed, most civil law orders), is not referred to as criminal.[28] People trying to keep a roof over their families' heads and maintaining stability for their children and elders, are thus associated with thugs and thieves. Second, it is a fundamental twin principle of discrimination law that those in similar situations should be treated the same,

---

22 Mail on Sunday, July 10, 2011 Sunday

23 The Express, August 31, 2011.

24 The Sunday Telegraph, June 12, 2011 pp, 1, 6.

25 The Sunday Telegraph, October 16, pp 4,5.

26 Hansard HC vol 532 col 353 (7 September, 2011). See also Royce Turner, 'Gypsies and British Parliamentary language: an analysis', (2002) 12 Romani Studies, pp 1-34, who summarises that they are portrayed in Parliament as: 'dishonest, criminal, dirty'. For an account of the Coalition's 'offensive' on Gypsies and travellers, see J. Grayson, 'Playing the Gypsy 'race card'' (2010) Institute of Race Relations June 4, 2010, < http://www.irr.org.uk/2010/june/ha000020.html (accessed 01.01.11).

27 There was an inevitable ancillary offence of failing to remove the hard standing and reseed the ground: R (Sheridan and McCarthy) v Basildon DC [2011] EWHC 2938 (Admin) [17].

28 See e.g. the coverage of Robert Fidler's clandestine 'castle' built without planning permission: http://news.bbc.co.uk/1/hi/england/surrey/8495412.stm.

whilst those in different situations should be treated differently.[29] Romany Travelers are in a different situation to most, yet the politicians, and with them, the media,[30] harp on about obeying the *same* law, as if that alone exonerated anyone from discrimination. Third, although within the Green Belt, the site actually was on a disused scrapyard, which was not quite the image portrayed by the Prime Minister of criminal tinkers and travellers despoiling England's green and pleasant land.

Words and the Law

It is not just the politicians who make the law. Judges interpret statutes and create common law, thus setting precedents. These decisions, and perhaps their accompanying comments, can also make a difference. Their record is mixed, with some dreadful low points.

Back in 1983, in *Mandla v Dowell Lee*,[31] the rules of a private school dictated that boys had to wear the school uniform (including a cap), and keep their hair cut 'so as not to touch the collar'. The school refused Gurinder Singh admission as a pupil because he would not comply with those rules. As an orthodox Sikh, he was obliged not to cut his hair, and to restrain it by wearing a turban; so he could not wear the school cap. The Court of Appeal held that as Sikhs could show no common biological characteristic, they did not form a racial group for the claim to proceed.[32] This scientific approach is completely at odds with multiculturalism. Further, the Court attacked the Commission for Racial Equality for supporting the case, whilst one appeal judge told Mandla (and no doubt 'foreigners' in general): 'If persons wish to insist on wearing bathing suits they cannot reasonably insist on admission to a nudist colony...'[33] The House of Lords reversed on all counts. Nonetheless, it shows senior judges deciding an accusation of discrimination by standards completely at odds with multiculturalism.

In the same year, a differently constituted Court of Appeal was again trying to

---

29 See e.g. DH v Czech Republic (2008) 47 E.H.R.R. 3 [175]: 'The Court has also accepted that a general policy or measure that has disproportionately prejudicial effects on a particular group may be considered discriminatory notwithstanding that it is not specifically aimed at that group...'; Griggs v Duke Power 401 US 424 (US Supreme Court), 431: 'The [Civil Rights] Act proscribes not only overt discrimination but also practices that are fair in form, but discriminatory in operation.'

30 In 2001, the national newspapers used the terms 'Dale Farm' and 'illegal' in 406 stories. The BBC was just as culpable: a Google search of BBC news reveals 273 hits for these combined terms for the year 2011.

31 [1983] 2 AC 548 HL

32 [1983] QB 1, at 10F (Lord Denning MR), 15H (Oliver, LJ,), 22D (Kerr, LJ,).

33 [1983] 1 QB 1, at 21C (Kerr, LJ).

restrict the law's potential to improve intercultural relations , this time successfully, with no reversal by the House of Lords. In *Perera v Civil Service Commission (no. 2)*,[34] an advertisement for a legal assistant stated that candidates with a good command of the English language, experience in the UK and with British nationality, would be at an 'advantage'. It was held that these 'mere preferences' did not amount to a *requirement or condition* within the meaning of the Race Relations Act 1976. To come within the Act, the Court stated, an employer should elevate the preference to a requirement or 'absolute bar' which *has* to be complied with, in order to qualify for the job. Stephenson, LJ justified the decision thus:

> ... a brilliant man whose personal qualities made him suitable as a legal assistant might well have been sent forward... in spite of being, perhaps, below standard on his knowledge of English...[35]

Of course, a court willing to see the purpose of the statute fulfilled would have reasoned that it was a *requirement* to have any of those characteristics to achieve the 'advantage'. But Stephenson's LJ seemingly undramatic comment reveals a far more serious problem underlying British cultural relations. If a candidate has to be 'brilliant' to compensate for a nationality-based 'weakness' then he is at a disadvantage because of his nationality. A 'brilliant foreigner' will obtain a post otherwise suitable for an 'average Englishman'. The comment disguises this bigotry to outsiders by suggesting that Britain is a fair place where any 'brilliant' person can 'make it', no matter what their race.

A few years later, the Court of Appeal stuck to its guns, in *Meer v London Borough of Tower Hamlets*.[36] Here, the employer attached twelve 'selection criteria' to an advertised post. One of these was experience in the Tower Hamlets district. That put persons of Indian origin (including Mr Meer) at a disadvantage because a higher than average proportion of them were new to the area. The Court of Appeal rejected Meer's claim of indirect discrimination holding that the criterion was again a *mere preference*. Staughton, LJ justified this decision by considering the alternative: the law of indirect discrimination 'would have such an extraordinarily wide and capricious effect'. It did not occur to the judge that the law would only have that effect if indirect discrimination were *extraordinarily wide and capricious*. Of course, the sub-text is that discrimination like this is not the problem; the problem is discrimination *law*, which should not be allowed to get out of control. It took EU

---

34 [1983] ICR 428. The Federal Court of Western Australia refused to follow Perera in Secretary of Department of Foreign Affairs and Trade and: Styles (1989) 88 ALR 621, see also Waters v Public Transport Corporation (1991) 173 CLR 349, (High Court of Australia).

35 Ibid, at 437H-438A

36 [1988] IRLR 399 (CA).

Directives effectively to reverse *Perera* and *Meer*, by replacing the statutory phrase *requirement or condition* with the more liberal *provision criterion or practice*.[37]

More openly expressed opinions followed. In *Khan v Chief Constable of West Yorkshire*,[38] Lord Woolf MR, (as he then was) stated: 'To regard a person as acting unlawfully when he had not been motivated either consciously or unconsciously by any discriminatory motive is hardly likely to assist the objective of promoting harmonious racial relations.' In *Nagarajan v London Regional Transport*,[39] Lord Browne-Wilkinson dissented: 'To introduce something akin to strict liability into the Acts which will lead to individuals being stamped as racially discriminatory... where these matters were not consciously in their minds when they acted is unlikely to recommend the legislation to the public as being fair and proper protection for the minorities that they are seeking to protect.'

These comments do not actually represent the law, which covers unintentional as well as intentional discrimination. But the message is that perceived public opinion should not be challenged. The law should go as far as challenging patent bigotry, but not 'innocent' or subconscious causes of disadvantage (where of course, most problems begin), for fear causing resentment by the general public. As well as the matter of presuming that all British people share this opinion, and that a judge considers himself to be in touch with public opinion, these comments undermine the ambition of equality law and policy.

In sum, the cases suggest that anti-discrimination law should provide equality by the standards of the 'white Englishman', do no more than provide for the 'brilliant foreigner', not venture into potentially 'wide and capricious' areas of inequality, nor the beyond general public's perception of inequality, which is confined to patent bigotry.

The judges' comments have a lot in common with the political and media comments highlighted above. First, they were factually incorrect, or misleading. Second, they were populist, suggesting that Britain is a fair country, and foreigners and minorities 'had nothing to complain about'. Third, they reinforce the suggestion that this 'fairness' is to be judged from the perspective of the 'white Englishman' Fourth, in suggesting that the law should require no more than avoiding patent bigotry, they do nothing to educate the legal world, and the broader population, about the subtleties of discrimination the law actually seeks to address.

---

37 See e.g. Framework Directive 2000/78/EC, art 2(2)(b); Race Directive 2000/43/EC, art 2(2)(b); Recast Directive 2006/54/EC, art 2(1)(b); Equality Act 2010, s 19.

38 [2000] ICR 1169 (CA), [14]. reversed, but not on this point, [2008] UKHL 48.

39 [2000] 1 AC 501 (HL), at 510.

Finally, there is the legal aspect of the Dale Farm eviction and the illegal/unlawful dichotomy.[40] In the last case confirming the eviction, the High Court referred to the criminal law 30 times. It was expressed as a major factor in its reasoning. By comparison, in a well-publicised planning case involving a large house built without permission by deceit (behind a screen of straw bales), the High Court, in confirming its demolition for breach of planning law, did not refer to the criminal law once.[41] The implication is that 'outsiders' and minorities who breach planning law are criminals, whilst white men simply run into a minor civil matter. They are regarded as 'cheeky', 'daring', and 'maverick'.

Where is the Compassion?

Most of North America and Western Europe has assumed a policy of multiculturalism. Inherent in this a celebration of difference, and tolerance.[42] This suggests that the key is psychological, or emotional, rather than formal. Human rights law originates, partly at least, from human compassion, or the milk of human kindness. People generally have a sense of compassion, especially for the underdog. This appears at odds with the resistance by ordinary (so presumably decent) people to much discrimination law, especially positive action programmes[43] and the truism that anti-discrimination laws are enacted to combat prejudices in mainstream society. The comments highlighted above - all devoid of compassion, celebrations of difference, and tolerance - reveal that the general public's perception is important in defining, interpreting, and implementing, the law. But in complex societies where so much disadvantage is invisible to an uninformed public, relying on public perception is no more useful than asking for a jury's opinion after providing it with newspapers instead of the evidence. It becomes obvious that there is a *duty* on politicians and judges to educate the public in the hard truths behind a asylum seeker's plight and the real disadvantages that exist in society, so triggering their innate human compassion. The neglect of this duty breeds cynicism rather than compassion, which in turn feeds into the political, media, and legal statements and decisions.

---

40 See e.g. the coverage of Robert Fidler's clandestine 'castle' built without planning permission: http://news.bbc.co.uk/1/hi/england/surrey/8495412.stm. See now, [2011] EWCA Civ 1159.

41 [2010] EWCH 143 (Admin); for the refusal of leave to appeal, see [2011] EWCA Civ 1159.

42 See R. Wasserstrom,, 'Racism, sexism and preferential treatment: an approach to the topics' (1977) 24 UCLA L Rev 581, pp 585–589.

43 In the 2004 general election, in a core Labour constituency, Peter Law resigned from the Labour Party in protest at the selection of a candidate from an all-women short-list. He stood as an independent and overturned the Labour majority of 19,000 votes, winning with a majority of 9,000 (The Times April 6, 2004). In 2006, the Labour Party issued an apology to the electorate 'for getting it wrong'. (The Independent May 8, 2006).

The judiciary can take a particular lead. For the law to be structured around human compassion is not as fanciful as it first seems. The Canadian Supreme Court has developed its human rights jurisprudence around the theme of 'human dignity'.[44] Indeed, this principle can be detected in most human rights discourses and even is expressed in Britain's Equality Acts and the equality directives.[45] There is no doubt it can resolve issues in discrimination law,[46] even if it is not the single guiding principle.[47]

With a similar flavour, the US Supreme Court fixes the level of scrutiny of allegedly discriminatory state and federal actions according to the suffering of the group question; it looks for a history of purposeful and invidious discrimination, based on prejudice or inaccurate stereotypes, against a class without political power.[48] These observations about the state of groups in society are as loaded with compassion as they are with intellectual rigour. They show that positive human emotions can be identified and realised in law.

---

44 Law v Canada [1999] 1 S.C.R. 497 (SCC). For a discussion of dignity in English law, see D. Feldman, "Human dignity as a legal value", Part I [1999] PL 682, Part II [2000] PL 61. For a discussion on the role that dignity can play in discrimination law, see G. Moon and R. Allen, 'Dignity discourse in discrimination law: a better route to equality?' (2006) 6 E.H.R.L.R. 610.

45 By Equality Act 2006, s 3(c). the Commission for Equality and Human Rights is charged to carry out its duties, inter alia, 'with a view to encouraging and supporting the development of a society in which there is respect for the dignity and worth of each individual.' By the Equality Directives (2006/54/EC, 2000/78/EC, 2000/43/EC) and the Equality Act 2010, s 26(1)(b), harassment can occur when conduct has the purpose or effect of 'violating' the victim's 'dignity'. See also English v Thomas Sanderson Blinds [2009] ICR 543 (CA), especially [37].

46 Eight specific issues are considered by G. Moon and R. Allen, "Dignity discourse in discrimination law: a better route to equality? (2006) 6 E.H.R.L.R. 610.

47 R. v Kapp [2008] 2 S.C.R. 483 (SCC) [19]-[24]. See also, Rory O'Connell, 'The role of dignity in equality law: lessons from Canada and South Africa': I.J.C.L. 2008, 6(2), 267-286.

48 Accordingly, racial groups are afforded more protection than age groups. The Supreme Court has not refined the matter much further though, as, somewhat perversely, whites are afforded the same equal protection as other racial groups: Adarand Constructors v Pena 515 US 200 (1995).

Conclusion

Human rights and equality laws are rooted in compassion. Politicians and judges create equality laws, yet their public pronouncements often undermine these same laws. Left alone, at best, our equality law can only manage to *enforce* a celebration of difference and tolerance, which of course, is a miserable and mean-spirited way of going about things. Given active support, our equality law could *facilitate* such achievements, a far more worthwhile goal.

Bibliography

Civil Liberty Briefing No 5, Liberty, London, June 1987.

Gezer v Secretary of State for the Home Department [2004] EWHC Civ 1730.

http://www.conservatives.com/News/Speeches/2011/10/May_Conservative_values_to_fight_crime_and_cut_immigration.aspx (accessed 23.12.11).

Hansard HC vol 532 col 353 (7 September, 2011).

Royce Turner, 'Gypsies and British Parliamentary language: an analysis', (2002) 12 Romani Studies, pp 1-34.

J. Grayson, 'Playing the Gypsy 'race card'' (2010) Institute of Race Relations June 4, 2010, < http://www.irr.org.uk/2010/june/ha000020.html (accessed 01.01.11).

R (Sheridan and McCarthy) v Basildon DC [2011] EWHC 2938 (Admin) [17].

http://news.bbc.co.uk/1/hi/england/surrey/8495412.stm.

DH v Czech Republic (2008) 47 E.H.R.R. 3.

Griggs v Duke Power 401 US 424 (US Supreme Court).

Secretary of Department of Foreign Affairs and Trade and: Styles (1989) 88 ALR 621.

Waters v Public Transport Corporation (1991) 173 CLR 349, (High Court of Australia).

Framework Directive 2000/78/EC.

Race Directive 2000/43/EC.

Recast Directive 2006/54/EC.

R. Wasserstrom,, 'Racism, sexism and preferential treatment: an approach to the topics' (1977) 24 UCLA L Rev 581.

Law v Canada [1999] 1 S.C.R. 497 (SCC).

D. Feldman, "Human dignity as a legal value", Part I [1999] PL 682, Part II [2000] PL 61.

G. Moon and R. Allen, 'Dignity discourse in discrimination law: a better route to equality?' (2006) 6 E.H.R.L.R. 610.

Equality Act 2006.

English v Thomas Sanderson Blinds [2009] ICR 543 (CA).

R. v Kapp [2008] 2 S.C.R. 483 (SCC) [19]-[24].

Rory O'Connell, 'The role of dignity in equality law: lessons from Canada and South Africa': I.J.C.L. 2008, 6(2), 267-286.

Adarand Constructors v Pena 515 US 200 (1995).

Mandla v Dowell Lee [1983] 2 AC 548 (HL).

Perera v CSC [1983] ICR 428.

Meer v Tower Hamlets LB [1988] IRLR 399 (CA).

Khan v Chief Constable West Yorkshire [2000] ICR 1169 (CA), [14], reversed, [2008] UKHL 48.

Nagarajan v LRT [2000] 1 AC 501 (HL).

The End of Multiculturalism? A Riposte

Paul Weller [49]

Multicultural Societies as Societies of Diversity

Societies that are composed of many ethnicities, cultures and religions are not a new phenomenon, but have a long global history. Historically speaking, especially the political and military formations with wide geographical reach and known as "empires" (for example, the Roman, the Ottoman and the British empires) contained a great variety of ethnicities, cultures, and religions even if among the rulers there was a dominant ethnicity, culture and/or religion. Such empires often incorporated pre-existing and more ancient civilisations that were themselves often also the outcome of the interplay between a particular dynamic of forces in relation to a plurality of ethnicities, cultures and religions.

In this sense, the phenomenon of multicultural societies and the challenges and opportunities presented by their characteristics is by no means a new one in human social, political and religious history. At the same time, it is arguable the advent and development in the late twentieth century of the phenomenon of globalisation has brought with it new dimensions to these older equations. Such globalisation has occurred by means of what the historian Arnold Toynbee called the 'annihilation of distance' (Toynbee, 1958: 87) that was brought about by modern means of transportation, communications technology and the post-Second World War upheavals of decolonisation and associated mass labour migration and refugee movements of peoples. In concert with Toynbee's early insight into this changed situation, Fethullah Gülen has also observed that,

---

49 Paul Weller is Professor of Inter-Religious Relations, University of Derby; and Visiting Fellow, Oxford Centre for Christianity and Culture at Regent's Park College, University of Oxford. He is author of (2005) Time for a Change: Reconfiguring Religion, State and Society, T & T Clark, London; (2008), , Continuum, London; (2009) A Mirror for our Times Religious Diversity in the UK: Contours and Issues? "The Rushdie Affair" and the Future of Multiculturalism, Continuum, London; and (2011), Religious Discrimination in Britain: A Review of Research Evidence, 2000-2010, Equality and Human Rights Commission, Manchester. He is co-editor, with Ihsan Yilmaz (2012) of European Muslims, Civility and Public Life: Perspectives on and from the Gülen Movement (Continuum: London). Until its abolition by the Coalition Government, he was a member of the expert advisory panel on faith to the Minister of State, Ministers and Civil Servants in the UK's Department for Communities and Local Government.

Modern means of communication and transportation have transformed the world into a large, global village. So, those who expect that any radical changes in a country will be determined by that country alone and remain limited to it, are unaware of current realities. This time is a period of interactive relations. Nations and people are more in need of and dependent on each other, which causes closeness in mutual relations. (Gülen, 2004a: 230).

As a result of all this, already by the middle of the twenty-first century in his book *An Historian's Approach to Religion*, Arnold Toynbee had begun arguing that:

The adherents of each religion...seem likely to come gradually to be distributed all over the Oikoumenê, but it may also be expected that, in the process, they will come to be intermingled everywhere with adherents of all other faiths..... As a result, the appearance of the religious map of the Oikoumenê may be expected to change from a pattern of a patchwork quilt to the texture of a piece of shot silk. (Toynbee, 1956: 139).

Multiculturalism as a Political Project

However, in addition to change from the 'patchwork quilt' to the 'shot silk' pattern of ethnic, cultural and religious groups, in more recent times the notion of 'multicultural' has come to be used not only to describe the plural composition of societies developed as a result of the migratory and refugee movements of peoples, but has also been adopted as a terminology for a particular kind of social and political project for dealing with such plurality. Thus in the United Kingdom, from the mid-1960s until what I have elsewhere called the 'social policy shock' (see Weller, 1998: 195) delivered by the 7/7 London bombings, a specific vision of 'multiculturalism' shaped social policy and the broad political consensus of successive British Governments of whatever political colour. The approach underlying this had been classically articulated by the former Labour Government Home Secretary, Roy (now Lord) Jenkins, whose original line of argument that informed what became this broadly bi-partisan approach was that, 'I do not think that we need in this country a melting-pot, which will turn everybody out in a common mould, as one of a series of someone's misplaced vision of the stereotyped Englishman' (Jenkins, 1967: 269)

Jenkins explained, rather, that the policy aim should be that of 'integration' (understood in those days clearly to be the opposite of 'assimilation'), defined as '...equal opportunity, coupled with cultural diversity, in an atmosphere of mutual tolerance.' (Jenkins, 1967: 269) The high water mark of such an approach was, arguably, the report of the Runnymede Trust's Commission on the Future of Multi-Ethnic Britain (2000). Chaired by the political scientist (now Lord) Bhikhu Parekh, the report produced by this Commission (which is sometimes known by the shorthand name of the 'Parekh Report') set out a vision of Britain as a 'community of communities'.

The Satanic Verses Affair and Questioning the Multicultural Project

Even a decade prior to the Parekh Report, the so-called Satanic Verses controversy around Salman Rushdie's (1988) book of the same name had sown seeds that led to a questioning the underlying consensus. Because of this my own book, looking back on that controversy from twenty years later, and published in 2009, is called *A Mirror for our Times: 'The Rushdie Affair' and the Future of Multiculturalism*. In many ways, the fall-out from 'the Rushdie affair' gave licence for views strongly opposed to multiculturalism to surface into more mainstream discourse than had been possible following the 1968 sacking of the Conservative Shadow Cabinet Minister Enoch Powell following his (in)famous 'rivers of blood' speech in which he stated, with reference to the transformation of England into a more plural society and against the background of the Parliamentary debate on the 1968 Race Relations Bill which embodied Jenkins' approach, that: 'As I look ahead, I am filled with foreboding; like the Roman, I seem to see 'the River Tiber foaming with much blood.'

Thus in the context of the Rushdie controversy, the Conservative Member of Parliament for Bridlington, John Townend (quoted in *The Guardian*, 29.8.90), stated that 'England must be reconquered for the English'. He argued that, 'When Muslims say they cannot live in a country when Salman Rushdie is free to express his views, they should be told they have the answer in their own hands - go back from whence you came.' Townend went on to complain of what had happened to what he called 'this green and pleasant land' and identified the two sources of the problem. First of all he referred to immigration and, second, what he called 'the pernicious doctrine of multi-culturalism', in relation to the latter he argued that, 'The British people were never consulted as to whether they would change from being a homogenous society to a multi-racial society.' From more within the (then) Thatcherite political mainstream, Norman (now Lord) Tebbit suggested that minorities would find his now famous 'cricket test' difficult to pass on the basis that their real loyalties lay elsewhere rather than in England (*The Guardian*, 21.4.90).

As might have been expected, politicians and social commentators within that kind of tradition claimed that 'the Rushdie affair' had proved them to be right all along about the dangers of New Commonwealth immigration. After the controversy and, even more so, following the emergence of terror violence associated with Muslims and Islam, such questioning of 'multiculturalism' as a viable basis for social cohesion in a plural society was not only limited to the political tendency of which Townend is a representative example. So an early indication of the coming changes in the tone and parameters of the debate can be seen in an Independent article with the significant title, 'Xenophobia as a survival mechanism' that was penned by the otherwise politically liberal columnist, Jill Tweedie (1989). Another example was the 18th February 1989 editorial under the title "Limits to mutual tolerance" and published in the generally liberal UK newspaper, *The Independent*. This noted with regard to the 'multicultural' policy approach original espoused by Roy Jenkins that:

> Roy Jenkins' philosophy was predicated on the expectation that the minorities would also demonstrate tolerance, and the implicit belief that all manifestations of cultural diversity would be benign. It is becoming disturbingly apparent that this is not the case. The time has therefore come for an examination of how a tolerant, multi-cultural society should handle the intolerant behaviour on the part of a minority.

In fact, in response to *The Satanic Verses* controversy even Roy Jenkins (1989) himself had been recorded as saying, 'In retrospect, we might have been more cautious about allowing the creation in the 1950s of substantial Muslim communities here'. Reflecting on the same controversy, the writer Fay Weldon (1989: 31) had put it even more starkly in her book, *Sacred Cows: A Portrait of Britain, Post-Rushdie, Pre-Utopia*, claiming that, 'Our attempt at multiculturalism has failed. The Rushdie Affair demonstrates it' and advocated what she identified as the more 'uni-culturalist' (Weldon, 1989: 32) approach of the USA in terms of a more assimilationist 'melting pot'. Therefore, the seeds for a retreat from a commitment to the social and political project of multiculturalism were clearly being sown even a decade before the high water mark of its articulation in the so-called Parekh Report from the Runnymede Trust.

Bombings and the Social Policy Shock to Multiculturalism

However, during the intervening decade in many ways, and especially at local levels and in the fields of politics and popular culture, the UK arguably became increasingly even more 'multicultural' when the word is understood in its descriptive sense, in terms of the permeation into popular life, the media, business, governance and other areas of a range of people with diverse national, ethic, cultural and religious backgrounds. Therefore, while *The Satanic Verses* controversy presented an 'early warning' for multiculturalism as a social and political project, it took the combined effects of the international shock-waves from the events of September 11th 2001 in the USA and the domestic impact of the immediately preceding summer 2001 northern English mill town disturbances involving youth of Muslim background, to set in motion the articulation and development of a different kind of vision and associated political project to at least rival, if not initially, at least, supplant that of the social and political vision and project of 'multiculturalism'.

The outline of this new vision and the basis for this project was supplied in government commissioned reports by John Denham (2001) and Ted Cantle (2001) that followed the northern mill town disturbances – the former being a report from within government and entitled *Cohesive Communities*, and the latter being commissioned by government by undertaken by an academic and entitled *Community Cohesion*. While having containing differences in focus and emphasis, both reports gave impetus towards the new social policy goals and associated language of 'social cohesion' that, thereafter, came to rival and gradually supplant notions of 'multiculturalism' in the remaining periods of Government of the New Labour political project.

But it was especially in the context of the atmosphere of heightened tension following the 7th July 2005 bombings in London, that developments took place in British society that led to what appears to have been an official retreat from the previous bi-partisan approach to multiculturalism. That approach had, since the mid-1960s, shaped the social policy and political consensus in the UK. It had informed the equality and diversity policies of central and local government and other significant social institutions, and had shaped the development of law in this field. But in the light of the 'social policy shock' (Weller, 2008: 195) of 9/11 in the USA, of 11/3 in Madrid, Spain, and 7/7 in London, UK, a new social policy language began to coalesce around the previous theme of 'social cohesion', supplemented now by such themes as 'shared values' and 'Britishness' all being looked at through the lense of intense concerns about 'security' and the challenge presented by 'radicalisation' and 'extremism'. The extent and reach of this overall change of approach affected even those who had an official role to play in the promotion of 'multiculturalism' - as can be illustrated in a 22nd September 2005 statement released by the Chair of the former Commission for Racial Equality (and Chair now of the Equality and Human Rights Commission), Trevor Phillips. In this statement Phillips (2005) argued that, '….the aftermath of 7/7 forces us to assess where we are. And here is where I think we are: we are sleepwalking our way to segregation. We are becoming strangers to each other, and we are leaving communities to be marooned outside the mainstream.'

At a Government level, following a 2006 Cabinet reshuffle, the emphasis on "cohesion" led to the establishment of a Race, Cohesion and Faiths Directorate in what was then the newly created Department for Communities and Local Government (DCLG). The new Directorate continued the work initiated by the former Faith Communities Unit in the Home Office, but it linked this to the wider agendas of race and cohesion, and in 2006 it set up a Commission on Integration and Cohesion that reported in the following year (Commission on Integration and Cohesion, 2007). Significantly, the Directorate was also made responsible for tackling racism, extremism, and hate, as well as for promoting inter-faith activity in England and Wales. Thus, on the other side of 7/7, the earlier concerns around 'social cohesion' have, in many ways, coalesced with concerns around countering 'religious radicalism' and/or 'religious extremism', leading to a very close relationship being established between the policy aims, objectives and instruments of 'social cohesion' and 'security'.

Multiculturalism, Coalition Government, and Wider European Developments

By the time the new Conservative-Liberal Coalition came to power in 2010, the future of 'multiculturalism' was being widely questioned across the political spectrum in the UK, while in the wider European environment, the Netherlands increasingly saw the emergence of voices challenging the previous consensus that had, perhaps, of all the EU countries, been closest to that of the UK. In France, the wearing of the burkah in public places became outlawed. In Germany, its Chancellor Angela Merkel, pronounced the death of what in Germany is known as 'Multikulti' when in 2010 she spoke about the 'utter failure of multiculturalism' in Germany – although from my perspective as a British citizen with family in Germany and who has made many visits there over the last quarter of a century, I have to say that I am not sure it can really be said that multiculturalism was ever yet tried there!

On 5 February 2011, at a Security Conference in Munich, Germany, the UK Prime Minister, David Cameron, felt sufficiently emboldened to challenge what he called 'the doctrine of state multiculturalism', arguing that this had 'encouraged different cultures to live separate lives, apart from each other and the mainstream'. Cameron also went on to say that 'we' had 'failed to provide a vision of society to which [the different cultures] … feel they want to belong. We've even tolerated these segregated communities behaving in ways that run completely counter to our values'. Very pointedly, the remainder of the speech was an outline by Cameron of his vision for the more successful integration, specifically, of Muslims and Islam in Britain, through a combination of what he called 'muscular liberalism', 'active participation in society', and a side-lining of extremism.

While it is arguable that David Cameron's statement did mark yet another step in the long march of retreat from UK officialdom's comfort with the concept of multiculturalism, it is important to note that although much of the media gave his speech the headline 'failure of multiculturalism', Cameron did not himself use this phrase, speaking rather of 'state multiculturalism' (underling mine). In fact, it is arguable that what might be called the 'multicultural' flavour of British life (in comparison with what can be found in the majority of other European countries) has now gone so far and so deep that it would be politically damaging for any governing party to attempt to retreat too much from that. So it criticising 'state multiculturalism' Cameron could be consistent with the Tory Party's instinctive dislike for, and wish to roll back, the competence of the state, as well as the Liberal Party's preference for the state not to interfere too much in social questions, without running too great a risk of alienating black, ethnic and religious minority members, supporters and voters for either party.

It therefore remains unclear just how far the retreat from 'multiculturalism' as a political project might continue to go in the UK. In a time of economic crisis - when the dangers of social fragmentation becoming aligned with strongly negative attitudes towards minorities of all kinds arguably can emerge more strongly than in times of relative prosperity - it is to be hoped that the descriptively multicultural realities of British social life might act as a brake on any tendency on the part of the political mainstream to yet further roll back on the gains made by 'multiculturalism' as a political project. As Fethullah Gülen (2004: 249-250) warns, it is an illusion that the uncomfortable plurality of the modern world can be wished away:

> The desire for all humanity to be similar to one another is nothing more than wishing for the impossible. For this reason, the peace of this (global) village lies in ensuring that people appreciate these differences. Otherwise it is understandable that the world will devour itself in a web of conflicts, disputes, fights and bloodiest of wars, thus preparing the way for its own end.

However, one of the reasons that at least some aspects of the critique of 'multiculturalism' must be seriously engaged with has been the concern that particular 'takes' on 'multiculturalism' may lead to the creation and reinforcement of 'parallel' societies. It is for this reason that the Republican ideal in France has so strongly struggled against the notion, either in France itself and on a wider European Union level, of the notion of 'multiculturalism' In the Republican vision, the ideal is that citizens are citizens who should all enjoy the rights and responsibilities that come from Liberté, Equalité and Fraternité, regardless in principle of their ethnic, national or religious backgrounds or current other belongings.

One can, of course, understand the ideals that inform such an approach, and which are often contrasted with a British approach that is said to remain strongly reflective of the British Empire's ways of dealing with ethnic, cultural and religious diversity by the cultivation of 'clientellist' individuals and bodies to mediate between the state and individuals of diverse national, ethnic and religious groups. Approached theoretically, both systems have apparent strengths and weaknesses. In actual practice it may be that, in their results, they are not as far apart as the contrasting theoretical approaches may suggest. Indeed, there is even a case that, ironically, the baneulieux of the French citizens of minority ethnic and religious backgrounds are at least, if not more, segregated from 'mainstream' French life than is the case in the UK.

This is not to argue that everything in the UK is without problems. Particularly in areas where there is an indigenous white and historically Christian population alongside a largely single background ethnic and religious minority group – as with the predominantly Muslim and Pakistani heritage presence in a number of the northern English former mill towns - the degree of 'parallel' living without meaningful interaction that has sometimes developed can indeed be a cause for concern. But whatever ideal model is articulated and adopted it is important for it to be measured against the actual social realities of each context.

Multiculturalism, Ottoman Heritage and Modern Turkey

There will be other papers in this seminar which will address 'multiculturalism' in relation to Turkey. So I will not at this point attempt to unpack any detailed argument, leaving that to others with closer and more detailed knowledge than I have of contemporary Turkey and, before it, of Ottoman history and polity. However, broadly speaking, it is arguable that in the case of Turkey, through the emergence of a more modern Turkish nationalism and the influence within that of French Republican ideals and perspectives, a more exclusive form of Turkish nationalism developed in comparison with the older, more inclusive and pluriform Ottoman heritage.

As argued by Benedict Anderson (1983), modern ideas of nationhood originally evolved around 'ethnicity', which is a concept that is the subject of a substantial social scientific theoretical literature (Bacal, 1991). And in the course of constructing his theory of nation-states as 'imagined communities', Anderson suggested that the nation state was a competitive concept relative to religion, secularising previous ideas of primary belonging that were defined more in religious terms. As can clearly be seen in examples from the recent European history of the disintegration of ethnically diverse states such as the former Yugoslavia, ethnic and religious diversity can - and often does - pose challenges to the concept of the nation state.

Another part of the emergence of a more 'singular' Turkish form of nationalism relates, of course, to the external military, political and economic pressures under which the remains of the Ottoman Empire found itself at the start of the twentieth century and out the reaction to which the modern Turkish state was born. Unlike most Muslim majority countries, Turkey was never colonised. But these pressures were real and it is undoubtedly the case that, at the time, foreign powers with ties of ethnic and religious kinship to the substantial Greek and Armenian Christian populations tried to exploit the position of these minorities in order to try and weaken the internal political and military position of the country, both before and after Mustafa Kemal Ataturk's national revolution.

The outcome of these struggles led to human tragedies experienced by many thousands of individuals and families in the population transfers and exchanges between Greek Christian minorities in Turkey and Turkish Muslim minorities from Greek lands. These pressures also contributed to the large scale loss of so many Armenian Christian lives in events that, still to this day in Turkey, are difficult to confront in terms of the free examination of historical evidence and open debate on the responsibilities of that period.

The legacy of this early twentieth century period in Turkey - both in terms of pressures brought to bear from without as well as policies pursued from within - has resulted in a contemporary Turkey that (at least apparently) has a much more attenuated religious and ethnic diversity than the country's population of only a century ago. Nevertheless, even contemporary Turkey, with its apparently relatively monochrome religious composition and linguistic dominance of the modern Turkish language, is also an example of how what have been called 'essentialised' identities and labels can be misleading in relation to the actual degree of diversity that can exist below the surface of an apparently more homogenous surface. Thus, while the Christian population of Turkey is indeed now miniscule compared with the position of around a century ago, even though there are many things held in common between them, the religious diversity between Sunni Muslims and Alevis should not be overlooked. And, as part of an ongoing linguistic, political and military conflict, there remains the position of the Kurdish population, especially in the south east of the country.

Multiculturalism and the Dangers of Communalism and Sectarianism

Turkey's own history therefore, and the example of many other countries in Europe - not least in more recent times in the Balkans – but also in other parts of the world, such as the events that accompanied the creation of the modern states of India, Pakistan and Bangladesh, and outbreaks of communalism that have continued since then, stand as a reminder of the dangers that can occur when a particular kind of 'multiculturalism' becomes 'set' into forms that create deep social and political cleavages out of difference. Writing in 1974 in an essay on 'Communalism and the Social Structure of Religion', but perhaps with even more relevance today, Trevor Ling (1974: 59) stated that, 'Among the dangers to the peace of the world today religious communalism might appear to rank as one of the more serious.' In presenting this analysis, Ling's argument to some extent prefigured a leitmotif of the historian of religion Wilfred Cantwell Smith's (1978) book *The Meaning and End of Religion* that protested against the reification into entities such as 'Islam' and 'Christianity', of what Cantwell Smith felt it was more accurate to refer to as the products of an interplay between 'personal faith' and 'cumulative tradition'. Ling (1974: 61) himself argued that:

> The fact that such terms have been invented and have gained currency is no guarantee that they refer to real objective recognisable entities, each possessing a sufficiently high degree of internal unity to justify the degree of external differentiation which the terms imply.

Furthermore, he argued (Ling, 1974: 66) argued that such constructions of sharply defined religious identities usually '....arise out of concealed quasi-nationalisms, and they advance concealed quasi-nationalistic causes.' Taking a brief look at the implications of this in another part of the world, in his 1987 book *Communal Violence in India*, P.R. Rajagopal records that during the 1950s, 381 communal riots took place, which resulted in 153 people being killed. In the 1960s there were 2,689 riots in which 3,247 people were killed. In the 1970s there were 2,608 riots with 1,108 people killed; and, for the first five years alone of the 1980s, there were 2,771 riots with 2,772 people killed. At the close of the twentieth century and the beginning of the twenty-first century, a rise in Hindu nationalism and the impact of Islamic militancy in relation to Kashmir, led to further outbreaks of violent communalism.

In the experience of the Indo-Pakistan sub-continent these dangers are described and analysed in terms of 'communalism'. In an article entitled 'On the Varieties of Communalism in India', T.K. Oommen (1991: 12) differentiates between six different types of 'communalism' and argues that '…the six varieties of communalism that I have talked about are qualitatively different. We need to specify the attributes of each type of communalism and its implications for the society and polity in India.' Briefly – but as are discussed at more length in the chapter concerned, these types and some of their characteristics as identified by Oommen can be summarised as follows:

1. 'Assimilationist communalism' (Oommen, 1991: 7): in India, this is expressed in terms of 'devices to identify non-Hindus as Hindus'.

2. 'Welfarist communalism' (Oommen, 1991: 8): in which communal actions intended to bring benefit to one's community, as a 'resultant of co-terminality between caste and class'.

3. 'Retreatist communalism' (Oommen 1991: 9): which entails withdrawal from political activity in which 'presumed non-action is action'.

4. 'Retaliatory communalism' (Oommen, 1991: 9): in which celebrations which are 'provocations' that involve 'hurting the feelings or sentiments of others'.

5. 'Separatist communalism' (Oommen, 1991: 10): which is a kind of 'cultural nationalism' within the state.

6. 'Sucessionist communalism' (Oomen, 1991:11): which 'insists that a religious group is a political entity, and therefore it should have a separate political roof, an independent sovereign polity'.

And as Oommen (1991: 13) also argues:

> If we really want to arrive at authentic solutions we must identify the different dimensions of the phenomenon under analysis. I believe the very existence of different varieties of communalism does indicate different causes. And the different causes will have to be dealt with separately rather than treated together. This is the first step in any meaningful analysis.

Closer to home in the United Kingdom, phenomena that share some of these characteristics are known as 'sectarianism' and are found classically in Northern Ireland, but also to some degree in Scotland. in their instructive book *Moving Beyond Sectarianism: Religion, Conflict and Reconciliation in Northern Ireland*, Joseph Liechty and Cecelia Clegg (2001: 245) identify what they call a 'scale of sectarian danger' through which the conflictual temperature and destructive potential of 'sectarianism' is escalated by words and by actions in the following kind of way:

1. We are different, we behave differently

2. We are right

3. We are right and you are wrong

4. You are a less adequate version of what we are

5. You are not what you say you are

6. We are in fact what you say you are

7. What you are doing is evil

8. You are so wrong that you forfeit ordinary rights

9. You are less than human

10. You are evil

11. You are demonic

It does therefore need to be taken seriously that 'communalistic' and 'sectarian' tendencies emerge in societies when ethnic and religious groups slip into a form of identity politics in which their own identity and rights become more important to them than universal human rights, and when religions become reduced to a means of transmitting and/or securing the interests of a particular group rather than as offering a blessing to humankind, which is the aim of spirituality in the religions. Fethullah Gülen (in Ünal and Williams, eds., 2000: 248) warns of such dangers among people of Muslim background when he argues that:

> When those who have adopted Islam as a political ideology, rather than a religion in its true sense and function, review their self-proclaimed Islamic activities and attitudes, especially their political ones, they will discover that the driving force is usually personal or national anger, hostility or similar motives. If this is the case, we must accept Islam and adopt an Islamic attitude as the fundamental starting-point for action, rather than the existing oppressive situation.

Of Mosaics, Patchwork Quilts and Shot Silk

At the beginning of this essay, I noted that 'multiculture' can be found in the history of empires. Indeed, some Muslims seek to draw on such historical models as a rationale and apologia for contemporary Muslim support for multicultural societies. Fethullah Gülen himself, for example, has referred to the Ottomans in this way when reflecting on the current state of Balkan societies. Gülen (2004: 42) is certainly not apologetic about the achievements of Ottoman civilisation and, in particular, highlights the religiously informed realism of the Ottoman rulers in dealing with the cultural and religious diversity of their Empire, including in the Balkans region:

> .....our glorious ancestors captured the hearts of people by means of tolerance and became the protectors of the general peace. The longest period of peace in the Balkans and the Middle East, which have always been volatile areas, was realized with the enduring tolerance of our ancestors. From the moment that tolerance and those great representatives left history, this region became void of peace and contentment.

Narratives about historic Muslim polities are, in fact, often appealed to by Muslims and continue to exercise a strong influence upon the contemporary Muslim imagination today. In parts of the world where Islam has had particularly strong influence, such as in the Middle East, the image of a 'mosaic' has historically been invoked as one that can perhaps best accommodate national, cultural and religious plurality, with one of the classical expressions of this being the 'millet system' of the Ottoman Empire. Relative to the history of Christendom patterns exemplified by the Holy Roman Empire and the Papacy, or the later pattern of cujus regio, ejus religio, it the traditional Islamic approach is claimed to have been relatively successful within the boundaries of the predominantly Muslim societies in which it operated. At the same time, there remained a gap between ideal and reality (see M. Ma'oz, 1978: 115-42), with Christians and Jews often being treated by the state and the majority population as inferior members of the Islamic empires.

In the nineteenth century, Ottoman Empire reforms officially granted Christians and Jews equality within the political community, but those who insisted on their legal rights of emancipation were often bitterly opposed. It is also the case that, within the Islamic Empires, groups other than the majority Sunnis, such as the Shi'as, Ismailis, 'Alawis and Druzes, have been even more strongly opposed since they were viewed as being unorthodox or, at best heterodox. They were therefore sometimes seen as more of a threat to the unity of the 'ummah' than religious traditions and communities that were completely distinct from the household of Islam. However, the contemporary position of the Middle Eastern Christian communities is one in which, as minorities, they have suffered considerable social and demographic pressure and consequent population attrition in their key areas of historic geographic presence in Syria, Turkey and other similar countries where the ancient Christian Churches have been struggling to maintain a social foothold (see Wessels, 1995).

Notwithstanding this, many Muslims still appeal to a traditional 'mosaic' model as a basis for accommodating a variety of religious beliefs and practices in public life. And in contemporary Europe there are some adaptations of this classic 'treaty-based' approach that might to some extent resonate with what Muslims might realistically hope for within a European context where they are in the minority rather than majority position. An example of this can be found in the not widely known but significant Acuerdo de Cooperacíon del Estado Español con las Comisíon islamica de España (in English translation: 'Co-Operation Agreement of the Spanish State with the Islamic Commission of Spain' - see Antes, 1994) that, in 1992, was ratified by the Spanish Parliament. This is an agreement between the Spanish state and its Islamic communities that is parallel to other treaties of a similar kind established with both Protestant Christian and Jewish communities. This agreement guarantees a range of rights for minority Muslims such as civil recognition of religious marriages and the declaration of mosques as inviolable. As Peter Antes (1994: 50) commented, 'The treaty is the most comprehensive recognition of Muslim rights signed in Europe so far'.

The difficulty with this, however, is that while this traditional 'mosaic' model might be able to claim some historical success in relation to diverse populations of broadly settled geographies, its weakness is that it admits of little movement or change. It is therefore questionable how adequate it is in the context of globalised population movements and the highly mixed societies that result from physical migration and the globalisation that is characterised by the almost instantaneous transmission of ideas and influence and are reflected in Toynbee's image of 'shot silk' as compared with the more traditional 'patchwork quilt' of the 'mosaics' that have historically formed the backcloth for such traditional Muslim approaches.

In Conclusion: On Not Abandoning Multiculturalism, But Developing It

I understand the arguments of those who, from a commitment to pluralism (rather than its reverse), want to argue for an approach that goes 'beyond multiculturalism'. This is because there is a form of dangerous identity politics that can be encouraged by a particular kind of 'multiculturalism'. Concluding a 1994 essay on religion and politics in Britain since 1945 Gerald Parsons (1994: 154) issued a warning that without an effort on the part of religious leaders and politicians, political parties and religious groups to '.....understand the subtleties and complexities of the interactions to which their various commitments give rise' then 'the alternative is the reduction of increasingly complex issues to the convenient slogans of competing religious-cum-political pressure groups - a bleak and unhappy prospect indeed.'

However, while I recognise that such a danger is real, I also want to argue that to abandon 'multiculturalism' presents too high a risk of losing the important gains that its vision has secured and which I would want to argue, especially in the United Kingdom's historic version of 'multiculturalism', outweigh the downsides.. To abandon a vision and political project of 'multiculturalism' in a global social, political, cultural and religious context where 'mosaic' and 'patchwork' patterns are no longer adequate to reality is likely to lead to an emphasis on 'integration' into a dominant culture and religion which, in contrast with the 'integrationism' of Roy Jenkins' original vision for the polity of the United Kingdom is likely, rather, to become an assimilationist project that will carry the seeds of its own destruction in its denial of plural realities.

But in arguing for keeping faith with 'multiculturalism' as a political project, I want to argue for a ***developed*** form of it along the lines of what might be called a 'dynamic multiculturalism' rather than a more 'static' form – in other words one that does not reify essentialised communities into static social, political and religious formations that can too easily play into the hands of identity politics, but which instead promotes the interplay of cultures. Such an approach could be characterised in terms of a translation into a social and political democratic multiculturalism of what the historian of religion and theologian Wilfred Cantwell Smith in his book *Towards a World Theology* spoke about with reference to developments in the more circumscribed field of the study of religion. This he identified as a process of engaging with the otherness of 'the other' that culminates in when a 'we all' are talking with each other about 'us':

> The traditional form of Western scholarship in the study of other men's religion was that of an impersonal presentation of an 'it'. The first great innovation in recent times has been the personalisation of the faiths observed, so that one finds a discussion of a 'they'. Presently the observer becomes personally involved, so that the situation is one of a 'we' talking about a 'they'. The next step is dialogue, where 'we' talk to 'you'. If there is listening and mutuality, this may become that 'we' talk with 'you'. The culmination of this process is when 'we all' are talking with each other about 'us'. (Smith, 1981: 101)

In this context, it is important to note that European Union policy documents tend to speak more of 'inter-cultural relations' than of 'multiculturalism'. For myself I would rather not set one against the other, but argue that both create the conditions for a healthy form of the other – in other words, a dynamic and democratic multiculturalism, the difficulties of maintaining and developing which should not be underestimated, but the alternatives to which lead only backwards in a world where the challenges of living with plurality and with 'otherness' are only likely to grow in both their ubiquity and their importance. Therefore, in terms of political science and social practice, I would continue to argue strongly in support of this version of 'multiculturalism' against those who argue that 'multiculturalism' has failed in the past or present and/or offers nothing for the future. And finally, within the overall form of this argument and the social and political commitment which it continues to undergird, from within the religious sphere I would also argue strongly that within a multicultural polity, instead of the religious people pursuing the interests of their own group, they should each defend and promote the interests of other religious groups and that, together with all people of goodwill whether of religious faith or not, they should reach towards the transcendent horizon to which the religions are called to point and for which reason they ultimately exist.

Bibliography

Anderson, B. (1983), *Imagined Communities: Reflections on the Origin and Spread of Nationalism*, London: Verso.

Antes, P. (1994), "Islam in Europe", in S. Gill, G. D'Costa, and U. King (eds.), *Religion in Europe: Contemporary Perspectives*, Kampen, Kok Pharos, pp. 49–50.

Bacal, A. (1981), *Ethnicity in the Social Sciences: A View and Review of the Literature on Ethnicity (Reprint Paper on Ethnic Relations, No.3)*, Coventry: Centre for Research in Ethnic Relations, University of Warwick.

Cameron, David (2011). "PM's speech at Munich Security Conference", 05.02.11, at www.Number10.gov.uk the official website of the Prime Minister's Office, downloadable from: http://www.number10.gov.uk/news/speeches-and-transcripts/2011/02/pms-speech-at-munich-security-conference-60293

Cantle, T. and the Community Cohesion Team (2001), *Community Cohesion: A Report of the Independent Review Chaired by Ted Cantle*, London: Home Office

Commission on Integration and Cohesion (2007*), Our Shared Future*, London: Commission on Integration and Cohesion.

Commission on the Future of Multi-Ethnic Britain (2000), *The Future of Multi-Ethnic Britain: The Parekh Report*, London: Profile Books.

Denham, J. and the Ministerial Group on Public Order and Community Cohesion (2001), *Building Cohesive Communities: A Report of the Ministerial Group on Public Order and Community Cohesion*, London: The Home Office.

Gülen, F. (2004), *Towards a Global Civilization of Love and Tolerance*, New Jersey: The Light.

Jenkins, R., (1967), *Essays and Speeches*, Collins: London.

Jenkins, R. (1989), 'On race relations and the Rushdie affair', in *The Independent Magazine*, 14.3.89.

Rushdie, S. (1988), *The Satanic Verses*, London: Viking Penguin.

Guardian, The (1990), [White, M.], "Tebbit's test match swipe goes over the racial boundary for irate Asian community", in *The Guardian*, 21.4.90.

Guardian, The (1990), [Wintour, P.], "MP in furore over 'Muslims go home' ", in *The Guardian*, 29.8.90.

Independent, The (1989), "Limits to mutual tolerance" (editorial), in *The Independent*, 18.2.89

Liechty, J. and Clegg, C. (2001), *Moving Beyond Sectarianism: Religion, Conflict and Reconciliation in Northern Ireland*, Dublin: The Colomba Press.

Ling, T. (1974), 'Communalism and the social structure of religion', in J. Hick, (ed.), *Truth and Dialogue: The Relationship Between World Religions*, London: Sheldon Press, pp. 59-76.

Ma'oz, M. (1978), "Islamic-Arabism versus Pluralism: The Failure of Intergroup Accommodation in the Middle East", in N. Rhoodie (ed.), *Intergroup Accommodation in Plural Societies* London: MacMillan, pp. 115–42.

Ooommen, T.K. (1991), S. Arokiasamy (ed.) *Responding to Communalism: The Task of Religions and Theology*, Anand: Gujarat Sahitya Prakash, pp. 3-13.

Parsons, G. (1994, "Introduction: Deciding How Far You Can Go", in G. Parsons, (ed.), The Growth *of Religious Diversity: Britain From 1945. Volume II: Issues*, London: Routledge, pp. 5-21.

Phillips, T., (2005), 'After 7/7: sleepwalking to segregation'. *Commission for Racial Equality*, 22, September.

Rajagopal, P. (1987), *Communal Violence in India*, New Delhi: Uppal Publishing House.

Smith, W. C. (1978), *The Meaning and End of Religion*, London: SPCK.

Toynbee, A (1956), *An Historian's Approach to Religion*, London: Oxford University Press.

Toynbee, A (1958), *Christianity Among the Religions of the World*, London: Oxford University Press.

Tweedie, J. (1989), "Xenophobia as a social mechanism", in *The Guardian*, 27.2.89.

Ünal, A. and Williams, A., ed. (2000), *Advocate of Dialogue*. Fairfax, Virginia: The Fountain.

Weldon, F. (1989), *Sacred Cows: A Portrait of Britain, Post-Rushdie, Pre-Utopia*, London: Chatto and Windus.

Weller, P. (2008), *Religious Diversity in the UK: Contours and Issues*, London: Continuum.

Weller, P. (2009), *A Mirror for our Times: "The Rushdie Affair" and the Future of Multiculturalism*, London: Continuum.

Wessels, A (1995), *Arab and Christian? Christians in the Middle East*, Kampen, Kok Pharos, 1995.

So What's Wrong With Multiculturalism?

Marie Macey [50]

Introduction

In this paper I critically analyse the theory and practice of the type of multiculturalism that has been dominant in Britain and other western European societies for nearly half a century, and which is itself strongly influenced by such societies as Australia and Canada (Macey, 2006). The popularity of multiculturalism is such that it has spread – and continues to spread – to very disparate societies such as the US and Turkey (Köker, 2010). Indeed, Kymlicka has stated that there is no clear alternative to multiculturalism, which is the dominant, and accepted, approach to cultural and religious diversity around the world (1998, 2001a,b).

I profoundly disagree with Kymlicka because I believe that the theory, policy and practice of 'western' multiculturalism are fundamentally flawed. My conviction grew out of reviewing the literature for a book aimed at criticising the effects of multiculturalism on minority ethnic women (Macey 2009). This made me realise that it was not only minority women who suffered from multiculturalism, but men as well as women, majorities as well as minorities and, indeed, liberal democratic society as a whole.

Lack of space prevents me developing more than one aspect of the above (other than in the final section), so I concentrate only on the negative effects of multiculturalism

---

50 Dr. Marie Macey is a Senior Research Fellow in the Centre for Applied Social Research, University of Bradford. Her main research interests centre around ethnicity, gender and religion. Marie has worked with academic colleagues and local organisations/community groups on projects funded by the Centre for Public Scrutiny, the Department of Communities and Local Government [1. Faiths in Action, 2. The Interfaith Network, 3. Neighbourhood Renewal], the Economic and Social Research Council [ESRC], the Equality and Human Rights Commission [EHRC], the Joseph Rowntree Foundation, the National Institute for Health and Clinical Excellence [Health Action Zone]. Marie published booklets/ monographs, chapters in books and articles in international, national and overseas journals and is on the Advisory Board of The Pakistan Journal of Women's Studies. Her recent publications include: Negotiating Boundaries? Identities, Sexualities, Diversities (2007) [edited with C.Beckett and O.Heathcote]; Multiculturalism, Religion and Women: Doing Harm by Doing Good? (2009) and Ethnic, Racial and Religious Inequalities: The Perils of Subjectivity (2010) [with A.Carling].

on minority ethnic and religious groups in Britain, particularly people of Mirpuri[51] heritage and Muslim faith in Bradford, West Yorkshire [see appendix], because: (1) a key aim of multiculturalism is the achievement of ethnic equality, yet empirical research shows this group (along with Bangladeshis) to be the most consistently deprived in society (Modood et al., 1997, Berthoud 2000, Beckford et al., 2006, Platt 2002, 2007a,b,c); (2) a second objective of multiculturalism concerns inclusion and participation in society, and deprivation militates against this (Macey 2009); (3) it is arguable that the *extent* of the differences between minority groups and others is a factor in both social and self-exclusion, and (4) the Mirpuri population in Bradford remains a 'closed' community whose members practise the culture and religion of the homeland; (5) this community is one of the largest in Britain relative to the size of the 'native' population.

It is important to say at the outset that nothing that I say should be read as implying that multiculturalism *causes* any of the examples of culturally rooted behaviour that I give. But I do suggest that it *facilitate* it, both directly and indirectly, in a number of ways – by positively encouraging minority groups to maintain the culture and language of the 'homeland' to the point of 'locking' them into this, and at a different level, by creating a culture of fear among majorities such that they are afraid to intervene in case they are accused of racism. Before developing my arguments, I should state that these stem from the facts that: (a) I am a Feminist Sociologist; (b) in addition to my research I have worked extensively with South Asian women – particularly in relation to domestic abuse, and South Asian young people of both genders – in relation to forced marriage; (c) being opposed to multiculturalism as policy and practice does not imply criticism of normative multiculturalism or the struggle to achieve universal human rights: quite the reverse!

Why Multiculturalism(s)?

Multiculturalism was a response to the cultural and religious diversity that began to characterise Western Europe after the Second World War [WWII] as a consequence of needing to recruit overseas labour to replace workers who died in the war as well as extensive restructuring/economic development after it, and in Britain, the demands by ex-servicemen that the government honour its pledge to provide them with a better life.[52] This meant that most migrant workers were recruited into jobs

---

51 Mirpur is a rural, isolated, conservative area of [Azad] Kashmir whose people are generally uneducated and who practise a highly traditional variant of Islam. The area has historically been one of the poorest in Pakistan, though this has changed in recent years due largely to UK settlers sending large-scale cash remittances 'home'. Lack of investment in infrastructure, however, means that demand for migration continues since greater prosperity has not effected a change in most Mirpuris' lives (Ballard, 2003).

52 Together with an ideology that saw women's place as being in the home, replenishing the population, and freeing up the 'male' jobs which women did during the war!

at the bottom end of the labour market, with poor pay and conditions. Much overseas recruitment took place in colonies and former colonies – for Britain, the Caribbean, then India, Pakistan and Bangladesh (Allen and Macey 1994). For African Caribbeans, Britain was 'the Motherland' and their aim was to settle here permanently (Green 1990). South Asians intended to remain only as long as it took to earn enough money to improve their conditions back home: they had no desire to remain in an alien environment – culturally, linguistically and religiously – and one of which they morally disapproved (Ballard 1994). Both groups experienced widespread racism,[53] and this, together with their different orientations to British society, had short and long-term effects on their openness to integration and their willingness to adapt their cultures.

The initial structural location of the early settlers set in train a cycle of disadvantage at the micro level that continues to the present day, and which in some countries mirrored that at the macro level due to lack of citizenship rights (Hammer 1985). And though migrants to Britain had full citizenship, the racism they experienced at all levels of British society emphasises the importance of Brubaker's (1992) distinction between formal and substantive citizenship.

The above situation was not improved by the fact that the British Government made no provision for its newly arrived citizens; nor did it develop any policies towards them until the families of the early migrants began to arrive in the 1960s. It was then decided that 'something had to be done' – at least about non-English speaking children in British schools. This began a series of government interventions, particularly in education, that were based on ideologies of 'assimilation', 'integration' and 'cultural pluralism' (Mullard 1982), and were expressed through various forms of cultural pluralism, multiculturism, anti-racism, and a subsequent form of multiculturalism claiming to incorporate anti-racism. The current – and first official – government position is 'cohesion' (Cantle 2001, 2005, 2007) which will not be discussed in any detail here.[54]

---

53 For racial discrimination in: politics, see Ballard (2007), Gabriel and Ben Tovin (1982); health, Gordon and Newnham (1986); housing, Brown and Gay (1985), Association of Metropolitan Authorities (1985) Greater London Action for Race Equality (1987) education All Faiths for One Race (1982, DES [Swann] (1983), All London Teachers Against Racism and Fascism (1984), Troyna and Williams (1986); employment, Allen, et al. (1977), Association of Metropolitan Authorities (1985), London Association of Community Relations Councils (1985), Newnham (1986), Brennan and McGeevor (1987) Gifford et al. (1989); social services and social security, Gordon and Newnham (1985), Connelly (1987), Rooney (1988); the criminal justice system, Gilroy (1982); Racially motivated violence, Commission for Racial Equality [CRE] (1987), Home Office (1981), Pilger (1988).

54 The various strands of 'cohesion' have been greeted by many as rejecting multiculturalism, but I would argue that writers on cohesion (including Cantle, 2008 and Singh, 2007) can be located firmly within a multicultural ideology (see Macey and Carling, 2011).

What Multiculturalism(s)?

It is necessary to clarify how the term 'multiculturalism' is used in Britain – a distinctly problematic exercise, since it is a contested concept which changes over time (and place). Multicultural advocates clearly share this problem: Kukathas (1986, 1992, 1996, 1997) suggests that: 'What exactly multiculturalism amounts to … is not so clear, since policies bearing that name vary, and principled defences of multiculturalism do not always defend the same thing.' (2001:85). Modood (1994, 2001, 2005) says: 'multiculturalism is conceived differently in different countries and is given varied institutional expression depending upon the local and national political culture.' (1997:4). Athias comments: 'there are as many varieties [of multiculturalism] as Heinz or blossoms'. (2002:279). Cantle states that the lack of definitional agreement means that: '[multiculturalism] no longer has any real meaning, other than at a very generalised level and in political terms.' (2008:68). But perhaps Phillips takes the ultimate stance in titling her 2007 book: 'Multiculturalism *without* Culture'. However, all these writers then proceed to laud multiculturalism as if acknowledging definitional problems has solved them!

Notwithstanding the lack of a single definition, there appear to be a number of areas of agreement, for instance: comments below suggest at least some level of shared understanding of the concept, which:

- deals with diversity via accommodation, not exclusion (Kukathas, 2001);
- is based on respecting diversity and valuing cultural difference (Meeto and Mirza, 2007);
- is a policy agenda designed to redress unequal treatment and "culture-racism" (Phillips, 2007);
- is a political, social and cultural movement that respects a multiplicity of diverging perspectives outside of dominant traditions (Willett, 1998, Parekh, 2000a,b);
- involves a range of rights, different foci, including political representation, affirmative action, exemptions from laws, recognition of traditional legal codes, etc. (Kalev, 2004);
- the belief that all cultures are equal in value; every individual and every culture in which individuals participate, as being equally valuable (Minogue, 2005);
- the political idea of multiculturalism – the recognition of group differences within the political sphere of laws, policies, democratic discourses and the terms of a shared citizenship (Modood, 2007), and,
- a shift to true multiculturalism … would involve the abandonment of cultural hegemony by the native Britons. (Melotti, 1997).

Despite being a contested concept, all multiculturalism involves policies and practices designed to cope with non-Western cultural and religious diversity in society. But of major significance is that we are not simply talking about accepting and respecting differences, but incorporating these into the public arena (see Modood and Melotti above). This could present radical challenges to conventional ways of running liberal democratic societies, as well as privileging minorities over majorities in terms of rights.[55] The question for this paper is, what are the effects of this on minority groups themselves? And the answer is that the greatest impact has been on 'minorities within minorities' (Carling, 2008), for it is older men, often self-styled leaders, who have claimed the right to determine community wants/needs:

> What multiculturalism does (in return for information and votes) is to concede some measure of autonomy to community leaders to govern their communities. In reality this means that community leaders have most control over the family, women and children. Together with the state, community leaders define the needs of the minority communities then limit and separate progressive voices on the grounds of these being inauthentic and westernised. More radical elements of our community are labelled as extremists. This is the result of multi-cultural policies. They have had an enormous and devastating impact on women's autonomy and rights. (Patel 1998: 22)

Some Problems With Multiculturalism

Theory

I believe that the theoretical and practical problems inherent within multiculturalism render it damaging and dangerous to its supposed beneficiaries. Thus, a moment's thought about the holocaust or apartheid, for instance, illustrates that one of the central planks of multiculturalism, *Cultural relativism* – the notion that all cultures are equally positive – is nonsense. It is also rather unseemly to find that *Racialisation* permeates multiculturalism since apparently only non-white cultures need attention; and this indiscriminately, no matter how similar they are to white ones – or, indeed, how different some white minorities are to white majorities. *Essentialism* is inherent in multiculturalism, yet it is surely racist to view minority groups as being – unlike majority ones – undifferentiated on such bases as age, class and gender (and therefore power). *Culture* itself is treated as static (apparently only white cultures are dynamic), and *identities* are singular, or at best hierarchical,

---

55 An example of exemption from the law is allowing halal and kosher slaughter which significantly increases animal suffering (Singer, 1991). An example of an extension is allowing Muslims to take more than one wife while non-Muslims would be jailed for bigamy for the same action (Wynne-Jones, 2008).

with 'race' and ethnicity being prioritised over all aspects of a person's identity. There is, too, the fact that supporters of multiculturalism spend so much time extolling the virtues of cultural and religious diversity that they fail to acknowledge the existence of *conflict*, despite its reality (Gutmann 2003). Finally, as the world becomes increasingly global/universal on all dimensions, multiculturalism insists that the correct orientation is the *particular/local*.

Policy and Practice

Multicultural policy varies widely across Britain, as does understanding of what it should look like in practice, and whilst some multicultural (and anti-racist) thinking is enshrined in the law, much of it is not. Examples of formal/legal requirements sometimes centre around what is viewed as equal opportunities, e.g. in the workplace and the criminal justice system; informal/ideological multicultural policy permeates most of the public sector services – education, the police, social services, etc. (for details, see Macey and Carling 2011). And here, one of the most negative effects of multiculturalism has been on professional practice with teachers, social workers and police officers afraid that intervening in 'community' affairs will lead to accusations of racism (Johal 2003). The women participants in the Saheli Project criticised the government and professionals for enabling violence and oppression to go unchallenged (Mahoney and Taj 2006).[56] The other side of the coin is where professionals from minority groups privilege the community over the needs of individuals, as with police officers who report the whereabouts of young people fleeing forced marriage (Allen, in Sawyer 2008). Nor is it always minority ethnic officers who fail the vulnerable – there is the case of the murdered young women whose fears of, and evidence for, threats to her life were ignored by the police (Marshall 2007). Social workers, too, whether due to ethnic loyalty or ignorance have reported the whereabouts of runaways, and have tended to see family mediation as an appropriate way of handling forced marriage – with disastrous consequences (Khanum 2008). And there are doctors whose 'understanding' of multiculturalism has led to them stereotyping South Asian women, and reporting domestic violence to husbands and community leaders (Puri 2005).

Reality

The importance of the above issues cannot be over-stated because they have devastating effects on the lives – and deaths – of real people, particularly women:

> Around the world, women and girls continue to be victims of countless acts of violence. It is indeed a grim reality that the range of gender-based violence

---

56 The participants in this project talked of women from eleven to sixty-five disappearing; forced marriage; domestic violence; 'honour' related violence, including murder; paedophilia; sexual abuse in homes and mosques; incest and rape.

is devastating, occurring quite literally from womb to tomb. (UN General Assembly, 2001)

Okin (1989, 1997, 1998, 1999) suggests that minority ethnic women are more vulnerable to oppression and violence than their western counterparts, and Akpinar (2003) says that the reasons for this are rooted in patriarchal cultures imported from the 'homeland'. These include *female genital mutilation* [FGM] (Stewart 1998, CIMEL/INTERIGHTS 2001, Dorkenoo et al., 2006); *forced and false marriage* (Southall Black Sisters 2001, Mahoney and Taj 2006, Khanum 2008, Muslim Arbitration 2010) – tellingly termed 'statutory rape' by Idrus and Bennett (2003);[57] *sex selective abortions* (Waldby 2003, Saharso 2005, Puri 2007, Solomon 2007, Thapar-Björkert 2007); so-called *honour crimes* – including murder (Meeto and Mirza 2007, Macey 2007, 2008, 2009, Brandon and Hafez 2008, Home Affairs Select Committee 2008) and *domestic violence*. The latter is the only example given here which has not entered Britain (and wider Europe) via migration, but minority women experiencing abuse are often prevented from seeking help for such reasons as uncertain immigration status (Dilday 2007) and the fear of deportation (Meeto and Mirza 2007), lack of access to English, lack of qualifications and skills (Macey 2008), lack of service provision (Burman and Chantler 2004), lack of professional intervention due to fear of being accused of racism (Patel 1998, Refugee Women's Association 2003, Samaroo 2005, Levitt and Ware 2006, Home Office 2007); and, of course, ethno-religious prohibitions on divorce.

Summary

In this paper I have analysed what I see as some of the main theoretical and practical problems inherent in multiculturalism from the perspective of a feminist sociologist, focusing on the impact of these on minority ethnic groups, particularly 'minorities within minorities'. In the process, my criticisms have ranged across theory, policy and practice without clearly delineating between these. Nor have I considered the significant differences that actually exist between multicultural theorists, though I would justify this on the grounds that my concern is to examine multiculturalism as it impacts on *real people in the real world*.

My conclusion is that multicultural theory is fraught with tensions and contradictions of an order that make it highly unlikely that it could ever have achieved its aims. But it is the empirical evidence on multiculturalism in practice that really highlights its inadequacies, for multiculturalism has failed the people it

---

57 The centrality of intercontinental 'arranged' marriages – the vast majority of which involve some element of coercion (Muslim Arbitration Tribunal, 2008) – to Pakistani social structure and organisation in Britain should not be underestimated (Shaw, 1994). Such marriages are viewed as key to preserving family forms and networks and maintaining the 'purity of bloodlines' (Bhatti, 2007).

was meant to benefit. It has not enhanced equality and may actually have increased inequality by detracting from anti-racism (Bannerji 2000) and by encouraging the maintenance of traditions that are dysfunctional in the modern (or post-modern) context. It has penalised both minorities and majorities because it is antithetical to genuine equality of opportunity (Barry 2001). And – though not specifically discussed in this paper – in encouraging separation, if not separatism, it has had a negative impact on society as a whole, operating against social cohesion and posing a threat to liberal democracy. *My argument, then, is that for all these reasons, multiculturalism has to go. But it also has to go because in the current globalised – universal – world, multiculturalism is an illogical, unachievable and anachronistic project.*

What I have not done so far is to propose an alternative approach to multiculturalism that is fit for today's globalised world. It is a world of economic and political inter-dependence in which nation-states are significantly influenced by international factors and much legislation cuts across national boundaries (including that relating to human rights). Advanced information and communications technology is also a major influence so that global cultures strongly influence national ones. *In other words, the world as we know it is universal.*

Conclusion: Where Do We Go From Here?

Berlant and Warner (1994) and Nye (2007) argue that the above aspects of globalisation suggest an increased need for debate on diversity, if not the actual strengthening of multicultural policy and practice. I would argue, however, that not only is this *not* the case, but that in such a context, multiculturalism is little short of an anachronism in both theoretical and practical terms. My criticisms in this paper have hopefully served to illustrate why, and how, I have reached this conclusion, but in purely pragmatic terms I would flag up the lack of logic and practical impossibility of maintaining a local, culturally relativist, multicultural stance in a globalised world. And even if we could, I would argue that this would be doing a disservice to those minority ethnic and religious communities that are already alienated from the mainstream.[58]

However, the empirical evidence suggests that multiculturalism is so deeply institutionalised in British society that it has become 'received wisdom' which permeates thinking, policy and practice to an extent that precludes critical analysis. This has had a range of unforeseen consequences – from the suppression and/or denial of research findings, through the reluctance of professionals to intervene in 'community affairs', to the development of contradictory and potentially highly

---

58 See Macey (1999b, 2002, 2005, 2007 and Bolognani, 2007a,b) on Bradford young Mirpuri men's involvement in crime, rioting and terrorism.

damaging policies, such as setting employment targets that almost by definition lead to illegal discrimination against white people in favour of visible minorities and defining racially motivated crime in ways that rely on perceptions rather than proof.

Time after time, we have acceded to the (sometimes-violent) demands of ethno-religious minorities for special treatment, thereby encouraging such unacceptable behaviour as cruelty to animals and anti-democratic forms of protest, such as rioting (Carling et al., 2001; Macey, 2009). Simultaneously, we have *refused* to introduce legislation, or to put into practice that which already exists, when it comes to violence against women, such as forced marriage, female genital mutilation and domestic violence. And we have allowed organisations such as the Muslim Arbitration Tribunal to exploit legal loopholes to implement *shar'ia* law in Britain that has far-reaching, potentially negative consequences for Muslim women's rights. All this is legitimated by the belief that multiculturalists hold the high moral ground in their concern for the welfare of minorities. *However, my argument in this paper has been that as soon as one ceases to essentialise minority communities, one is forced to accept that multiculturalism is only good for older men, and that only in the short term – in the longer term, it is bad for minorities as a whole.*

Throughout all this, both proponents of multiculturalism and the government have maintained the stance that diversity is always and everywhere positive, i.e. of benefit to British society. But this position can only be maintained by ignoring the huge economic and social costs to the diverse people who make up the white majority. The economic costs alone include the payment of benefits that result from widespread unemployment among some minorities due to lack of education or skills (including those who continue to enter the country as 'marriage' partners); the payment of full benefits to bigamous families; the provision of interpreters and translators; the increasing number of Muslim men in prisons; the demands on the health service due to large families, disabled children (linked to first cousin marriages) and the long-term physical and mental health consequences suffered by women who experience domestic abuse, forced marriage and FGM, and, of course, the millions of pounds that are now being spent on consultations and special programmes directed at Muslims because of the involvement of a tiny minority of them in terrorism. It is difficult to resist the conclusion that the resistance to acknowledging that diversity is always and everywhere positive when linked to multiculturalism, is an extreme example of 'the emperors' new clothes' syndrome. And when it is also linked to the cohesion agenda, multiculturalism has had serious negative effects on both minority women's groups (Patel and Siddiqui, 2010) and on inter-ethnic relations, particularly in places where minorities have become majorities and the neglect, if not displacement, of British culture is most profound.

Thus, the argument in this paper is that multiculturalism is not only bad for minorities, but for majorities and, indeed, for British society as a whole.

The Way Forward: Back to the Future?

So what would replace multiculturalism as a means of coping with highly diverse societies? And my answer to this is – nothing new; it is, rather, that we return to the days before we thought it necessary to 'cope with' or 'manage' diversity as a characteristic of *visible* ethnic or religious minorities only. For this rests on the assumption that having a brown skin or wearing the *hijab* indicate such significant difference as to require special treatment – and this is both patronising and potentially racist, as well as sometimes just plain wrong.

My suggestion, then, is that we renew our efforts to achieve a genuine liberal democracy that would, by definition, include the promotion of equality of opportunity and the elimination of all forms of discrimination based on such criteria as age, class, ethnicity, gender, race, religion or sexuality. It would also involve the acceptance of liberal values that, arguably, are not narrowly British, but universal, as Gutmann argues:

> some basic human goods span the considerable diversity of modern cultures and support a set of ethical standards that are universal at least for the world as we know it and human beings as we know them. (Gutmann 1993 p. 193)

Notwithstanding this, since universal values are implemented in a national context, there is a requirement for a shared national identity, sense of citizenship, and commitment to the common good that transcends narrowly individual, ethnic, religious, or local community concerns. And this is where liberalism must part company with multiculturalism, for it implies the (re)assertion of certain core values over the minority ethnic and religious ones imported into Britain (as advocated by the current Prime Minister, David Cameron). People *choose* to come to this country, and while the cultures and religions of their countries of origin continue to influence their lives – both public and private – they should also be free to adapt and change as they see fit. This applies particularly, perhaps, to young people, especially those born and/or educated in this country: at what point do we allow them to cease being defined as an ethnic minority? It is also reasonable that in cases of conflict, it is the established culture of the society in which migrants have opted to settle that should take precedence over those of other countries.

But how are we move from the current situation in which multicultural ideology has resulted in some ethno-religious groups living 'parallel lives' (Ouseley, 2001) and some young people being alienated from both their own communities *and* British society? I would suggest that the first thing we need to do is to reject the multicultural view of universalism as a dirty word, and liberal values as either Eurocentric or racist:

> we need to revive a sense of direction, shared purpose and confidence in British society. One way to tackle this is to bring to an end the institutional attacks on national identity—the counterproductive cancellation of Christian festivities, the neurotic bans on displays of national symbols, and the sometimes crude anti-Western bias of history lessons—which can create feelings of defensiveness and resentment. We need to work together, as a society, to develop a renewed sense of collectivity that asserts our shared British identity and Western values. (Mirza et al., 2007 p. 7)

A number of writers have pointed to the need for a clearer conception of shared citizenship, nationality, or sense of the common good. However, this may not be simple task:

> The problem is ... that the criteria for membership in the British nation may be so undemanding as to render membership incapable of providing the foundation of common identity that is needed for the stability and justice of liberal democratic politics. (Barry, 2001: 83)

There are just two aspects of this enterprise of which I am convinced. The first is that it is urgent for everybody's sake, for all the reasons given in this paper The second is that multiculturalism has nothing to contribute to it – Britain is a European society, albeit one that is a member of the international community. And, who knows, it may not be such a difficult task as we assume, for:

> Perhaps a growing sense that 'when in Rome, do as the Romans do' has not been outlived as a maxim of immigrant integration, precisely because the contemporary 'Romes' are polyglot places in which the ties that bind are increasingly procedural and universalistic. (Joppke, 2004: 255)

Postscript

What Messages Are There From the British Experience of Multiculturalism for the Turkish One?

No system or ideology lends itself to direct transfer from one society to another, but it *is* possible to learn from others' experiences – what works and what doesn't work (amended as appropriate); what to avoid at all costs and what is essential to make multicultural societies positive, successful and inclusive of all their diverse citizens. In this endeavour, the macro, mezzo and micro levels of society require attention and planned action.

It seems to me that a first imperative is for Turkish democracy to be as fully developed as possible, offering equality of opportunity and a stake in the 'common good' to all its citizens:

> Democracy is more than a licence to celebrate (and exaggerate) difference. ... It is a political system of mutual reliance and common moral obligations ... If multiculturalism is not tempered by a stake in the commons, then centrifugal energy overwhelms any commitment to a larger good. This is where multiculturalism has proved a trap even – or especially – for people in the name of whom the partisans of identity politics purport to speak. (Gitlin, 1995: 236)

To achieve this, it may be necessary to implement a clear definition of the concept of citizenship, as well as the rights *and* responsibilities that accompany this. Legislation at state level may be necessary to ensure genuine equality of opportunity for all citizens as well as clearly thought through policies at the mezzo level aimed at enhancing knowledge, understanding, and – above all –promoting the social mixing at the micro level that is a prerequisite of intercultural dialogue.

Residential and social segregation in parts of Britain, such as Bradford, has prevented this from happening, including in schools, which are as ethnically and religiously separated (segregated) as are homes. It is currently possible for children of Mirpuri heritage in Bradford to grow up without seeing a white face, other than that of their schoolteacher (Ousely 2001) so that racialised stereotypes abound. A 'Linking Schools' project is currently having some success in encouraging intercultural mixing and dialogue among children (Raw 2006, Department for Communities and Local Government 2007a), but avoidance of the need for such projects is obviously to be preferred if possible.

Nevertheless, educational initiatives around intercultural dialogue and social cohesion can be highly productive, and here it is possible that Turkish women – like their British and international counterparts – will be keen to encourage dialogue across socially constructed ethnic and religious boundaries.

Multiculturalism – whether in Britain or Turkey – is about more than improving the economic and/or social situation of minorities, or trying to persuade people to respect others' cultures and religions. In the final analysis, it is about how multicultural and multi-faith societies as a whole can learn to function in a peaceful, collaborative and cohesive way, to the benefit of all.

Bibliography

Akpinar, A. (2003) 'The Honour/Shame Complex Revisited: Violence Against Women in the Migration Context', *Women's Studies International Forum*, 26 (5): 425-42.

Allen, S. (1971) *New Minorities Old Conflicts: Asian and West Indian Migrants in Britain*, New York: Random House.

Allen, S. (2008) in P. Sawyer, 'Forced Marriage Victims Betrayed by Doctors', *The Telegraph*, 29 June.

Allen, S., Bentley, S. and Bornat, J. (1977) *Work, Race and Immigration*, Bradford: University of Bradford.

Allen, S. and Macey, M. (1990) 'Race and Ethnicity in the European Context', *British Journal of Sociology*, 41 (3): 375-93.

Allen, S. and Macey, M. (1994) 'Some Issues of Race and Ethnicity in the "New" Europe: Rethinking Sociological Paradigms', in P. Brown and R. Crompton [eds] *The New Europe: Economic Restructuring and Social Exclusion*, London: UCL Press Ltd.

All Faiths for One Race (1982) *Talking Chalk: Black Pupils, Parents and Teachers Speak About Education*, Birmingham: AFFOR.

All London Teachers Against Racism and Fascism (1984) *Challenging Racism*, London: ALTARF.

Anthias, F. (2002) 'Beyond Feminism and Multiculturalism: Locating Difference and the Politics of Location', *Women's Studies International Forum*, 25 (3): 275-86.

Association of Metropolitan Authorities (1985) *Housing and Race: Policy and Practice in Local Authorities*, London: AMA.

Ballard, R. [ed] (1994) *Desh Pardesh. The South Asian Presence in Britain*, London: C. Hurst and Co.

Ballard, R. (2003) *Remittances and Economic Development*, written evidence to the Select Committee on International Development, London: The United Kingdom Parliament.

Ballard, R. (2007) 'Living with Difference: A Forgotten Art in Urgent Need of Revival?' in J. Hinnells [ed], *Religious Reconstruction in the South Asian Diasporas*, Basingstoke: Palgrave Macmillan.

Bannerji, H. (2000) *The Dark Side of the Nation: Essays on Multiculturalism, Nationalism and Gender*, Toronto: Canadian Scholars' Press.

Barry, B. (2001) *Culture and Equality: An Egalitarian Critique of Multiculturalism*, Cambridge: Polity Press.

Beckett, C. and Macey, M. (2001) 'Race, Gender and Sexuality: The Oppression of Multiculturalism', *Women's Studies International Forum*, 24 (3/4): 309-19.

Beckford, J., Gale, R., Owen, D., Peach, C. and Weller, P. (2006) *Review of the Evidence Base on Faith Communities*, London: ODPM.

Ben-Tovim, G. and Gabriel, J. (1987) 'The Politics of Race in Britain, 1962-79: A Review of the Major Trends and of Recent Debates', in C. Husband [ed], *'RACE' in Britain: Continuity and Change*, London: Hutchinson [2nd Edition].

Berlant, L. and Warner, M. (1994) 'Introduction to Critical Multiculturalism', in D.T. Goldberg [ed] *Multiculturalism: A Critical Reader,* Oxford: Blackwell.

Berthoud, R. (2000) 'Ethnic Employment Penalties in Britain', *Journal of Ethnic and Migration Studies*, 26: 389-416.

Bhatti, M. (2007) *Victim of Tradition: my painful journey through a forced marriage,* Bradford: MA Thesis.

Bolognani, M. (2007a) 'Community Perceptions of Moral Education as a Response to Crime by Young Pakistani Males in Bradford', *Journal of Moral Education,* 36 (3): 357-69.

Bolognani, M. (2007b) 'The Myth of Return: Dismissal, Survival or Revival? A Bradford Example of Transnationalism as a Political Instrument', *Journal of Ethnic and Migration Studies,* 33 (1): 59-76.

Brandon J. and Hafez S. (2008) *Crimes of the Community: Honour-Based Violence in the UK,* London: Centre for Social Cohesion.

Brennan, J. and McGeevor, P. (1987) *Employment of Graduates from Ethnic Minorities*, London: CRE.

Brown, C. and Gay, P. (1985) *Racial Discrimination: 17 years after the Act*, London: Policy Studies Institute.

Browne, A. (2006) *The Retreat of Reason: Political Correctness and the Corruption of Public Debate in Modern Britain,* London: Civitas.

Brubaker, W.R. (1992) *Citizenship and Nationhood in France and Germany,* Cambridge, MA: Harvard University Press.

Burman, E. and Chantler, K. (2004) 'There's No Place Like Home: Emotional Geographies of Researching 'Race' and Refuge Provision in Britain, *Gender, Place and Culture,* 11 (3): 375-97.

Cantle, T. (2001) *Community Cohesion: A Report of the Independent Review Team,* London: Home Office.

Cantle, T. (2005) *Community Cohesion: A New Framework for Race and Diversity,* Basingstoke: Palgrave Macmillan.

Cantle, T. (2007) *Community Cohesion: A New Framework for Race and Diversity,* Revised and Updated Edition, Basingstoke: Palgrave Macmillan.

Carling, A.H. (2008) 'The Curious Case of the Mis-claimed Myth Claims: Ethnic Segregation, Polarization and the Future of Bradford', *Urban Studies,* 45 (3): 553-89.

Carling, A., Davies, D., Fernandes-Bakshi, A., Jarman, N. and Nias, P. (2001) *Fair Justice for All? The Response of the Criminal Justice System to the Bradford Disturbances of July 2001,* Bradford: Programme for a Peaceful City/Joseph Rowntree Charitable Trust.

Cimel/Interights (2001) *Roundtable on Strategies to Address 'Crimes of Honour',* Women Living Under Muslim Laws, Occasional Paper No. 12, London: CIMEL.

City of Bradford Metropolitan Council [CBMDC] (1996) *Bradford and District Demographic Profile,* Bradford: Educational Policy & Information Unit.

Cohen, R. (1988) *The New Helots: Migrants in the International Division of Labour,* Aldershot: Gower Publishing Company.

Commission for Racial Equality (1987) *Living in Terror: A Report on Racial Violence and Harassment in Housing,* London: CRE.

Connelly, N. (1987) *Social Services Departments and Race: A Discussion Paper,* London: Policy Studies Institute.

Department of Education and Science [DES] (1985) *Education for All, [The Swann Report].* London: HMSO.

Department for Communities and Local Government (2007) *Face to Face and Side by Side: A Framework for Interfaith Dialogue and Social Action,* London: DCLG.

Dilday, K.A. (2007) 'Language, Immigration and Citizenship', *Open Democracy,* www.opendemocracy.net

Dorkenoo, E., Morison, L. and Macfarlane, A. (2006) *A Statistical Study to Estimate the Prevalence of Female Genital Mutilation in England and Wales.* Summary Report. London: FORWARD.

Elam, G., De Souza-Thomas, L. and Ward, H. (2006) 'HIV and AIDS in the United Kingdom African Communities: Guidelines Produced for Prevention and Care, *Eurosurveillance Weekly Release,* 11 (1).

European Commission (1985) *Europe Without Frontiers – Completing the Internal Market* [White Paper], European Documentation 2/1988, June.

Farnell, R., Furbey, R., Hills S.Al-H., Macey, M. and Smith, G. (2003) *'Faith' in Urban Regeneration? Engaging Faith Communities in Urban Regeneration,* Bristol: The Policy Press/Joseph Rowntree Foundation.

Gifford, (Lord), Brown, W. and Bundey, R. (1989) *Loosen the Shackles: First Report of the Inquiry into Race Relations in Liverpool,* Liverpool: Liverpool Law Centre/London: Karia Press.

Gilroy, P. (1982) 'Police and Thieves' in Centre for Contemporary Cultural Studies, *The Empire Strikes Back,* London: Hutchinson.

Gilroy, P. (1987) *There Ain't No Black in the Union Jack,* London: Hutchinson.

Gitlin, T. (1995) *The Twilight of Common Dreams: Why America is Wracked by Culture Wars,* New York: Henry Holt.

Gordon, P. and Newnham, A. (1985) *Passport to Benefits? Racism in Social Security,* London: The Runnymede Trust.

Gordon. P. and Newnham, A. (1986) *Different Worlds: Racism and Discrimination in Britain,* [2nd Edition], London: The Runnymede Trust.

Greater London Action for Race Equality (1987) *The Face of Injustice,* London:

Glare.

Green, J. (1990) *THEM: Voices from the Immigrant Community in Contemporary Britain*, London: Secker and Warburg.

Gutmann, A. (1993) 'The Challenge of Multiculturalism in Political Ethics', in *Philosophy and Public Affairs*, 22: 171-206.

Hammer, T. [ed] (1985) *European Immigration Policy: A Comparative Study*, Cambridge: Cambridge University Press.

Home Office (1981) *Racial Attacks*, London: HMSO.

Home Affairs Select Committee (2008) *Domestic Violence, Forced Marriage and "Honour"-Based Violence*. Sixth Report of Session 2007-08, London: The Stationery Office Ltd.

Idrus, N. and Bennett, L. (2003) 'Presumed Consent: Marital Violence in Bugis Society', in L. Manderson and L. Bennett [eds] *Violence Against Women in Asian Societies*, London: Routledge Curzon.

Johal, A. (2003) 'Struggle not Submission: Domestic Violence in the 1990s', in R. Gupta [ed] *From Home Breakers to Jail Breakers*, London: Zed Press.

Joint Council for the Welfare of Immigrants [JCWI] (1989) *Unequal Migrants: The European Community's unequal treatment of migrants and refugees*, London: E.S.R.C. Policy Paper No.13.

Joppke, C. (2004) 'The Retreat of Multiculturalism in the Liberal State: Theory and Policy', *British Journal of Sociology*, 55 (2): 237-57.

Just W.D. (1989) 'Ethnic Minorities on the West European Labour Market', *Christian Action Journal*, Summer: 21-23.

Kalev, H.D. (2004) 'Cultural Rights or Human Rights: The Case of Female Genital Mutilation', *Sex Roles*, 51 (5/6): 339-48.

Khanum N. (2008) *Forced Marriage, Family Cohesion and Community Engagement: National Learning Through a Case Study of Luton*, Luton: Equality in Diversity.

Köker, L. 2010) 'A Key to the "Democratic Opening": Rethinking Citizenship, Ethnicity and Turkish Nation-State, *Insight Turkey*, 12 (2): 49-69.

Kukathas, C. (1986) 'Liberalism and its Critics', *Humane Studies Review*, Winter: 1-110.

Kukathas, C. (1992) 'Are there any Cultural Rights?' *Political Theory*, 20 (1): 105-39.

Kukathas, C. (1996) 'Liberalism, Communitarianism and Political Community', *Social Philosophy and Policy*, 13 (1): 80-105.

Kukathas, C. (1997) 'Cultural Toleration', in W. Kymlicka and I. Shapiro [eds] *Ethnicity and Group Rights*, New York: New York University Press.

Kukathas, C. (2001) 'Is Feminism Bad for Multiculturalism?' *Public Affairs Quarterly*, 15 (2): 83-98.

Kymlicka, W. (1998) 'Introduction: An Emerging Consensus?', *Ethical Theory and Moral Practice*, 1: 143-57.

Kymlicka, W. (2001a) *Politics in the Vernacular: Nationalism, Multiculturalism and Citizenship,* New York: Oxford University Press.

Kymlicka, W. (2001b) 'Western Political Theory and Ethnic Relations in Eastern Europe', in W. Kymlicka and M. Opalski [eds] *Can Liberal Pluralism Be Exported?* New York: Oxford University Press.

Kymlicka, W. (2007) *Multicultural Odysseys: Navigating the New International Politics of Diversity:* Oxford: Oxford University Press.

Lewis, P. (2002) [2nd ed.] *Islamic Britain: Religion, Politics and Identity among British Muslims,* London: I.B. Tauris.

Lewis, P. (2004) *After September 11: Bradford—More Than A Race War,* Diocese of Bradford, www.bradford.anglican.org

Lewis, P. (2006) 'Imams, Ulema and Sufis: Providers of Bridging Social Capital for British Pakistanis? *Contemporary South Asia,* 15 (3): 273-87.

Levitt, H. and Ware, K. (2006) 'Anything with Two Heads is a Monster: Religious Leaders' Perspectives on Marital Equality and Domestic Violence', *Violence Against Women,* 12 (2): 1169-90.

London Association of Community Relations Councils (1985) *In a Critical Condition: a survey of equal opportunities in employment in London's health authorities,* London: LACRC.

Macey, M. (2003) 'From Assimilation to the Celebration of Diversity?' in V. Smékol, H. Gray and C.A. Lewis [eds] *Together We Will Learn: Ethnic Minorities and Education,* Brno, Czech Republic: Barrister and Principal.

Macey, M. (2006) 'South Asian Migrants in Britain', in A.H. Carling [ed] *Globalization and Identity: Development and Integration in a Changing World,* London: I.B. Taurus.

Macey, M. (2007) 'Ethnicity, Gender and Boundaries of Choice in Minority Ethnic Communities', in C. Beckett, O. Heathcote and M. Macey [eds] *Negotiating Boundaries? Identities, Sexualities, Diversities,* Newcastle: Cambridge Scholars Press.

Macey, M. (2008) 'Transcontinental Marriage Between British and Pakistani Citizens: Arranged or Forced? *Pakistan Journal of Women's Studies: Alam-e-Niswan,* 15 (2): 1-28

Macey, M. (2009) *Multiculturalism, Religion and Women: Doing Harm by Doing Good?* Basingstoke: Palgrave Macmillan.

Macey, M. and Carling, A. (2010) *Ethnic, Racial and Religious Inequalities: The Perils of Subjectivity,* Basingstoke: Palgrave Macmillan.

Mahoney, M. and Taj, S. (2006) *Muslim Women Talk Wales: Saheli Project Report,* Cardiff: Welsh Assembly Government.

Marshall, C. (2007) 'Killed for Loving the Wrong Man'. BBC News, 11 June.

Meeto, V. and Mirza, H.S. (2007) 'There is Nothing 'Honourable' about Honour Killings: Gender, Violence and the Limits of Multiculturalism', *Women's Studies*

International Forum, 30: 187-200.

Melotti, U. (1997) 'International Migration in Europe: Social Projects and Political Cultures'. in T. Modood and P. Werbner [eds] *The Politics of Multiculturalism in the New Europe: Racism, Identity and Community,* London: Zed Books Ltd.

Minogue, K. (2005) 'Introduction: Multiculturalism: A Dictatorship of Virtue', in West, P. *The Poverty of Multiculturalism,* London: Civitas.

Mirza, M., Senthikumaran, A. and Ja'far, Z. (2007) *Living Apart Together: British Muslims and the Paradox of Multiculturalism,* London: The Policy Exchange.

Modood, T. (1994) 'Establishment, Multiculturalism and British Citizenship', *The Political Quarterley,* 65 (1): 53-73.

Modood, T. (1997) 'Introduction: The Politics of Multiculturalism in the New Europe', in T. Modood and P. Werbner [eds] *The Politics of Multiculturalism in the New Europe: Racism, Identity and Community,* London: Zed Books Ltd.

Modood, T. (2001) 'Multiculturalism', in J. Kreiger [ed] *The Oxford Companion to Politics in the World,* Oxford: Oxford University Press.

Modood, T. (2005) *Multicultural Politics: Racism, Ethnicity and Muslims in Britain,* Edinburgh: Edinburgh University Press.

Modood, T. (2007) *Multiculturalism: A Civic idea,* Cambridge: Polity Press.

Modood, T., Bethoud, R., Lakey, J., Nazroo, J., Smith, P, Virdee, S. and Beishon, S. (1997) *Ethnic Minorities in Britain: Diversity and Disadvantage,* London, Policy Studies Institute.

Mullard, C. (1982) 'Multiracial education in Britain: from assimilation to cultural pluralism' in J. Tierney [ed], *Race, Migration and Schooling,* New York: Holt, Rinehart and Winston.

Muslim Arbitration Tribunal (2008) *Liberation from Forced Marriage.* www.matribunal.com

National Statistics (2003) *The 2001 Census,* www.statistics.gov.uk/census2001.

Newnham, A. (1986) *Employment, Unemployment and Black People,* London: The Runnymede Trust.

Nye, M. (2007) 'The Challenges of Multiculturalism', *Culture and Religion,* 8 (2): 109-23.

Okin, S. Moller (1989) *Justice, Gender and the Family,* New York: Basic Books.

Okin, S. Moller (1997) 'Is Multiculturalism Bad for Women?' *Boston Review,* 22: 25-8.

Okin, S. Moller (1998) 'Feminism and Multiculturalism: Some Tensions', *Ethics,* 108: 661-84.

Okin, S. Moller (1999) *Is Multiculturalism Bad for Women?* in J. Cohen, M. Howard and M.C. Nussbaum [eds] Susan Moller Okin (with respondents) *Is Multiculturalism Bad for Women?* Princeton, NJ: Princeton University Press.

Ouseley, Sir H. (2001) *Community Pride not Prejudice: Making Diversity Work in Bradford* [The Ouseley Report], Bradford: Bradford Vision.

Parekh, B. (2000a) *The Future of Multi-Ethnic Britain,* London: Profile Books.

Parekh, B. (2000b) *Rethinking Multiculturalism,* Basingstoke: Macmillan.

Patel, P. (1998) 'Southall Black Sisters', Keynote Address to the Conference on *Domestic Violence in Asian Communities,* Bradford: Keighley Domestic Violence Forum [KDVF]/ University of Bradford.

Patel, P. and Siddiqui, H. (2010) 'Shrinking Secular Spaces: Asian Women at the Intersect of Race, Religion and Gender', in R.K. Thiara and A.K. Gill [eds], *Violence Against Women in South Asian Communities: Issues for Policy and Practice,* London: Jessica Kingsley Publishers.

Phillips, A. (2007) *Multiculturalism Without Culture,* Princeton, NJ: Princeton University Press.

Pilger, J. (1988) 'Foreword' in Tompson, K. *Under Siege: Racial Violence in Britain Today,* Harmondsworth: Penguin.

Platt, L. (2002) *Parallel Lives? Poverty Among Ethnic Minority Groups in Britain.* London: Child Poverty Action Group.

Platt, L. (2007a) *Moving on Up? Pay Gaps: The Position of Ethnic Minority Men and Women,* Manchester: EOC.

Platt, L. (2007b) *Migration and Social Mobility: The Life Chances of Britain's Minority Ethnic Communities,* York: Joseph Rowntree Foundation.

Platt, L. (2007c) *Poverty and Ethnicity in the UK,* York: Joseph Rowntree Foundation.

Puri, S. (2005) 'Rhetoric v. Reality: The Effect of 'Multiculturalism' on Doctors' Responses to Battered South Asian Women in the United States and Britain', *Patterns of Prejudice,* 39 (4): 416-30.

Puri, S. (2007) 'There is No Such Thing as Too Many Daughters, but Not Too Many Sons: The Interaction of Medical Technology, Son Preference and Sex Selection Among South Asian Immigrants in the United States', Paper presented to the *Second National Bioethics Conference,* Bangalore, India, December.

Raw, A. (2006) *Schools Linking Project 2005-06: Full Final Evaluation Report,* Bradford: Education Bradford.

Refugee Women's Association (2003) *Refugee Women's News,* June/July, Issue 23, RWA.

Rooney, B. (1988) 'Some Obstacles to Change in Social Work and Social Work Organization', in S. Allen and M. Macey [eds] *Race and Social Policy,* London: ESRC.

Saharso, S. (2005) 'Sex Selective Abortion: Gender, Culture and Dutch Public Policy', *Ethnicities,* 5 (2): 248-281.

Samaroo, A. (2005) Cultural Influences on Domestic Violence in Asian Communities in Britain: Service Providers' Perspective on the Relationship between Cultural Practices and Domestic Violence, University of Bradford: MPhil Thesis.

Shaw, A. (1994) 'The Pakistani Community in Oxford', in Ballard (1994) op.cit .

Singer, P. (1991) *Animal Liberation,* London: Harper Collins.

Singh, D. (2007) *Our Shared Future,* Commission on Integration and Cohesion, London: DCLG. www.integrationandcohesion.org.uk

Sniderman, P.M. and Hagendoorn, L. (2007) *When Ways of Life Collide,* Princeton, NJ: Princeton University Press.

Solomon, S. (2007) 'Sex Selective Abortion Comes to Canada', *National Review of Medicine,* 4 (15), 18 September.

Sookhdeom, P. (2005) 'Will London burn too?' *London Spectator,* 11 November.

Southall Black Sisters [SBC] (2001) *Forced Marriages: An Abuse of Human Rights – One Year After 'A Choice By Right',* London: SBS.

Stewart, D.E. (1998). *Female Genital Mutilation: The Midwifery Case,* Bradford: University of Bradford MA Dissertation.

Thapar-Björkert, S. (2007) *State Policy, Strategies and Implementation in Combating Patriarchal Violence, Focusing on "Honour Related" Violence,* Norrköping: Integratiönsverkets Stencilserie.

Troyna, B. and Williams, J. (1986) *Racism, Education and the State,* Beckenham: Croom Helm.

UNFPA (2000) *The State of the World Population: Ending Violence Against Women and Girls,* New York: UN.

UNICEF (2005) *Female Genital Mutilation/Cutting: A Statistical Exploration,* New York: UNICEF.

UNICEF (2006) *Child Protection Information Sheet: Female Genital Mutilation/ Cutting,* New York: UNICEF.

Waldby, C. (2003) *Literature Review and Annotated Bibliography: Social and Ethical Aspects of Sex Selection,* London: Human Fertilisation and Embryology Authority.

Willett, C. [ed] (1998) *Theorizing Multiculturalism: A Guide to the Current Debate,* Malden, Mass: Blackwell Publishers.

Wynne-Jones, J. (2008) 'Multiples Wives will mean Multiple Benefits', *The Telegraph,* 18 April.

The Origins, History and Development of Multiculturalism in the UK

Mohammed Abdul Aziz [59]

Introduction

The origins, history and development of multiculturalism in the UK are complex and contested. How one describes them depends much on whether one takes the broader or narrower conception of multiculturalism. Broader multiculturalism is taken here to refer to the new progressive politics of the 1960s and 70s centred on the 'politics of identity: being true to one's nature or heritage and seeking with others of the same kind public recognition for one's collectivity' (Modood, 2007, p.2). The broader conception accommodated difference on grounds of race, gender, sexuality and a host of other characteristics. This meaning of multiculturalism was prevalent in the US. The narrower conception of multiculturalism, as used in the UK and much of Europe, refers to a multiculturalism brought about 'not so much by the emergence of a political movement but by a more fundamental movement of peoples. By immigration – specifically, the immigration from outside Europe, of non-White peoples into predominantly white countries' (Modood, 2007, p.2). The narrower conception of multiculturalism is, therefore, limited specifically to accommodating differences in relation to immigrant communities, and from my perspective, is only a subset of the broader conception. This paper recognises these two conceptions of multiculturalism, but whereas many critics and advocates of multiculturalism have in more recent years sought to divorce the two conceptions, or at least seek a judicial separation between the two in their treatment of multiculturalism, this paper will make the argument that the two conceptions not only derive from the same key drivers and have had a symbiotic relationship in their history and development, but also that a focus solely on the latter, at the

---

59 Mohammed studied Law at the University of London and was called to the Bar in 1996. He was the founding CEO of the Forum Against Islamophobia & Racism. In 2004, he founded FaithWise, a religion and belief equality and human rights consultancy and worked as a Senior Advisor to the UK Government on Race, Faith & Cohesion until 2011. Mohammed has held numerous public appointments, including Commissioner at the Commission for Racial Equality, the Equal Opportunities Commission and the TUC's Commission on Vulnerable Employment. He was a Member of the Commission for Equality & Human Rights Steering Group, the Governments Review of Treasury Counsel Appointments and two Cabinet Office Honours Committees. Mohammed has also held many positions in the third sector: Council Member of Liberty, Vice Chair of the Equality & Diversity Forum, Trustee of the East London Mosque and Chair of the European Network Against Racism. Mohammed is currently a Visiting Fellow at Cambridge University.

expense of the former, whilst beneficial in some respects, much impoverishes and perhaps even endangers the goals to be achieved by the latter in other critical ways. This paper will, therefore – whilst ultimately primarily concerned with the UK, and by definition with the narrower approach – start with an exposition of multiculturalism in its wider context.

The Key Post-war Underlying Drivers for Multiculturalism in the UK

It is possible to argue that the drivers for multiculturalism are recent and pragmatic – particularly if one takes only the narrow meaning of multiculturalism. We suggest, however, that the drivers hail from far deeper movements in European and UK history and thought, and are therefore much more deeply embedded in the UK. It is possible to argue that the spirit of multiculturalism is embedded in both the very history and making of the UK – the Acts of Unions between England, Scotland and Ireland, allowing different established churches, laws and educational systems – even if these were primarily politically driven (see, for example, Paxman, 2007) and how it administered its vast empire – an empire on which the sun never set – most notably the multi-ethnic, multi-religious subcontinent of British India. The focus here, however, will be more modest: the paper will focus on only some of the most significant of the more recent of these drivers, namely, the post war rejection of the master race theory, the development of international standards of human rights, the impact of the Civil Rights Movement in the US on Black communities in the UK, and the mass migration of people, from all corners of the world, to the UK in the second half of the last century.

The Post-War Rejection of the Master Race Theory

The master race theory was, of course, at the heart of the period of European imperialism, as it was in most previous empire-building enterprises throughout history. In terms of its place in British imperial thinking, it was perhaps best encapsulated in the idea of 'the White Man's burden' (Kipling, 1899). Whereas in the pre-modern world, however, such beliefs had mostly led to the subjugation and slavery of vanquished peoples, European imperialism often also led to large-scale movements of peoples, holocausts, genocides and annihilations of entire populations. The ultimate European culmination of this trend was the Holocaust of millions in the heart of Europe itself during World War II. The origins of the Nazi version of the master race theory can be traced to 19th-century racial theories that propagated the idea that mixing distinct races resulted in degenerating their cultures (Biddiss, 1970, p514). It was believed at this time that Southern and Eastern Europeans had become racially mixed with Moors from across the Mediterranean, while Northern and Western Europeans had remained pure.

Proponents of this Nordic theory further refined previous Aryan superiority theories and argued that Nordic peoples had additionally developed certain innate qualities due to the challenging climate in which they lived (Schopenhauer, 2000, Vol. II, s.92). As such, Nazi policy not only stressed the superiority of the Nordic race, a sub-section of the white European Aryan race, but also that its purity had to be maintained and improved. It thus established a programme for systematically enhancing the Nordic/Germanic Aryans genetically through a programme of Nazi eugenics whilst simultaneously eliminating its 'defective' citizens from its ranks, as well as those considered to be racially inferior but with a potential to contaminate. Many of the consequential policies resulted in what eventually became known as the Holocaust. The absolute horrors of this Holocaust, as revealed at concentration and extermination camps like Auschwitz-Birkenau in the immediate aftermath of World War II, led to such a widespread revulsion against the master race theory that it quickly led to its complete moral rejection internationally.

The Development of International Standards of Human Rights

The modern concept of human rights has grown out of the medieval concept of natural rights and was initially formulated during the Enlightenment which helped secularise Judeo-Christian ethics in Europe (Ishay, 2008, p.64). The concept featured prominently in the political discourses of the American and French Revolutions and was further developed in the writings of philosophers such as Thomas Paine, John Stuart Mill and Georg Hegel (Paine, 2009; Mill, 2009; Hegel 1991). Whilst there are many examples of human rights documents that precede World War II, on the whole, these documents were agreed locally or nationally. The first international effort was in the aftermath of World War I, through the League of Nations established in 1919. However, many of the basic ideas that animate the human rights movement today were developed in the aftermath of World War II and the atrocities of the Holocaust mentioned above – through the newly created United Nations. The UN and its members have played a critical role in developing much of the discourse, the documents and the bodies of law that now make up international human rights law. Perhaps the most significant of the UN documents is the *Universal Declaration of Human Rights* (UDHR) adopted by the UN General Assembly in 1948. The document was structured to include the basic principles of dignity, liberty, equality and brotherhood in the first two articles, followed by rights pertaining to individuals; rights of individuals in relation to each other and to groups; civil and political rights; and economic, social and cultural rights. The final three articles place the rights in the context of limits, duties and the social and political order in which they are to be realised. The Declaration was subsequently bifurcated out into two separate covenants, the Covenant on Civil and Political Rights and the Covenant on Social, Economic and Cultural Rights. The documents are today almost universally recognised and serve as powerful standards through many regional and national structures. They are implemented in the UK through the European Convention on Human Rights, the European Court of Human Rights and the Human Rights Act 1998.

The Impact of the Civil Rights Movement in the US on Black Communities in the UK

If the European and international scene in the mid twentieth century was characterised by a wind of change with regards theories of racial equality and the humanity and dignity of individuals and groups, such a wind was also blowing fervently in many multi-ethnic nations. Movements by long-oppressed racial and religious minorities begun more rapidly to gather pace – not least among them was the African American Civil Rights Movement, primarily a nonviolent struggle to bring full civil rights and equality under the law to all Americans, including African Americans. The Civil Rights Movement was a continuation of the Abolition Movement. After the US Civil War, several constitutional amendments had extended certain legal rights to African Americans. However, the last quarter of the 19th century reversed the impact of these constitutional amendments in practice in the South, where segregation and discriminatory practices against African Americans was the legal norm until the landmark case of *Brown v. Board of Education* in 1954. The Brown Case proved to be a turning point for African Americans in the US. Invigorated by the *Brown* victory but frustrated by the lack of immediate practical effect, private citizens increasingly rejected gradualist, legalistic approaches as the primary tool to bring about desegregation. In defiance of the status quo, African Americans, led by such figures as the Revd Dr Martin Luther King Jr, adopted a combined strategy of direct action with nonviolent resistance known as civil disobedience. The new strategy paid off in the form of the Civil Rights Act 1964, the Voting Rights Act 1965, the Immigration and Nationality Services Act 1965, and the Fair Housing Act 1968. African Americans re-entered politics in the South and across the country they were to be treated as equal citizens again, at least in terms of the law. This was not just a new era of hope for young Blacks in the US but an inspiration for Black minorities across the Atlantic. The emergence of the Black Power Movement, from around 1966 to 1975, which brought figures such as Malcolm X to national prominence, enlarged the aims of the Black Civil Rights Movement to include racial pride, economic and political self-sufficiency, and freedom from more subtle forms of oppression.

The Mass Migration of People to Britain from All Corners of the World

Whilst there had been small waves of migration into the UK throughout the first half of the 20th century, it was the acute labour shortage following the end of World War II that led to the British Nationality Act 1948, which allowed the 800 million subjects in the British Empire at the time to live and work in the United Kingdom without needing a visa. These people were to fill a gap in the UK labour market for unskilled jobs, and many were brought to the UK specifically for this purpose on ships such as the *Empire Windrush*. Immigrants from the Indian subcontinent began arriving in the UK shortly after their country gained independence in 1947. The flow of Indian immigrants peaked between 1965 and 1972, boosted in particular by East African Indians fleeing from the Africanisation politics and policies in Uganda and Kenya. This Commonwealth immigration, made up largely of economic migrants, rose from 3,000 per year in 1953 to 46,800 in 1956 and 136,400 in 1961. This heavy numbers of migrants arriving in the UK each year soon became heavily politicised, such that from as early as the early 60s there seems to have grown an inverse relationship between rhetoric and legislation on the one hand, and reality and practice on the other. Since the early 60s, successive pieces of legislation have sought to restrict immigration: the Commonwealth Immigrants Act 1962, the Commonwealth Immigrants Act 1968, Immigration Act 1972, and the British Nationality Act 1981. Further legislation in 1993, 1996 and 1999 gradually decreased the rights and benefits given to those claiming refugee status ('asylum seekers'). Notwithstanding the new restrictions, however, throughout the 1970s, an average of 72,000 immigrants were settling in the UK every year from the Commonwealth; this decreased in the 1980s and early 1990s to around 54,000 per year, only to rise again to around 97,000 by 1999. Further, since the expansion of the EU in 2004, the UK has accepted immigrants from Central and Eastern Europe. Research conducted by the Migration Policy Institute for the Equality and Human Rights Commission suggests that, between May 2004 and September 2009, net migration from the new EU member states to the UK was approximately 700,000 people (Sumption and Somerville, 2010, p.13).

My argument here is that the above were some of the key underlying drivers and ingredients to seeding, influencing, inspiring and creating a backdrop context in post-war UK that promised the possibility of allowing the assertion of individual and group identities and differences by those oppressed with a demand for the same dignity, equality and respect as enjoyed by the majority and/or dominant group or groups. The widespread rejection of biological determinism and the master race theory allowed this possibility not just for different ethnic groups but also others, not least women; the development of international human rights standards ensured that in asserting individual and group identities and differences, individual and group dignity, equality and respect did not by implication have to be compromised but would be protected; the US Civil Rights Movement evidenced the struggle required to bring these ideas home but also provided the lessons and inspiration required to achieve that goal; and the mass migration of people from all corners of the world provided the numbers, the issues and the momentum for the change to take effect in the UK. However, if the backdrop and stage had been set for multiculturalism, the work towards realising and embedding it into the fabric of UK institutions, society and narrative was still at hand. This was to be achieved by a number of converging movements.

The Emergence of the Specific Movements and Their Achievements

If the above were the key post war driving forces for multiculturalism, then its development, consolidation and embedding took place in the second half of the 20th century in the context of and through at least three key movements in the arena of the politics of identity and difference: race, gender and sexual orientation – each undertaken by representatives of a collective with a distinctively different social location that had hitherto been neglected or suppressed. It is argued here that multiculturalism as it gained salience was possible because of the contributions of each of these movements towards shifting the mind-sets of opinion shapers and policy and law makers, and through them, ultimately, the general public.

The Race Equality Movement

The newly arrived Black and Asian populations of the late 40s and 50s occupied certain labour market positions and lived in particular areas. They were some of the most oppressed and exploited sections of society, working and living in the worst conditions (Bassi, 2007). However, antagonism against 'coloured' immigrants was never far from the surface and emerged into full public view in 1958 when 'race riots' took place in Nottingham and London's Notting Hill (Choudhury, 2011, p110). The riots led to the emergence of an anti-racism and race equality movement in the UK, which found friends in many mainstream politicians of this era, who recognised and publicly condemned the racism and racial discrimination that existed, and through the Race Relations Act 1965 outlawed public discrimination and established the Race Relations Board. Further Acts in 1968 and 1976 outlawed discrimination in employment, housing and social services, and replaced the Race Relations Board with the Commission for Racial Equality. In many ways, that policy framework created in response to that period continues to shape the UK approach to racism, equality and multiculturalism today. In the early 1980s, however, persisting societal racism, along with perceptions of powerlessness and oppressive policing, sparked a new series of riots. The Scarman Report in 1981, following the Brixton riots identified both racial 'discrimination' and 'disadvantage' in the UK, and concluded that urgent action was needed to prevent these issues becoming an 'endemic, ineradicable disease threatening the very survival of our society' (Scarman, 1981). There followed little government action, however, and despite new legislation on incitement to racial hatred, the era witnessed continued high levels of attacks on Black people. In 1985, after six years of enquiry, examining racism and educational attainment, the Swann Report advocated a multicultural education system for all schools (Swann, 1985). But again, the report found little concerted and sustained support from central government and its concept of a multicultural education for all was abandoned at the national level only three years later by the Education Reform Act 1988, which favoured a more assimilationist approach. However, despite this gloomy picture at the national level, both Scarman and Swann left a lasting impact at the local level, particularly in relation to many local authorities' education departments. They also contributed to a thriving anti-racism and race equality movement at the grassroots of BME communities – in particular, through the efforts of the Commission for Racial Equality and a national network of local Race Equality Councils, many policy and activist NGOs, such as the Runnymede Trust and the 1990 Trust, and many city and local authorities with high concentrations of ethnic minorities, for example, the Greater London Council and many inner London local authorities. One area of particular concern that remained, however, was that of institutional racism – both in terms of employment and services. This was brought to the fore in the aftermath of the murder of Stephen Lawrence, a black teenager, in 1993, and was eventually addressed through the McPherson Report 1999 and the Race Relations (Amendment) Act 2000.

The Gender Equality Movement

The movement towards gender equality began with the suffragette movement of the late-19th century, which made some significant gains in terms of women's rights to property and their right to vote. As women had made a significant contribution to the war efforts in both the World Wars, however, the gender equality movement gained a new 'second wave' impetus in the post war years. Aided by the emerging understanding of dignity, equality and human rights, the movement began to challenge more forcefully previously held beliefs about biological supremacy and gender determinism, and by the 60s, a more general movement for gender equality had gathered pace based on women's liberation and feminism. By the mid 70s, the gender equality movement had achieved two important pieces of legislation: the Equal Pay Act 1970 and the Sex Discrimination Act 1975. The latter also established the Equal Opportunities Commission, which made two critical contributions. Firstly, it brought a large number of cases to the courts under both pieces of legislation and thereby spawned a very large body of gender equality jurisprudence; and secondly, it helped to change public attitudes towards gender equality in many areas – for example, attitudes to equality in education opportunities for boys and girls and equality of access to different occupations for both men and women. This has made it possible today for women to serve in the armed forces, the fire brigade and the police service, and for men to work as nurses. Some changes, however, could only be achieved in the short term through more affirmative legislation and action – for example, women in higher levels of politics. The gender movement achieved one of the rare examples in the UK of positive discrimination in the form of the

Sex Discrimination (Election Candidates) Act 2002, which allowed only women shortlists for elections. Institutional gender discrimination is more regularly to be addressed, however, through the public sector gender equality duty as achieved by the movement in the Equality Act 2006.

The Gay Rights Movement

In the post-war period Alfred Kinsey in the US published two important studies on sexual behaviour (1948 and 1953) stating that 4% of American men and 2% of women identified themselves as exclusively homosexual. In 1954, the Wolfenden Committee was appointed to consider the law in the UK relating to homosexual offences. It was not until the Sexual Offences Act 1967, however, that homosexual acts between two men over 21 years of age and 'in private' was decriminalised in England and Wales. Attitudes in relation to sexual orientation have been very slow in changing on both sides of the Atlantic. However, when on 27 June 1969 the Stonewall riot began in New York, this ignited a more public and assertive gay rights movement. Within a very short time several energetic new organisations were set up in the US and UK that started to organise large scale public events for the first time: launches of gay liberation manifestos, lesbian and gay pride marches, demonstrations and rallies, gay dancing events and carnivals, and gay rights conferences. A decade later, the movement had also become prolific in the important area of media and popular culture – launching gay newspapers and TV and radio programmes. Success for the movement, however, has been slow in coming, and it was the Human Rights Act of 1998 that finally provided a breakthrough. The Act was successfully used by Stonewall to achieve equality in the armed forces, immigration, criminal law, co-habitation, fostering and adoption, succession, and claim to damages in fatal accident cases. The turn of the millennium saw a wave of primary legislation: the Employment Equality (Sexual Orientation) Regulations 2003; the Criminal Justice Act 2003; the Local Government Act 2003; the Civil Partnership Act 2004; the Equality Act 2006; the Equality Act (Sexual Orientation) Regulations 2007; the Criminal Justice and Immigration Act 2008; the Human Fertilisation and Embryology Act 2008; and the Equality Act 2010. Further, this legislation has now begun to spawn a new body of case law. However, attitudes towards homosexuals still remain a concern in the UK. On 30 April 1999, a bomb exploded in a gay pub in London's Soho area, the third in a series of bombs targeted at minorities by a lone extremist, which killed three and injured several others. This has resulted in further criminal law provisions against incitement and aggravated offences on grounds of sexual orientation. An allied concern is that of homophobic bullying in schools that continues to show little sign of abating.

The point of rehearsing the development and achievements of these movements or identity based political formations is to suggest that together, in light of their common experiences of injustice and oppression and given the opportunity of a particular context in the post war decades formed from the driving forces already discussed, they irreversibly changed the very fabric and narrative of the UK; they changed its national sub-conscience from a mono-cultural to a multicultural entity. To our mind, this was achieved through the following five concrete changes. Firstly, the movements helped to define and articulate more clearly the injustices and oppressions that are experienced by certain social groups and their members on grounds of identity and difference in a language more readily understood and accepted by the wider post war UK society (Heyes, 2000). These injustices and oppressions are manifold and have now been variously typologised by leading activists and academics in both the UK and US, but most notably by Iris Young as: cultural imperialism, exploitation, marginalisation, violence and powerlessness (Young, 1990, pp.48-63). Secondly, the movements helped to nurture the view that such injustices and oppressions have no place in a modern UK and that society as a whole and its institutions must commit to revaluing oppressed identities and changing dominant patterns of thinking and behaviour that oppress certain groups (Taylor, 1994; Gutmann, 2003). This has been done mostly through the law, the education system and promotional work more generally. Thirdly, the movements were able to assert that they and their members should no longer be characterised by stigmatising oppressive outsider accounts and sought variously to reclaim, redescribe or transform the ways their distinctiveness was understood which was more self-determined and authentic. This allowed members of these movements to acquire something that members of the dominant groups were able to access from the inception of modernity: a freer quest towards the nature of subjectivity and the self (Taylor, 1989), which in turn would impact their sense of self and community that they would then project and seek recognition for from wider society (Gutmann, 2003). Fourthly, the movements were able to at least partly embed the idea that if identity and difference should not be used for oppression, then neither should sameness and equality. This was a critique of the social ontology borne from the liberal political theory that citizens be conceptualised as essentially similar individuals, as for example in John Rawls famous thought experiment using the 'original position' (Rawls, 1971). The movements argued that this formal and shallow approach to equality leads to its own injustices and oppressions and a deeper equality approach was required for the recognition, respect and accommodation of difference (Kymlicka, 1995). Fifthly, the movements seeded the idea that the long histories of injustices and oppressions have left behind large legacies of structural economic and political disadvantages for certain social groups and their members that need to be specifically addressed and tackled (Song, 2007).

It is argued here that it is these five changes of identifying and defining the relevant group injustices and oppressions, recognition and commitment to rectification of them by wider society, the self-description of their distinctiveness by relevant groups, the demand for respect and accommodation of these differences and a commitment to redress the historical disadvantages of oppressed groups that make up the core elements of multiculturalism in the UK. Multiculturalism as such was not therefore planned, campaigned for and achieved as a single programme – but emerged as the result of multiple efforts by multiple groups and converging movements – all driven by certain underlying forces, openings and opportunities that prevailed in the post war period. UK multiculturalism then is much like the UK's unwritten constitution – it has evolved in the background in the face of the vicissitudes of a particular time and set of events and remains undefined in any concrete shape or form, although its practitioners have sufficient understanding of its salient parts to know that it exists, is embedded and works. The narrower version of multiculturalism, as more commonly used in the UK and much of Europe, referring to multiculturalism resulting from migration from outside Europe, of non-White peoples into predominantly white countries, is a subset of this larger picture.

The Tensions and Fractions Between and Within the Movements

We have already noted that multiculturalism in the UK was not the project or achievement of a single movement – but the outcome of the efforts of a number of coalescing movements, groups and interests. However, these movements were rarely co-working or co-operating. In fact, whilst these movements were moving towards a common goal, relations between and within them were fraught with difficulties. For example, whilst minority ethnic communities were experiencing the worst forms of injustices and oppressions their own characterisations of gay communities and attitudes in terms of gender were no better than the most oppressive attitudes and behaviour towards these groups from the dominant groups in society. In some ways this has not changed at all – thus, for example, the first conviction in the UK against incitement on grounds of sexual orientation, pronounced this year, was against three young Asian men. Within the gender movement, there are now whole bodies of literature around the Eurocentrism of the gender equality campaigns or the negative impact of cultural accommodation on women's rights (see, for example, Phillips, 2007, for a very interesting analysis of the full spectrum of this literature). The race movement provides perhaps the most stark examples of these tensions and fractions. We have already noted some of the tensions between this and the other movements, but even within the movement itself enormous tensions were brewing, first between Blacks and Asians, and then within the Asian category itself – between Indians, Pakistanis and Bangladeshis or Hindus, Muslims and Sikhs.

There were many reasons for these schisms between and within the groups. First, whilst they were actually involved in a common struggle, they nonetheless had very different starting points, histories, cultures of operation and prejudices of their own, and did not have much previous experience of working together. Their most significant achievements in many ways only reinforced their separateness – for example, whilst the Sex Discrimination Act and the Race Relations Act were written about the same time, by the same author, addressing similar issues, they were separately passed by Parliament establishing separate laws and institutions (the Commission for Racial Equality and the Equal Opportunities Commission) to help and assist their constituencies completely separately. Secondly, at a very critical point in the development of multiculturalism in the UK, the 80/90s, the Conservative Governments of the day had little interest in these struggles – if anything, in some instances, it was decidedly ideologically and politically hostile to these struggles in line with its positions on family values, public morality, anti-immigration and Britishness. This combined with the Thatcherite approach of 'no society, only individuals' meant that there was very little public space or resources for these movements, and whatever little of it that was available attracted ruthless competition. Thirdly, institutions that could have provided a common platform for these movements and subsequently did, for example, the Trade Unions, had been severely weakened by the Thatcher Government just as these movements were beginning to take off in the late 70s and early 80s.

There have, however, been two currents that have run against the above pattern of tensions and fractions. First, the picture at the city or local level has been somewhat different. Where city or local authorities were more receptive to these struggles, mostly those controlled by Labour, there was at least a semblance of co-working, at least in the town halls if not on the ground. Many such city or local authorities established Diversity & Equality Units and simultaneously funded, for example, Gay History Month events alongside Black History Month events, as well as awareness-raising events on domestic violence. This ensured a thriving diversity and equality or multiculturalism movement at the local level. Second, when New Labour was elected into Government in 1997, it not only brought with it more women, ethnic minorities and openly gay politicians, it also set into motion developments at the national level that would over the course of its stay in power not only embolden multiculturalism into the UK fabric and narrative, but also strengthen the solidarity between its various champions and beneficiaries. The result was numerous taskforces and steering groups, white and green papers, primary and secondary legislation that would ultimately lead to a single equality body, the Equality & Human Rights Commission, a single equality act, the Equality Act 2010, and a single Government Equality Office. The success in strengthening the solidarity between the various protagonists and beneficiaries are best witnessed in the development, achievements and the current operation of the Equality & Diversity Forum. But these relatively strong currents were not in the end sufficient to gel the different movements into one, who saw their achievements as one and labelled the same. One major implication of this was for the definition of multiculturalism in the UK: whilst the content of multiculturalism was achieved and embedded in the UK by the efforts of diverse groups, and its benefits shared by all these groups, the label of multiculturalism was narrowed to apply to only the migration related aspects of this phenomenon.

The Narrowing Discourse on Multiculturalism and Its Proliferation Into New Discourses

The narrowing discourse on multiculturalism started around the turn of the millennium with two key events – the disturbances in the Northern English cities in the Spring of 2001 and then the terrorist atrocities of 9/11 in the US later that same year. The narrowing discourse resulted from three simultaneous responses to events. Firstly, the response of long term detractors of multiculturalism whose reaction to the 2001 events was to reduce multiculturalism to that enjoyed by immigrant communities, and more specifically Muslim communities; to caricature that multiculturalism based on its extremes; and to attack it for its role in identity based politics and the violence with which this was expressed. Secondly, the response of certain left of centre politicians, media professionals and even some social justice campaigners to this criticism, which was on the whole to support it. Notable in this category was the then Chair of the Commission for Racial Equality, Trevor Phillips, whose speech on 'sleepwalking into segregation' made many headlines, and due to his role added much credibility to this argument. And thirdly, the response of the champions and beneficiaries of the wider conception of multiculturalism, who sought to cut their losses by distancing themselves from a soiled label, and those they perceived to have soiled that label, whilst protecting the content of that label – albeit under a different language, for example, diversity, inclusion, equality and human rights.

The response of New Labour as a Government in its second term to this development was to begin a twin track approach: on the one hand, it continued to enrich and embed the content of the broader notion of multiculturalism through its work under the inclusion, equality and human rights agendas, mainly led by the Women & Equality Unit (initially housed in the Department for Trade & Industry, and then at the Department for Communities and Local Government) and subsequently the Government Equalities Office, whilst simultaneously it amplified its rhetoric against the narrower conception of multiculturalism through a newly energised discourse on belonging, cohesion, citizenship, Britishness, loyalty and shared values, mainly led by the Home Office. This twin track approach continued into its third term, except that after the atrocities of 7/7 in 2005, its rhetoric against the narrower conception of multiculturalism was additionally delivered through its Preventing

Violent Extremism and Anti-Terrorism agendas split between various Government Departments. This twin track approach reinforces the argument that the content of the broader conception of multiculturalism is now locked into the UK fabric and narrative, even if plenty of rhetoric remains prevalent with regards to some parts of its application to certain pariah groups. However, this bifurcation of the broader conception from the narrower labelling, along with a difference between rhetoric and application, actually proliferated into four distinct (albeit overlapping) discussions and policy areas by the end of New Labour's term in government: equality/human rights, social exclusion/community cohesion, migration/integration and preventing extremism. We do not have the space here to discuss these individually, but hope to do this later in a longer version of this paper.

The Coalition Government and the Future of Multiculturalism

The new Coalition Government has inherited this large and complex reality and discussion on multiculturalism, and has on the whole, despite the rhetoric and various knee-jerk initiatives, continued in the footsteps of the previous Government – as the only option available. This is evidenced in a public exchange on this subject last year between the current Prime Minister and Deputy Prime Minister. In a speech at a security conference in February 2011 the Prime Minister stated: "…we have allowed the weakening of our collective identity. Under the doctrine of state multiculturalism, we have encouraged different cultures to live separate lives, apart from each other and apart from the mainstream. We've failed to provide a vision of society to which they feel they want to belong. We've even tolerated these segregated communities behaving in ways that run completely counter to our values." Three weeks later, his Deputy responded as follows: "For me, multiculturalism has to be seen as a process by which people respect and communicate with each other, rather than build walls between each other. Welcoming diversity but resisting division: that's the kind of multiculturalism of an open, confident society. And the cultures in a multicultural society are not just ethnic or religious. Many of the cultural issues of the day cut right across these boundaries: gay rights; the role of women; identities across national borders; differing attitudes to marriage; the list goes on. Cultural disagreements are much more complex than much of the debate implies. If you will forgive the phrase, they are not quite so black and white." Both men spoke about 'muscular liberalism' – but the first as an attack against the narrow conception of multiculturalism whilst the latter as a home for the broader conception of multiculturalism.

There is, however, perhaps one difference between the previous Labour government and the current Conservative-Liberal Coalition government. Whilst the previous government made the distinction between the two conceptions of multiculturalism and publicly distanced itself from the second whilst still promoting the first, it did not prevent the constituencies of the second from benefitting from the fruits of the first. Thus, for example, even in its dying days, despite the difficulties involved, the previous Government included religion and belief (sought in particular by British Muslims) in the public sector equality duty in the Equality Act 2010. The new Coalition Government, however, over four revisions witnessed by this author, systematically reduced the mention of race and practically obliterated the mention of religion and belief in its Equality Strategy published last year. And herein lies the main point we want to make in this chapter. The separation and demonization of the narrower version of multiculturalism, and depriving its constituencies of the rights and liberties enjoyed by other citizens under the broader conception, is an unfortunate development not just for the constituencies of the narrower version but also for all the beneficiaries of the larger conception. Two weeks before the Prime Minister's speech mentioned above, the Chair of his Party, Baroness Sayeeda Warsi, in discussing how Islamophobia had crossed the threshold of middle class respectability and passed the dinner-table-test in the UK, stated: "Ultimately, Islamophobia challenges our basic British identity. One of the most important aspects of our identity is our belief in equality before the law. But deep, entrenched anti-Muslim bigotry challenges that tradition … because it implies that one section of society is less deserving of our protection than the rest." That one section of society, however, could very quickly become other stigmatised sections of society, and before long they could be the cause of not just narrowing and poorly resourcing the application of the Human Rights Act 1998 and the Equality Acts 2006 & 201010, but repealing them altogether – as desired by the leading partner in the Coalition Government. And this could be the beginning of the undoing of the larger conception of multiculturalism so painfully won by so many oppressed groups.

Conclusion

We have discussed in this paper how UK multiculturalism emerged out of various driving forces in the post war context and the efforts of various identity based movements. We have also discussed how a narrower conception of multiculturalism developed in the UK and the attacks against this conception. Our final point in this paper is simply that UK multiculturalism is strong and now woven into the British fabric and narrative by groups that are no longer in the margins of British society as they used to be – for example, women and gay people. There remains the danger, however, of disowning the label and applying it to the sins of minorities within pariah groups. This not only moves old injustices and oppressions onto new groups, but given the circumstances can come back to bite the old groups again – as we have seen in other parts of Europe, e.g., Denmark. The way forward is for the new groups, caught under the narrower conception of multiculturalism, to forge strong alliances with the older groups and to return multiculturalism to its broader conception to be applied to the benefit of all UK citizens.

Bibliography

Bassi, Camila Multiculturalism, racism and class in Britain today (2007)

Biddiss, Michael D. Father of Racist Ideology: Social and Political Thought of Count Gobineau M W Books (1970)

Choudhury, Tufyal *Evolving Models of Multiculturalism in the United Kingdom* in *Interculturalism: Europe and its Muslims in search of sound societal models (Ed. Michael Emerson)* Foreign and Security Policy/CEPS Paperbacks (2011)

Farrar, Max *Violent urban protest – identities, ethics and Islamism* in *Post-traditional ethnicities – Identities and values in a changing world (Ed.* Gargi Bhattacharyya) Ashgate (2009)

Gutmann, Amy *Identity in Democracy* Princeton University Press (2003)

Hegel, Georg W. F. Elements of the Philosophy of Right Cambridge University Press (1991).

Heyes, Cressida J. Line Drawings: Defining Women through Feminist Practice Cornell University Press (2000)

Ishay, Micheline R. The history of human rights: from ancient times to the globalization era University of California Press (2008)

Kinsey, Alfred *Sexual Behavior in the Human Male* was published in 1948 and *Sexual Behavior in the Human Female* in 1953

Kipling, Rudyard The White Man's Burden in McClure's Magazine 12 (Feb. 1899)

Kymlicka, Will Multicultural Citizenship: A Liberal Theory of Minority Rights Oxford University Press (1995)

Mill, John S. On Liberty eBooks@Adelaide (2009)

Modood, Tariq Multiculturalism Polity Press (2007)

Paine, Thomas The Rights of Man eBooks@Adelaide (2009)

Paxman, Jeremy The English: A Portrait of a People Penguin (2007)

Phillips, Anne Multiculturalism Without Culture Princeton University Press (2007)

Rawls, John A Theory of Justice Harvard University Press (1971)

Scarman, Leslie The Brixton Disorders: 10-12 April 1981 HMSO (1981)

Schopenhauer, Arthur Parerga and Paralipomena Clarendon Press (2000) Vol. II, Section 92.

Song, Sarah Justice, Gender and the Politics of Multiculturalism Cambridge University Press (2007)

Sumption, Madeleine and Somerville, Will *The UK's new Europeans: Progress and challenges five years after Accession* Equality & Human Rights Commission/ Migration Policy Institute (2010)

Swann, Michael Education for All HMSO (1985)

Taylor, Charles Sources of the Self: The Making of the Modern Identity Harvard University Press (1989)

Taylor, Charles "The Politics of Recognition" in *Multiculturalism: Examining the Politics of Recognition (Ed. Gutmann, Amy)* Princeton University Press (1994)

Young, Iris M. *Justice and the Politics of Difference* Princeton University Press (1990)

Part 2
INTERCULTURALISM VIS-À-VIS MULTICULTURALISM: STRENGTHS AND WEAKNESSES

Isms and Schisms: The Benefits and Practical Implications of Interculturalism in the UK

Asif Afridi [60]

Introduction

This chapter is based on a literature review and primary research conducted with twenty-two 'intercultural' projects shortlisted or awarded as part of the Baring Foundation's three-year awards programme, "Awards for Bridging Cultures" (www.bridgingcultures.org.uk). The paper summarises learning from a twelve-month project (currently ongoing) to research the Baring Foundation-funded projects and to promote intercultural thinking and practice in the UK. It also draws on the experience of brap (an equality and human rights charity) in preparing to develop a network for 'intercultural practitioners' which will be launched later in 2012.

Advocates of interculturalism believe it offers a progressive alternative and helps to address a number of 'problems' associated with previous approaches to social relations (e.g. that it allows for a more dynamic and less 'fixed' interpretation of

---

60 Asif Afridi is a published researcher with practical national and international human rights experience of promoting equality and human rights. He is Deputy CEO at brap, a national equality and human rights advisory organisation based in Birmingham. brap adopt an inclusive and rights based approach to equality, drawing on their twelve years of practical experience addressing inequality and promoting social justice in Birmingham. Since 2010 Mr Afridi has been co-chair of English Regions Equality and Human Rights Network (EREN) – a national network of regional equality charities and networks from across England In 2010 he was a member of advisory group on plans to implement the 'equality measurement framework' and 'human rights measurement framework' in the UK (CASE department at LSE). He continues to work on a national research project to extract learning from the 'Awards for Bridging Cultures'. He has also been part of a national research project to identify practical barriers/ successes in implementation of a human rights approach to equality in provision of cancer services (funded by Macmillan Cancer Care).

'culture', encourages a more sophisticated level of dialogue between groups, enables different groups to identify 'commonality' as well as 'difference' and focuses on shared humanity).

This chapter considers whether the potential benefits of interculturalism outweigh its disadvantages, or whether it is just another 'ism' the UK could do without. It argues that there are a number of significant challenges to 'multicultural' thinking and practice in a UK context and that new developments (demographic change, political change, economic change) are amplifying calls for an 'alternative' vision of social relations in the UK and explores whether interculturalism can yet be said to offer such an alternative vision.

Background

The history of race relations in Britain is a history of 'isms' (Afridi 2009). In the 1950s a policy of 'assimilationism' envisaged immigrants being 'assimilated' as swiftly as possible into the 'host' community. Some critics of the assimilationist view considered that it regarded immigrants as 'trainee whites' whose role was to become as close to white citizens as possible: foreign cultures would be transformed but England would remain 'imperiously impervious' (Alibhai-Brown 2001 pp. 164 and 226).

In the 1960s 'integrationism' recognised that some concessions to 'difference' might be required, such as targeted interventions which would help remove some of the structural barriers immigrants and ethnic minority people faced in achieving economic inclusion (Bourne 2001).

From the late 1960s onwards 'multiculturalism' emerged as a political term and policy in the UK, partly in response to an anti-immigrant discourse. This policy placed greater emphasis on anti-racism and respect for Britain's diverse cultural groups (Sivanandan 1976).

In recent years, however – particularly following the 2001 World Trade Centre attacks and the 2005 London tube and bus bombings and amidst growing concerns about Islamic extremism and radicalisation – there has been much heated debate about whether 'multiculturalism' has run its course in the UK. In 2005, for example, Trevor Phillips, chair of the then-Council for Racial Equality, said that multiculturalist policies were leading us 'sleepwalking into segregation' (Phillips 2005). And in early 2011, in his first major speech on race relations, the British Prime Minister David Cameron said, 'We have even tolerated segregated communities behaving in ways that run counter to our values' (Cameron 2011).

The UK Government has also signalled that it is keen to move away from previous approaches to equality that have focused on or encouraged 'identity politics'. Its most recent Equality Strategy states:

> This strategy sets out a new approach to equalities, moving away from the identity politics of the past and to an approach recognising people's individuality... No one should be held back because of who they are or their background. But, equally, no one should be defined simply by these characteristics. We want a society where people are recognised for who they are and what they achieve, not where they are from. (HMG 2010, p.6)

While in theory this affords policy-makers and academics new opportunities to reinvestigate and question orthodox approaches to equality and community relations, in practice efforts to reinvigorate these areas of public policy remain largely those associated with multiculturalism or successor policies such as community cohesion.

The remainder of this paper outlines what an approach to community relations should look like in modern Britain. It focuses on 'interculturalism', one of the alternative approaches put forward to improve community relations in the UK. Is interculturalism another 'ism' that the UK could do without, or do its benefits outweigh its disadvantages? Given the persistent nature of race inequality in the UK, the legacy of international and domestic terrorism and religious fundamentalism, and the pressure public sector cuts are exerting on the most vulnerable and excluded groups, understanding the benefit of alternative approaches to community relations is as pressing now as it has ever been.

About the Research and a Definition of Interculturalism

The arguments in this paper are based on empirical research undertaken in 2011 by brap and supported by the Baring Foundation. The research involved a review of relevant literature, interviews with prominent intercultural thinkers and interviews with practitioners involved in twenty-two intercultural projects awarded as part of the Baring Foundation's 'Awards for Bridging Cultures' programme.

Although the research included an international literature review, the interculturalism debate feels already too academic in its emphasis and language. For this reason, the focus of this paper is on the practical lessons of the ABC projects researched rather than a further summary of the academic and policy literature. Interested readers will find that Malcolm James's two earlier papers for the Baring Foundation (2008 and 2009) do an extremely good job of tracing the roots of some of the key concepts of interculturalism and include extensive bibliographies — especially the earlier paper.

Interculturalism is not a new concept. Malcolm James traces the roots of the concept to US anthropological thinkers in the 1950s and 1960s and to Dutch, French and Canadian responses in the 1980s and 1990s to increasing diversity (James 2008, pp.2-3). There are a number of differing definitions of interculturalism and intercultural dialogue. For reasons of consistency, the same working definition of interculturalism is used in this paper as was used when examining the Baring Foundation-funded projects (and which formed the Baring Foundation's primary criterion for judging applications):

> Interculturality is a dynamic process whereby people from different cultures interact to learn about and question their own and each other's cultures. Over time this may lead to cultural change. It recognises the inequalities at work in society and the need to overcome these. It is a process which requires mutual respect and acknowledges human rights. (Baring Foundation 2009)

This paper draws upon that prior research, literature review and wider reflection to examine the following issues:

- What does an intercultural approach look like in practice?
- What are the key ideas and principles underlying an intercultural approach to community relations?
- To what extent does interculturalism offer a viable alternative approach to improving community relations in modern Britain?

Interculturalism: Key Ideas, Principles

Interculturalism is an approach to community relations that involves people from different cultures interacting and engaging in dialogue in order to learn about and question their own and each other's cultures. Five of its key principles are summarised below, along with an indication of where interculturalism and intercultural dialogue differ from other approaches to community relations in the UK such as multiculturalism, or community cohesion.

1. The Importance of Open and Critical Dialogue

Multicultural approaches to dialogue generally involve either 'celebrating' difference, or raising awareness of cultures that are not being tolerated or respected equally (Kundnani 2002). Because of this focus on celebrating and tolerating other people's cultures, approaches to multicultural dialogue generally discourage discussion that questions an individual's or group's cultural boundaries, attitudes, or practices. This can lead, albeit unintentionally, to the perpetuating and reinforcement of cultural boundaries and relationships of power that some may wish to question or challenge in order to effect personal or social change (Afridi 2007).

Intercultural dialogue on the other hand recognises that open and honest discussion of culture is valuable and that the way culture is discussed is extremely important because it has the potential to shape and alter social relations. Rather than using 'fixed' notions such as geography or ethnicity, Intercultural dialogue emphasises more dynamic, fluid concepts such as history, lived experience, change and context (James 2009, p.4), using these to promote the freedom of people to sometimes challenge their own (and others') cultural views and practices. This is seen as important because it recognises that that people cannot act under the auspices of 'culture' in an unconditional way. It recognises that our cultural practices should be contingent on the ability of all to exercise their rights and freedoms in society. Though it should be noted that this is not a value stance that is universally shared by all thinkers in this field.

2. Dialogue Can Help to Identify Different and Shared Values

Some advocates of intercultural dialogue see it as particularly suited to discussing and critiquing cultural 'taboos' – for example, about gender roles or sexuality (Kandel 2005). Interculturalism acknowledges that some forms of conflict can be used constructively to help identify both differences and similarities in values and outlooks between different people or groups. By contrast, current approaches to community cohesion or integrationism (of the type now being actively being discussed by the UK Government, for example) seek to reduce or 'de-fuse' conflict and dialogue by promoting a preconceived notion of shared 'British values' that all can sign-up to and which constitute a benchmark for social acceptance. In early 2011, however, David Cameron went even further than this, calling for 'a lot less of the passive tolerance of recent years and a much more active, muscular liberalism' in defence of British values (Cameron 2011).

3. A Departure from 'Community Representation'

Intercultural dialogue rejects the idea that individuals can be completely 'representative' of a particular cultural community. This approach helps to avoid participants conforming to a particular role or acting within particular cultural boundaries that have been ascribed to them. Multicultural approaches have generally encouraged the opposite, emphasising the importance of cultural representation in decision-making and public policy development to ensure people's cultures are protected, tolerated and respected.

4. Assesses the Impact of 'Culture' on People's Ability to Exercise Their Freedoms

The multicultural model assumes that different cultures should be celebrated but that no single culture should dominate another. Scheffer (2011) says that multiculturalism 'attributes no explicatory value to culture' and that because of this the role culture might play (as one factor amongst many) in determining social or personal outcomes cannot be understood. So, even though there may be 'cultural' reasons for poor educational outcomes in young women from a particular culture (because their parents have cultural views that they shouldn't be educated), in a multicultural model discussing 'culture' as the cause is frowned upon. Conversely, the intercultural approach suggests that in some instances culture *can* be used to explain particular social outcomes. Used in this way, intercultural dialogue can help create the conditions in which culture can be discussed – sometimes in a critical way – and can help identify new approaches to improving people's access to or enjoyment of particular freedoms.

5. Creating the Conditions for Collective Social Action

Critics of the multicultural approach often focus on the 'divisive' nature of the 'identity politics' it is now seen as having promoted (Malik 2002, Sen 2006). Using cultural or ethnic identity as a 'lever' is an established approach to political lobbying in a multicultural model. Yet this can cause division within and between cultural groups that are actively 'competing' for influence or for resources. The intercultural approach, it is suggested, discourages people from 'invoking' their 'cultural identity' as a something that should be tolerated and protected whatever the cost. It encourages people to recognise that culture is an integral part of our *shared* humanity and can and should be discussed as part of broader considerations about how we live together.

Intercultural dialogue, it is said, can also help to reduce the divisions between people as cultural boundaries are discussed and challenged, helping people recognise that they may have more in common than they previously thought. Interculturalism is also seen as helping to unlock new forms of social solidarity – campaigns for social change that are shared by people from widely differing cultural backgrounds who nonetheless face a similar threat, or have similar goals, such as action against climate change, for instance, or economic globalisation.

Why Interculturalism?

Advocates of interculturalism believe that some of its aspects make it particularly relevant and useable as an approach to improving community relations in 21st century Britain. While far from exhaustive, some of these are explored below.

Responding to 'Super-Diversity'

Critiques of multiculturalism have consistently identified the model's inability to cope with and respond to 'super-diversity' (Vertovec 2006). Multicultural models of community engagement and dialogue have tended to rely on the appointment of 'representatives' – often community leaders and typically generally older, heterosexual and male – who it is assumed can speak on behalf of their entire cultural or ethnic group.

While aspects of this approach may have been viable when the number of different ethnic groups in a city could be counted on one hand and were arguably more distinct and homogenous, this is much less the case in areas of the UK that are 'super-diverse' with literally hundreds of 'communities' and moreover a growing number of 'mixed' communities. It is also much less the case when the voices of the historically dispossessed – women, young people, gays and lesbians, people with disabilities – are increasingly struggling to be recognised (Kofman 1998 Vertovec 2010).

In moving attention away from 'representation' as a primary aim, interculturalism can be seen to encourage a wider array of voices and a more inclusive conception of dialogue. And by doing this, interculturalism is arguably better equipped to recognise 'diversity within diversity'. It may also be less prone to what Amartya Sen has called 'cultural conservatism', by which he means the tendency of orthodox 'representative' models of multiculturalism to emphasise those practices or attitudes that conform most closely to society's preconceptions of whatever cultural heritage is in question. 'If multiculturalism is defended in the name of cultural freedom, then it can hardly be seen as demanding unwavering and unqualified support for staying steadfastly within one's inherited cultural tradition,' Sen has written (Sen 2006).

Responding to Pressure on Public Resources

In the past, significant public resources were invested in representative structures designed to assert the rights of minority ethnic groups in UK society (e.g. race equality councils and a range of associated local minority ethnic decision-making forums). This is no longer the case and many of these bodies and/or initiatives have closed or ceased operating. Similarly, a number of national and local government programmes intended to improve outcomes for minority ethnic and other disadvantaged groups – for example, the national Aim Higher education programme intended to raise achievement amongst those from disadvantaged backgrounds – have also been terminated.

But ideological shifts as much as austerity are also redrawing the equalities landscape. More recently, for example, government policy and equalities legislation has focused on broader 'pan-equality' approaches that emphasise the need to reduce inequality in a range of areas (gender, disability, race, sexual orientation, gender reassignment, age, religion or belief, pregnancy and maternity). The government has also sought to introduce reductions to 'single identity' funding that only benefits particular ethnic or cultural groups.

The present economic and public spending environment is an inhospitable one for multicultural models of community relations, which typically have always required additional discretionary spend, rarely less. Yet despite this, variations of a multicultural model based on identity politics still dominate some areas of policy at a local level. It not uncommon, for example, to find a local authority that feels it has met its race equality obligations by having an 'African', 'Chinese', 'African Caribbean', 'Indian', 'Pakistani' and an 'Irish' representative on its community forum.

In other words, there is a significant gap between the aspirations of some aspects of government policy and its implementation on the ground. While there is an interest in moving beyond 'identity politics' and in making better decisions about how to use limited resources more effectively policy-makers lack a framework within which alternative approaches can be tested. Arguably, an intercultural approach could go some way towards filling this gap, mainly by creating the conditions in which people can actively explore whether their 'claim' to public resources or to a particular public policy decision based on their 'cultural rights' is the most important one (when balanced against the rights of others).

By balancing people's 'right to culture' against the needs of the wider cultural or ethnic group – or indeed against the wider social good – interculturalism also has the potential to help people negotiate issues of conflicting rights or entitlements. Intercultural dialogue has already played a part in the UK in considering issues such as female genital mutilation and forced marriages. It should of course be recognised though that there has been widespread critique of these practices from a range of communities within a multicultural model too.

Interculturalism: Further Development, Greater Currency

And yet, despite some of the potential advantages of interculturalism outlined above, the research identified a number of significant challenges that will need to be overcome if intercultural thinking and practice is to offer a genuinely viable model of community relations in the future in the UK. These are summarised below.

Interculturalism in Practice

Of the Awards for Bridging Cultures projects considered, a significant proportion did not view the work they were undertaking as explicitly 'intercultural'. These drew heavily on existing paradigms of social relations – most notably community cohesion and multiculturalism. Although strong projects in their own right this suggests that more work is needed to establish a clear framework of intercultural techniques, methods and practice that can guide projects and activities in the future.

A number of activities that could be said to represent an 'intercultural' approach did emerge, however. It was also significant that some of the projects recognised that it was often necessary to combine two or more of these activities in order to achieve successful intercultural dialogue. The most important of these activities included:

- Questioning and challenging cultural boundaries: activities that help participants understand that concepts such as race, culture, ethnicity and religion are 'static', that culture is dynamic, and that stereotypes about particular groups are socially constructed and often ill-informed.
- Helping people respond to 'diversity': activities to build people's confidence and knowledge regarding their own culture and identity in order to help them discuss their own and others' cultures; activities to prevent and manage conflict within and between cultural/ethnic groups through dialogue.
- Creating intercultural dialogue 'spaces': activities to develop 'neutral' spaces where intercultural dialogue is more likely to take place (e.g. by purposefully inviting people from different cultures to undertake intercultural dialogue, or by developing spaces for interaction where intercultural dialogue might happen naturally).

These activities were more likely to succeed when supported by particular techniques. Successful, reinforcing techniques included:

- Strong and appropriately skilled facilitators to help people engage in dialogue on their own terms.
- Using a range of dialogue methods.
- Recognising the harmful effects of stereotypes.
- Encouraging artistic and creative methods of self-expression to help discuss emotive and personal issues; and
- Activities to build the trust of participants in the dialogue process and in each other.

Evaluating the Impact of Interculturalism Compared to Other Approaches to Community Relations

Proponents of intercultural dialogue often emphasise the inherent value of providing people with the freedom to re-imagine their own culture and to negotiate their relationship with that culture. Yet it is hard to find any empirical examples of where that type of 'cultural freedom' has led to direct improvements in the quality of life of those involved. More research is required to understand exactly how intercultural dialogue can enable people to enjoy cultural freedom and whether this enables them to exercise other previously unachievable freedoms. For example, can intercultural dialogue help women renegotiate their role in the family, the community and wider society? Can intercultural approaches promote the establishment and acceptance of new social norms and outcomes for women – better education, for example, or a stronger political voice, or employment opportunities? What is the relationship of interculturalism to personal autonomy and self-determination?

These are complex questions and comparative research to examine the *impact* of intercultural approaches *over and above* other approaches is in its infancy.

Demonstrating the Inclusive Nature of Interculturalism

A common criticism of multiculturalism and community cohesion has been their tendency to focus primarily on issues of race and faith. While community cohesion policy does emphasise encouraging people from different backgrounds to get along with each other, the 'background' referred to is mostly commonly defined by ethnicity or faith. Not only has this limited the appeal of these approaches, it has also had other more negative consequences. Far right groups, for example, have been swift to make political capital from this, and have used the evident dissatisfaction and dispossession of some poor white British working class communities to promote their own racist politics.

Interculturalism has the potential to go beyond this by adopting a more inclusive approach to community relations. The approach does focus heavily on 'culture' and ethnicity and religion are of course likely to be discussed as part of this, but inherent in interculturalism is a consideration of other issues that influence people's perceptions of culture and their place in society, such as sex, age, class, sexual orientation. In this regard, interculturalism has the potential to help white British people too to reflect upon their culture and how this interacts with other people's cultures. Intercultural dialogue could – and arguably should – involve both ethnic minority and majority people in open and honest discussions about how their cultural views and practices can perpetuate inequality and disadvantage. And yet this was relatively rare in the projects examined through this research and is rare too in the wider literature.

Responding to the 'Britishness' Debate

Successive UK Governments including the current administration have attempted to create a shared view of 'Britishness' and British values. This has often been done in an attempt to improve community relations or latterly in the name of community cohesion (McGhee 2003). These attempts have failed, partly because it has been hard to achieve consensus, but also because the idea of 'Britishness' as promulgated from Whitehall has appeared exclusive and largely irrelevant to large swathes of the population.

Intercultural dialogue has the potential to help create the conditions where people can discuss what some of those shared social norms, values and conventions should be in a way that is more engaging for a wider range of people. However, the research identified few practical examples of activities that would help participants consider which cultural practices are 'appropriate' in society or the shared social norms and values they would wish to live by. While a number of academics have focused on understanding how consensus is reached regarding social norms (Habermas 1984) there is merit in further exploring this in the context of how intercultural dialogue can help facilitate constructive debate regarding culture and identity and the social conflict and division these can cause.

Conclusions

1. Interculturalism has a number of key attributes that make it well suited to addressing not only some of the key challenges that modern Britain faces, but also some of the shortcomings of earlier multicultural and community cohesion approaches. Yet despite policy-makers' rhetoric, models for strengthening (or 'managing') community relations remain largely based on multiculturalism and community cohesion. The terms of reference of these policies remain the default position. Interculturalism, by contrast, has no widespread currency in political or policy circles and there is a long way yet to go before it does.

2. But perhaps more important than this, interculturalism has little popular understanding either. If models based on interculturalism and techniques that promote intercultural dialogue are to flourish then both a *political* understanding of the concept *and* a popular, grassroots understanding of its application are needed.

3. While civil society organisations are ideally placed to pioneer, promote and use interculturalism not just in their daily work but also in specialist projects, a framework to explain, support and identify good practice, successful techniques and useable methods is lacking. Civil society organisations could also use interculturalism to *interrogate* and change their own practices but currently there is little indication that this is happening. Even some of the Awards for Bridging Cultures (ABC) projects did not see that intercultural principles could help them question and change some of the 'fixed categories' they were employing in their conceptions of culture (James 2009, p.8).

4. There would then be merit in pursuing a number of areas of research and development in order to improve the 'currency' of interculturalism both in policy-making circles and amongst civil society and grassroots organisations. Perhaps the first step to achieving this would be a 'stock-take' of what we want from community relations policy in the future. There was rarely much clarity on the expected outcomes of previous approaches to community relations. Multiculturalism, for example, was seen as a good idea (and if not a good idea then at least an expedient one), but it was never really clear how we would judge whether it had worked or not.

5. There is some evidence to suggest (James 2009, p.10) that some of the ABCs did not see their work as explicitly intercultural. That is to say, they did not see themselves as engaging in activities which commenced from a new or different conceptual framework than that which previously motivated their views of inter-community engagement or community relations and this had an impact on the structuring of the projects or the activities (James 2009, p.10). For example, most projects were 'bounded' by geography or existing client groups/audiences and the ABC activity could thus be seen as an extension or continuation of existing work or priorities.

In the economic and funding climate that has prevailed for civil society organisations for several years now – but which is now reaching perfect storm proportions – it is perhaps not surprising that small voluntary organisations look first and foremost at how existing proven activities can be protected and extended. But the ABC programme offered a key opportunity to bring a truly global dimension to interculturalism (rather than a simply a neighbourhood, town or city emphasis). The of use virtual, mobile and social media technology could have helped do this and would also have offered a means of exploring new solidarities and international community relations, but was barely explored.

6. To date, the intercultural debate has been a primarily academic one. The Baring Foundation's ABC programme is to be applauded in its efforts to take this debate to the grassroots. It has illuminated an urgent need for popular 'tools', resources and materials that will help begin the process of giving interculturalism real and sustainable meaning amongst civil society organisations, community groups, practitioners and activists. It is from this perspective that brap will be launching a practitioner-based interculturalism network later this year.

Bibliography

Afridi, Asif (2007) *Community Cohesion & Deprivation: Report for the Commission on Integration and Cohesion*, London: HMSO

Afridi, Asif and Warmington, Joy (2009) *The Pied Piper: The BME third sector and UK race relations policy*, Birmingham: brap

Alibhai-Brown, Yasmin (2001) *Imagining the New Britain*, New York: Routledge

Baring Foundation (2009): Website information for applicants to the Awards for Bridging Cultures programme http://www.bridgingcultures.org.uk/Judging/CriteriaForJudging#criterion1

Bourne, Jenny (2001) 'The *Life and Times of Institutional* Racism in *Race and Class*, 43,2, pp.7-22

Cameron, D (2011) Speech delivered to Munich Security Conference 05/02/2011. http://www.number10.gov.uk/news/pms-speech-at-munich-security-conference/

Goldberg, David (Ed.) (1994) *Multiculturalism: A Critical Reader*, London: Blackwell

Habermas, Jurgen (1984) *The Theory of Communicative Action, Vol. 1: Reason and the Rationalization of Society*, Boston: Beacon Press

Habermas, Jurgen (1998) *Between Facts and Norms*, Boston: MIT Press

Hm Government (December 2010) *The Equality Strategy: Building a Fairer Britain*, London: HMSO

James, Malcolm (2008) *Interculturalism: Theory and policy*, London: Baring Foundation

James, Malcolm (2009): *Interculturalism: social policy and grassroots work*, London: Baring Foundation

Kandel, Johannes (2005): 'Dialog mit Muslimen – ein kritischer Zwischenruf' in Zehetmair, H *(ed.): Der Islam: Im Spannungsfeld von Konflikt und Dialog*, VS Verlag für Sozialwissenschaften, Weisbaden, pp. 321-333

Kofman, Eleanor (1998) 'Whose city? Gender, class, and immigrants in globalizing European cities' in *Cities of Difference*, R. Fincher and J.M. Jacobs (eds), New York: The Guilford Press, pp. 279-300

Kundnani, Arun (2002) '*The Death of Multiculturalism*' in *Race & Class*, 43,4, pp. 67- 72

Malik, Kenan (2002) 'Against Multiculturalism' in *New Humanist*, Summer 2002

Mcghee, Derek (2003) 'Moving to 'our' common ground: a critical examination of community cohesion discourse in twenty-first century Britain' in *Sociological Review*, 51,3, pp. 376-404

Phillips, Trevor (2005) *After 7/7: Sleepwalking into segregation*, speech delivered on 22/09/2005 at Manchester Council for Community Relations. http://www.humanities.manchester.ac.uk/socialchange/research/social-change/summer-workshops/documents/sleepwalking.pdf

Scheffer, Paul (2011) *Immigrant Nations*, Cambridge: Polity Press

Sen, Amartya (2006) 'The uses and abuses of multiculturalism – Chili and liberty' in *The New Republic*, issue 27/02/06. http://www.pierretristam.com/Bobst/library/wf-58.htm

Sen, Amartya (2006) *Identify and Violence*, London: Penguin

Sivanandan, Ambalavaner (1976) 'Race, class and the state: the black experience in Britain' in *Race and Class*, 17,4, pp. 347-368

Solomos, John, Back, Les, *Racism and Society*, London: Macmillan

Vertovec, Steven (2006) *The Emergence of Super-Diversity in Britain,* Centre on Migration, Policy and Society Working Papers, 25, Oxford: Oxford University

Vertovec, Steven (2007) 'Super-diversity and its implications' in *Ethnic and Racial Studies,* 30, 6, pp. 1024-1054

Vertovec, Steven (2010) 'Towards Post-Multiculturalism' in *International Social Science Journal,* 61, 199, pp.83-95

'Interculturalism' or 'Critical Multiculturalism': Which Discourse Works Best?

Max Farrar [61]

Introduction

This chapter takes up an argument I advanced elsewhere (Farrar 2012) which traced the contested history of multiculturalist discourse in the UK, and argued for a modified position called 'critical multiculturalism'. This chapter abridges much of the material in the earlier work, and engages more directly with the argument that 'multiculturalism' should be replaced by 'interculturalism'. While I still advocate 'critical multiculturalism', this is a friendly debate; indeed some of the advocates of 'interculturalism' are friends of mine whose work I hold in high regard. There are some signs that interculturalist discourse is being adopted by important policy-oriented bodies in the UK and Europe, and if it becomes hegemonic I will not protest, particularly if my own critique of liberal multiculturalism is absorbed by the interculturalists. The nub of my argument is that multiculturalism should be defended against those UK intellectuals and politicians who, especially since 1989, have unfairly attacked it, and that the discourse should be strengthened by adding an emphasis on radical democracy, dialogue and equality.

Multiculturalism – a Brief History of a Contested Discourse

Multiculturalism's recent critics often imply that they are standing against the tide when they rail against its deficiencies. Multiculturalist discourse emerged in the UK in the mid 1960s with an important speech in 1966 to the National Committee for Commonwealth Immigrants by the Labour government's Home Secretary Roy

---

61 Prof Max Farrar, a cultural sociologist, is an Emeritus Professor at Leeds Metropolitan University, where until 2010 he was the Head of Community Partnerships and Volunteering and Professor for Community Engagement. An adviser to several boards and organisations on the issue of race, Professor Farrar has previously lectured in sociology and written research papers on the subject. He is the author of a book about Chapeltown in Leeds, The Struggle for 'Community' in a British Multi-Ethnic Inner-City Area (Edwin Mellen Press, 2002). He is also co-author of Teaching Race in the Social Sciences. He has worked in adult and community education, at a community Law Centre, for a 'race' think-tank and as a freelance writer and photographer. His life-long interest, both as a scholar and as an activist, is in the movements for social justice emanating from the multi-cultural inner cities of the UK. His current research focuses on the rise of Islamism.

Jenkins. Although it did not acquire its name until 1971, when Canada described itself a multicultural society, the multiculturalist ethos was subjected to its sharpest critique by Enoch Powell in 1968. Powell was another prominent British politician, Health Minister in an earlier Conservative government, and his infamous 'rivers of blood' speech attracted massive popular support. While multiculturalism did become the dominant position in public debate by the early 1990s, over the next thirty years its critics increasingly appeared to overwhelm its surprisingly silent defenders. The emergence of interculturalist discourse perhaps represents a tactical retreat by multiculturalists in the face of the onslaught, which culminated in 2011 with a full-scale attack on 'state multiculturalism' by the new Conservative Prime Minister David Cameron.

Roy Jenkins spoke at a time of steadily rising racial tension in the UK. There had been violent assaults in 1958 on 'West Indians' (as people of African and Caribbean heritage were called) in Notting Hill, London, and black people fought back over several nights. The remnants of Oswald Moseley's fascist movement, and the British Ku Klux Klan sought to inflame public opinion even further. In 1964 the Conservative candidate in a Birmingham by-election gained election to Parliament after using the unconscionable slogan 'If you want a nigger neighbour, vote Labour'. Roy Jenkins had observed the rise of the civil rights movement in the USA during the 1960s, led by the Ghandi-influenced Martin Luther King, with its more militant wings led by Malcolm X and the Black Panther Party. He envisioned a harmonious British society in terms which deserve close study. Setting out a position that came to be definitive for liberal-progressive opinion, Jenkins advocated the integration, rather than assimilation, of the 'New Commonwealth' (i.e. Caribbean, African and South Asian) populations who had begun to settle in the UK since the mid-1950s. Significantly, Jenkins defined integration as the nation's goal, where integration is understood as 'not a flattening process of assimilation but as equal opportunity accompanied by cultural diversity, in an atmosphere of mutual tolerance' (Jenkins 1967 p.267). He was very explicit about what he did not regard as the nation's goal: 'I do not think that we need in this country a "melting pot", which will turn everybody out in a common mould, as one of a series of carbon-copies of someone's misplaced vision of the stereotypical Englishman . . . [this] would deprive us of most of the positive advantages of immigration, which . . . I believe to be very great indeed' (Jenkins 1967 p.267). Whether these immigrants were the Normans, or Jewish refugees of the 1930s, 'we have been constantly stimulated and jolted out of our natural lethargy by a whole series of immigrations'. He pointed to the advances immigrant brought to British businesses, universities, cultural centres and cities, none of whom would remain attractive if they were to turn inwards and only serve their own 'racial group'. In a clear statement of the positive existential shock of immigration, Jenkins stated: 'To live apart, for a person, a city, a country, is to lead a life of declining intellectual stimulation'. Furthermore, there is 'no overall rational basis for resentment of the coloured immigrant population in our midst. Far from hindering our successful national development, they positively help it' (Jenkins 1967 p.269). Acknowledging that there are irrational causes of resentment, and perhaps under-playing the racism already visible in Britain, he also argued that 'we have as yet no established habit of hostility or bitterness on either side of the colour frontier' (p.272). His use of 'frontier' spoke to a rather less optimistic scenario. Nevertheless, this speech was a landmark.

Key features of multiculturalist discourse are expressed here by Jenkins: immigrants are a positive force in society; cultural difference is not to be 'flattened', but tolerated; equal opportunity (to provide for social and economic progress) is to be offered to new populations as a means towards their integration into the wider society; assimilation (i.e. the submerging of difference, by jettisoning the culture of origin) is rejected. In light of more recent debate, what seems to be the problem in Jenkins's approach for the critics of multiculturalism is his stance against assimilation, and his willingness to embrace the integrity of the cultures that migrants bring with them to the UK. It is precisely this which I believe needs to be defended. Against the argument that this has led to the segregation of cultures in the UK, I suggest that it has been the platform upon which our relatively tolerant society has been built over the past fifty years. By not 'flattening' the newcomers' cultures, the host culture (itself a product of centuries of immigration) has, in the main, learned to respect the best features of those cultures. The interculturalist argument gains strength, however, when it points out that there is much more to be done in building dialogue across cultures and in countering those tendencies which promote the view that one culture is superior to another.

There is much to be learned from the debate that ensued in the UK as multiculturalist thinking gained ascendancy. Firstly, there were significant developments within conservative thinking and practice on race relations. Perhaps most important was the decision by Ted Heath, leader of the Conservative Party, to eject Enoch Powell from his Shadow Cabinet. Heath took advice from his senior colleagues, including 'one-nation' conservatives such as RA Butler and Edward Boyle who had supported Roy Jenkins' anti-discrimination legislation and the community relations councils that were established in the late 1960s. By aligning the Conservative Party with multiculturalism, rather than British nationalism, Heath laid the basis for a report that surprised radicals and liberals in the mid 1980s. The Swann Report (1985) laid the foundations for multiculturalism in British schools. Its chair, Lord Swann, had been appointed by Conservative Prime Minister Margaret Thatcher in what was thought at the time to be a move against the liberal direction signalled in an earlier education report, chaired by an appointee of the previous Labour government,

Lord Rampton. Just before she became Prime Minister, Margaret Thatcher, an implacable foe of Ted Heath, spoke for the Powellite rump in her party when she said:

> People are really rather afraid that this country might be rather swamped by people with a different culture . . . We are a British nation with British characteristics. Every country can take some small minorities and in many ways they add to the richness and variety of this country. The moment the minority threatens to become a big one, people get frightened . . . We are not in politics to ignore people's worries: we are in politics to deal with them. (Thatcher 1978)

Multiculturalists were outraged. Perhaps overlooking the 'richness and variety' phrase, they read 'British characteristics' as 'white characteristics' and they saw 'swamped' as a direct reference to Powell's vicious prognosis of white Britain becoming brown Britain. Thatcher – who famously adopted the politician's mantra 'Never apologise, never explain' – rode calmly over the storm this statement provoked as she built nationalist right wing of her party with the invasion of the Falkland Islands (the Malvinas) in 198... But Swann's report was a direct rebuttal of this type of thinking. comprehensively rejected racism. It proposed that one of the key features of a new educational programme in schools would be what it called 'the appreciation of diversity'. Swann puts its ambitions rather cautiously, but these are clearly infused with multiculturalist assumptions: 'a variety of ethnic groups, with their own distinct lifestyle and value systems' will be living together. Furthermore:

> It is also possible that there will be some degree of cultural interchange . . . A multi-cultural curriculum [will exist when] it is accepted by all sections of society that to draw on a diversity of cultural sources, and to incorporate a world perspective, was proper and unremarkable. (Swann 1985 p. 324)

Swann's prediction came into effect rather more quickly than he seems to have expected. By the 1990s such a curriculum was commonplace, and while not all sections of society found it unremarkable to draw on diverse cultural sources, most young people did, as did significant proportions of the older generation. When, in 1995, Conservative Prime Minister John Major submitted to the United Nations a commitment that Britain wanted to 'enable' ethnic minorities to 'maintain their own cultures, traditions, language and values' (Runnymede Trust 1997 p.31) it seemed that multiculturalism was firmly embedded in the UK.

The second development took place within liberal and socialist opinion. In brief, Marxists attacked multiculturalists in schools during the 1970s and 1980s for their liberal assumption that infusing children with 'saris, samosas and steel bands' would make a real difference in society. For the left, the crucial issue was to change the structures in society that generated racism. All London Teachers Against Racism and Fascism argued that teachers must 'challenge inside and outside the school, the racism, sexism and class structures that divide us'. The debate was occasionally vitriolic, but the left's view seemed to have been accepted when both the liberal National Association of Multiracial Education (NAME) and the National Union of Teachers adopted an anti-racist analysis in the early 1980s (Troyna and Williams 1986 p. 67). In 1999 Lord Macpherson, reporting on the police's turpitude over the murder of Steven Lawrence, pronounced that 'institutional racism' existed within the Metropolitan Police. As this concept had been central to both liberal and left discourse on race over the previous thirty years, it seemed as though the rapprochement signalled by NAME's agreement with the left over racism had born fruit in society as a whole.

Although multiculturalism became the common currency of Conservative and Labour governments, backed up by successive laws against racial discrimination and the (somewhat indolent) Commission for Racial Equality, its opponents had not disappeared. But their focus shifted from race to culture. Given their historic role as champions of multiculturalism it might be surprising to some that liberals were among the most strident critics of those Muslims who demonstrated against the publication of Salman Rushdie's *Satanic Verses* in 1988. The feminist novelist Fay Weldon wrote that the Qur'an is 'food for no thought . . . It is not a poem on which society can be safely or sensibly based . . . It gives weapons and strength to the thought police' (Weldon 1989 pp. 6-7). But the moral panic around Islam and British Muslims became fully apparent in the aftermath of the violent urban protest by Muslims living in four northern British towns in the early summer of 2001 and the attacks by Al Qaeda on New York and Washington in September of that year. The Cantle Report (2001) on the so-called 'riots' in three of these towns, had the negative effect of portraying British Muslims as leading 'parallel lives' to those of their white counterparts, and suggested that they actively engaged in 'self-segregation'. The door was now wide open for a full-scale assault on multiculturalism. From the centre left, the writer Neil Ascherson (2004) described multiculturalism as 'literally conservative' because it reinforced ethnic identities. Also from the left, Kenan Malik (2009) denounced multiculturalism for legitimating the sedimentation of Islamic identities ever since the Rushdie affair. In the spirit of New Labour, Trevor Phillips, head of the Commission for Racial Equality, interviewed by the *Times* newspaper in 2004 said of multiculturalism: 'The word is not useful any more'. Asked if it should be 'killed off', he replied: 'Yes, let's do that'. Completely departing from all that has been said in the past four decades about the virtues of multiculturalism as a platform for integration, but in line with the Cantle report, Phillips continued: 'Multiculturalism suggests separateness' (cited in Pitcher 2009 p. 164). If the centre left was rejecting multiculturalism, it is no surprise that the right was even more hostile. *Daily Mail* columnist Melanie Phillips (2006) blamed multiculturalism for the emergence of supporters of Al-Qaeda in the UK. By 2011, Conservative Prime Minister David Cameron appeared to abandon multiculturalism altogether when he argued that:

> Under the doctrine of state multiculturalism, we have encouraged different cultures to live separate lives, apart from each other and apart from the mainstream. We've failed to provide a vision of society to which they feel they want to belong. We've even tolerated these segregated communities behaving in ways that run completely counter to our values . . . instead of encouraging people to live apart, we need a clear sense of shared national identity that is open to everyone. (Cameron 2011)

Although Cameron was clearly aligning himself with multiculturalism's critics, it is important to note his more emollient statements. He completely rejected the hard right view that all Muslims were dangerous; he stressed that Western values and Islam can be 'entirely compatible'; he agreed that the underlying issues of poverty and British foreign policy are important and that racism is to be condemned; he acknowledged the multiplicity of identity positions, 'so people feel free to say, 'Yes, I am a Muslim, I am a Hindu, I am Christian, but I am also a Londonder or a Berliner too' (Cameron 2011). Thus Cameron appears to be jumping on a bandwagon moving away from multiculturalism – a wagon which previously had Labour Party leaders such as Tony Blair and Gordon Brown at the reins – while simultaneously riding the multiculturalist horse. Multiculturalist discourse thus remains at the heart of public discussion in the UK. As Ben Pitcher pointed out in his review of Labour's record on this issue:

> Despite a recent appetite for obituary writing, pronouncements of the death of multiculturalism are premature . . . what is being subjected to criticism is the rhetorical status of the term 'multiculturalism' *within that discourse* . . . The purpose of this rejection [of 'multiculturalism'] is to symbolise and benefit from popular anxiety about 'separateness', not to indicate a substantial change in policy and practice. (Pitcher 2009 p. 165, italics as in original)

Interculturalism as a Response to Multiculturalism

So far as I can see, the idea of interculturalism appeared in the early 2000s. Ireland's National Consultative Committee of on Racism and Interculturalism provided this definition in 2002:

> Interculturalism suggests the acceptance not only of principles of equality of rights, values and abilities, but also the development of policies to promote interaction, collaboration and exchange with people of different cultures, ethnicity or religion living in the same territory. Furthermore,

interculturalism is an approach that sees difference as something positive that can enrich a society and recognizes racism as an issue that needs to be tackled to create a more inclusive society. The concept of interculturalism has replaced earlier concepts of assimilation and multiculturalism. (Cited in Titley 2012)

The statement that it has 'replaced' multiculturalism was perhaps premature, at least for the UK, but others have discussed the term on the assumption that multiculturalism has failed. Leonie Sandercock argued for a 're-theorisation' of multiculturalism, applying Stuart Hall's sociology of the multiple identifications adopted in multicultural Britain. Writing the key-note chapter for the *Intercultural City Reader* she offered interculturalism as the replacement for multiculturalism (Sandercock 2004). Malcolm James (for the Baring Foundation) advocated interculturalism as a deliberate 'move away from models for post-colonial society based on sealed cultural groups (multiculturalism and community cohesion)' (James 2009 p.3). The context for these developments appears to be the spread across Europe of a critique of multiculturalism. Titley (2012) notes the hostility to multiculturalism mounted in Germany, the Netherlands, Sweden and the UK, while reminding us that France had never signed up in the first place. Ali Rattansi (2011 p.4), who has a long and distinguished career in the sociology of British race relations, has pointed out that most of the criticisms of multiculturalism made throughout Europe are 'either misguided or exaggerated', but he too supports the move to interculturalism as the preferred discourse in this period. The major European Commission/Council of Europe 'Intercultural Cities' programme, started in 2008, is an indicator of just how effective the campaign against multiculturalist discourse has been.

In that initiative, interculturalism was defined as 'a concept that promotes policies and practices that encourage interaction, understanding and respect between different cultures and ethnic groups' (Wood 2009 p.11). The programme was conceived of as 'part of our shared vision of an intercultural Europe which values human dignity, civic participation and respect for diversity as the foundation stones for socially and economically strong communities' (p.13). Further, the intercultural city is one which 'actively combats prejudice and discrimination and ensures equal opportunities for all' (p. 17). Ali Rattansi, having traced the achievements of multiculturalist thinking and practice, argued for the new concept in these terms:

> Use of the notion of interculturalism acts, instead, to undercut this essentialist tendency [in multiculturalism] – it cannot by itself completely prevent it – by building in a conception of connectedness, interaction, and interweaving between the beliefs, practices, and lifestyles of different (not separate) ethnic groups as part of national cultures that are in constant flux. (Rattansi 2011 p.153).

He continued:

> There is now an urgent need for a transformation of the vocabulary of multiculturalism into that of 'interculturalism', with a corresponding shift to underpinning premises which highlight the deep historical interconnectedness of cultures and an understanding of how conceptions of tolerance, liberty, rationality, and so forth are shared across 'civilizations', and in particular how non-Western cultures have made a vital contribution to the development of these ideas and their appropriate institutions. Modernity is not a uniquely Western phenomenon, but a shared Eurasian achievement. (Rattansi 2011 p.159).

None of this sounds very different from Roy Jenkins' statement in 1966, quoted above. Indeed, if we add Tariq Modood's authoritative definition of multiculturalism to Jenkins' original approach, it would be hard to see how interculturalism improves upon multiculturalism:

> Multiculturalism is where processes of integration are seen both as two-way and as working differently for different groups. In this understanding, each group is distinctive, and thus integration cannot consist of a single template (hence the 'multi') . . . 'culturalism' . . . refers to the understanding that the groups in question are likely to not just to be marked by newness or phenotype or socio-economic location but by certain forms of group identities. The latter point indeed suggests that a better, though longer, term might be "pluralistic integration". In the perspective of multiculturalism, the social requirement to treat these group identities with respect leads to a redefinition of the concept of equality. (Modood 2005)

What Modood provides here is the affirmation of group identities <u>and</u> the recognition that these group identities will change in response to each other over a period of time. Thus integration is achieved (as all the various groups, including the white-skinned ones) adjust their identifications. Intercultural dialogue is obviously one of the means by which these changes take place. Throughout his work, Modood has emphasised the role of equal opportunity and publicly legitimated opposition to racism as other aspects of the process. Malcolm James' definition wraps all these ideas together in this form, and again it is hard to see what the differences with multiculturalism actually are:

> Interculturality is a dynamic process whereby people from different cultures interact to learn about and question their own and each other's cultures. Over time this may lead to cultural change. It recognises the inequalities at work in society and the need to overcome these. It is a process which requires mutual respect and acknowledges human rights. (James 2007 p.2)

Interculturalists will no doubt stress that their approach is more active in promoting dialogue than some multiculturalists have been. Spearheaded by the European Year of Intercultural Dialogue in 2008, an interculturalist programme was developed in eleven cities, but none in Britain. The Baring Foundation sponsored a large programme of intercultural dialogue in Britain. In his review of the bids for Baring's funds, Malcolm James was unimpressed by the concepts offered by organisations aiming to deliver these programmes. He argued that their key concepts - 'community', 'culture', 'contact', 'parallel lives', and 'community cohesion' – were inappropriate because they

> are often based on fixed notions of ethnicity and geography which limit the possibility of facilitating intercultural relations through social policy because they restrict humans to the boundaries of neighbourhoods, skin colour and certain cultural practices. These limitations deny everything else that humans are – complex, contradictory, changing and socially structured. Until policy makers address these concerns and realities, oppressive and discriminatory ways of living will not be eradicated. (James 2009 pp. 2-3)

The argument that ethnic minorities in Britain – actually, the focus was on Muslims – were leading 'parallel lives' was one of the spurs for the further critique of multiculturalism in the aftermath of the violent urban protest in the northern cities in 2001. "Community cohesion' was the government policy that resulted from the reports into those so-called 'riots' (Farrar 2009). The 'contact hypothesis' – that prejudice decreases, and a sense of joint community rises, when rival cultures are brought into dialogue with each other – was the theory that underlay the community cohesion initiatives. So it is hardly surprising that intercultural programmes would replicate those ideas. But James went so far as to argue that all these ideas should be abandoned. Just as the Marxist anti-racists criticised the multiculturalists for ignoring racism and class oppression (see above), James argued for a notion of interculturalism that included (amongst other things):

- social action around all forms of discrimination and disadvantage, and in particular 'race', gender, sexuality, poverty, age and class
- that government take responsibility for structural inequalities [and]
- support for anti-racist methodologies that address histories of racism

(James 2009 p.16).

In my view, James is right to argue that interculturalist discourse should take the structural aspects of discrimination (in all sectors of society) into consideration, and should link itself to anti-racism, just as multiculturalism should.

Further critique of interculturalist thinking and practice in education and youth work in Europe has come from Gavan Titley. He describes this as a 'failed experiment'. It has failed because it sees culture in an essentialised and reductive form, thereby losing sight of the 'mixedness' and the diffusions that permeate culture. (This resonates with James' point that humans are 'complex, contradictory and changing' – so, therefore, are the cultures they create.) But Titley goes further than this. He argues that interculturalism rests upon racial categories that it holds in common with those it opposes. Thus, when the response to intercultural dialogue is 'We tried to talk with them but they just won't change' a hardening of positions take place and racism resurfaces. The clear implication of Titley's argument is that the very categories of 'race' and 'culture' must be unpicked. It is well known that 'race' has no validity as a scientific concept, but it is not so widely recognised that cultures have also been understood in essentialised terms and placed in a hierarchy (often embrocated with the spurious biology of 'race'). Culture thus works, as 'race' does, to categorise and differentiate human groups (Lentin and Titley 2011). The view that immigrants disturb and degrade 'our culture' is a type of common sense, and that people's fear of this process is natural, flows easily from the theory that cultures can be described in a ladder of value. It is just this 'non racial' viewpoint that the new right parties have developed over the past thirty years. Titley (2012) argues that intercultural learning programmes are vulnerable to challenge from the right precisely because they rest on similar assumptions about culture, and because they buy into the argument that multicultura.ism has failed. Since this argument itself has been motivated by increasingly hostile characterisations of Muslims ever since the Rushdie affair, it would seem essential to simultaneously defend the integrity of Islam and the rights of Muslims, and to offer a qualified defence of multiculturalism. Interculturalist discourse, at best, offers no real improvements on 'anti-racist' multiculturalism; at worst it plays into the hands of those who seek to valorise 'Western' culture (which, at its most extreme, means 'Aryan' culture) over all the others.

Critical Multiculturalism

Insofar as it contained simplistic, essentialised notions of identity and culture multiculturalism suffered from the defects of interculturalism. In its rapprochement with anti-racism, multiculturalism overcame its early weakness of neglecting the way that class, 'race' and gender structured the processes of discrimination faced by minority groups. As it embraced the theory that identities are unstable, multiple, developing and capable of melding, multiculturalist discourse, backed by legislation and equal opportunity programmes, helped shape the UK into a society which is widely recognised as being more tolerant of difference than any of its European neighbours. In the chapter referred to at the outset (Farrar 2012) I offered an outline of a new discourse – labelled critical multiculturalism – which I argue would provide a platform for further progressive development of UK. These are its components:

1. support for Bhikhu Parekh's version of Britain as a 'community of communities', where difference is respected;

2. support for Tariq Modood's notion of 'two-way integration', where the identities of all ethnic groups (including those that are white-skinned) undergo processes of change as the overarching national community emerges;

3. recognition that these two features entail a *negotiation* of diversity, rather than the uncritical celebration of diversity advocated by some liberal multiculturalists. Critical multiculturalists, for instance, would support homosexual rights, reject any type of coercion of women, and promote the sexual and geographical mixing of ethnic groups. But they would oppose the coalition government's refusal in 2011 even to talk to political Islamists. Instead, they would promote dialogue and debate on all points of difference between and among all ethnic groups;

4. adoption of a strong position on full legal rights for all ethnic minorities, and strict implementation of equal treatment regardless of ethnicity (as outlined by Will Kymlicka) – relentlessly opposing, therefore, discrimination in any form;

5. explicitly linking these integration processes to the discourse on radical democracy. Every ethnic group needs to be fully and meaningfully engaged in the civic life of the nation, which requires effective political power to be transferred from the centre to the localities;

6. recognition that economic discrimination is as important as cultural discrimination in the generation of disadvantage; thus critical multiculturalism advocates economic equality as well as legal and cultural equality.

Two of these points explicitly differentiate critical multiculturalism from liberal multiculturalism. Point (2) sets critical multiculturalism against cultural relativism: it aligns itself with those who take a radical view on the rights of sexual minorities. While not seeking make any claims for the cultural superiority of those nations which protest the rights of sexual minorities, it does stand up for those rights, and seeks actively to persuade others of their validity. Point (6) above moves the debate away from the cultural dimension of social life to the economic, and critical multiculturalism aligns itself with radical leftists who oppose neo-liberal capitalism and who support social democracy. Programmes of action which embody this type of thought would, it seems to me, provide a real basis for social progress.

Bibiography

Cameron, David (2011) Prime Minister's speech on radicalisation and Islamic extremism at the Munich Security Conference, 5th February 2011. www.number10.gov.uk/news/speeches-and-transcripts/2011/02/pms-speech-at-munich-security-conference-60293 Accessed 23.02.2011

Farrar, Max (2009) 'Violent Urban Protest – identities, ethics and Islamism' in Bhattacharyya, Gargi (ed.) (2009) *Ethnicities and Values in a Changing world,* Farnham: Ashgate.

Farrar, Max (2012 forthcoming) 'Multiculturalism in the UK – a contested discourse' in Farrar, Max, Simon Robinson, Yasmin Valli, and Paul Wetherly (eds) (2012, forthcoming) *'Islam' and 'the West' – Key issues in multiculturalism,* London: Palgrave.

James, Malcolm (2008) *Interculturalism: Theory and Practice*, London: Baring Foundation

James, Malcolm (2009) *Interculturalism: Social Policy and Grassroots Work*, London: Baring Foundation

Jenkins, Roy (1967) *Essays and Speeches*, London: Collins.

Lentin, Alana and Gavan Titley (2011) *The Crises of Multiculturalism: Racism in a Neoliberal Age.* London: Zed Books

Modood, Tariq (2005) 'Remaking Multicultrualism after 7/7' *OpenDemocracy* 28 Septmebr 2005, available at www.opendemocracy.net/conflict-terrorism/multiculturalism_2879.jsp Accessed 14.02.2012

Pitcher, Ben (2009) *The Politics of Multiculturalism – Race and racism in contemporary Britain,* Basingstoke: Palgrave Macmillan.

Rattaansi, Ali (2011) *Multiculturalism – A very short introduction*, Oxford: Oxford University Press.

Runnymede Trust (1997) *Islamophobia: A challenge to us all* by the Commission on British Muslims and Islamophobia, chaired by Professor Gordon Conway.

Sandercock, Leonie (2004) 'Reconsidering Multiculturalism: Towards and Intercutlrual Project' in Wood, Phil (ed.) (2004) *Intercultural City Reader*, Stroud: Comedia.

Swann, Lord (1985) *Education for All – the report of the committee of enquiry into the education of children from ethnic minority groups*, London: HMSO, Cmnd 9453.

Titley, Gavan (2012) 'After the failed experiment: intercultural learning in a multicultural crisis' in Yael, Ohana and Henrdik Otten (eds) (2012) *Where Do You Stand? Intercultural Learning and Political Education in Contemporary Europe,* Wiesbaden: VS Verlag.

Troyna, Barry & Williams, Jenny (1986) *Racism, Education and the State*, London: Routledge.

Weldon, Faye (1989) *Sacred Cows – a portrait of Britain post-Rushdie pre-utopia*, London; Chatto and Windus.

Wood, Phil (ed.) (2009) *Intercultural Cities – Towards a model for intercultural integration*, Strasburg: Council of Europe Publishing.

Interculturalism in Europe: Fact, Fad or Fiction – the Deconstruction of a Theoretical Idea

Ravinder Barn [62]

Introduction

The concept of interculturalism, particularly under the direction of the Council of Europe (CoE), in contemporary European societies is being seen as a useful tool to address marginalisation and achieve social cohesion. However, there is little theoretical and/or empirical development of this concept and how it differs from multiculturalism. This paper seeks to critically operationalise this idea to help disentangle the opacity which clouds key notions surrounding this concept. The paper is structured in three parts. Part one sets the scene to provide an overview of the notions of race and ethnicity, and racial and cultural diversity in Europe. Part two explores the notion of multiculturalism as this is arguably the model which interculturalism seeks to replace. Part three outlines the concept of interculturalism and considers the utility of this model. It is argued that the extent to which the concept of interculturalism can claim to be an empirical reality remains to be seen. Indeed, there is a real need for policy initiatives with measurable outcomes to obviate the concept of interculturalism being dismissed as a fad or fiction.

Although European societies have never been culturally homogeneous, it is evident that with the legacy of colonialism, slavery, impact of globalisation, economic disparities, and international wars and conflict, there is increasing racial and culturally heterogeneity. It is estimated that there are almost 21 million people of 'foreign' background living in European countries, comprising less than 3% of the aggregate population of Europe (Haug, Compton and Courbage 2002). Such diversity raises concerns about common values and norms, and ties that may bind

---

62 Ravinder Barn is Professor of Social Policy at Royal Holloway, University of London. She was awarded her PhD in Sociology in 1989 by the University of Warwick. She began her academic career at Middlesex University in 1988, and joined Royal Holloway, University of London in 1990. She has over 60 publications which includes 7 books. She is an experienced empirical mixed-methods researcher with a particular interest in migration, multiculturalism, social justice and human rights. As Principal Investigator, she has successfully led on a number of externally funded research studies for the Joseph Rowntree Foundation, the former Commission for Racial Equality, The Canadian High Commission, and the Department of Health. Her research is empirically and theoretically grounded and key findings are disseminated to a wide variety of potential beneficiaries ranging from academic researchers, central and local government, international organizations including the Council of Europe and the European Union, and third sector organizations.

disparate groups together. Moreover, there are other social changes as societies evolve. These may include the role of women, gender, family form, and sexuality. Such changes require negotiation in the context of modernity and diversity (Barn 2010).

The increasing racial and cultural heterogeneity found in modern contemporary societies has generated enormous political and academic debate about the best and most desirable ways to achieve racial harmony. The terms race and ethnicity are often, mistakenly, used interchangeably to mean the same thing. Writers in the field of social sciences make important distinctions. Whilst 'race' is discredited as a biological term, and is generally understood to be a social construct to understand the dynamics of racism, ethnicity is often defined 'as denoting socio-cultural factors such as shared histories, memories, myths, customs, sentiments and values' (Goulbourne and Solomos 2003).

With the growth of racial and ethnic pluralism in the European Union, there is an important and ongoing debate about the notion of citizenship and entitlement to social and political rights and a conferment of duties and responsibilities (Maiz and Requejo 2005). Concerns about the threat to the so-called host culture and to the welfare state from immigrant groups and asylum seekers are de rigour and regularly exploited by the far right and others (Sprague-Jones 2011). Such debates impact decisions about how notions of citizenship are conceptualised, understood and implemented. The dichotomy of 'us' and 'them', the process of 'otherisation, and the boundaries of belonging constitute the key dimensions of the citizenship debates. With the push and pull factors of immigration, the economic disparities between the advantaged north and the disadvantaged south and socio-economic concerns about the preservation of 'indigenous groups', there are severe implications for the social and political rights of migrant labour. Thus, whilst the affluent north requires migrant labour to meet its needs, it manifests insecurity about the concessions it can make to help migrants 'feel at home'.

Social scientists in Western societies have put forward various models of race relations to understand the process by which minority communities become absorbed or assimilated into mainstream society to which they migrate (Park 1914, Gordon 1964, Berry 1980). Such models have encompassed notions of separation and marginalisation to assimilation and integration. Politicians have advanced the policy arena in their articulation of the future and the way forward. Thus, in Britain whilst the conservative Minister and Member of Parliament, the late Enoch Powell, talked of 'rivers of blood' (Powell 1968), the former Labour Minister and Member of Parliament, the late Roy Jenkins, advocated integration and equal opportunity in an atmosphere of mutual tolerance (Jenkins 1967). Arguably, Roy Jenkins's form of integration could be viewed as an important cornerstone of British multiculturalism.

Multiculturalism

The notion of multiculturalism is relatively new as a policy objective in Western societies. Indeed, the term multiculturalism appears to have been initially employed in the context of a handful of nation states – Canada, Australia, Britain and the United States – primarily from the 1970s onwards. Modood (2007) notes that although these same countries had previously pursued a policy agenda of assimilation (conformity to dominant culture), they shifted their stance when it was no longer considered desirable to impose assimilation on people who were racially and cultural different. Indeed, Canadian society enshrined multiculturalism in its legal framework to provide recognition to discrete groups such as the First Nation Native people of Canada and the Quebeckers (Kymlicka 2003).

Whilst the reality of multiculturalism in terms of racial and cultural diversity is an undeniable fact in contemporary societies, the meanings associated with such a policy particularly in the context of aims, process and outcome can vary considerably (Alba and Nee 2003). For example, Meer and Modood (2011) argue that whilst Canadian multicultural policy was formulated within the values of liberalism, individual freedom, equal citizenship and non-discrimination; Australian multiculturalism by contrast was focused upon the need to integrate new immigrants. Moreover, the multiculturalism focus of Britain and the USA was initially largely in the field of education in the form of mother-tongue teaching, multi-faith recognition, halal food, ethnic dress and so on.

The term multiculturalism came to be associated with diversity and in particular how the state dealt with accommodating different religious and cultural groups in a way that provided equal opportunity, civic status, individual freedom, and group recognition.

Since the events of 9/11 in which almost 3,000 people were killed as a result of extremist violence in the USA, and other such acts including 7 July suicide bombings in London; the notion and practice of multiculturalism has become the subject of a critical gaze (Phillips 2006). More recently, the global fiscal crisis together with the growing tide in right wing extremism has led to mainstream politicians attacking the policy of multiculturalism. From the French President Nicolas Sarkozy who declared that newcomers should 'accept to melt in a single community', others including the British Prime Minister David Cameron and German Chancellor Angela Merkel have shown their displeasure about multiculturalism. Also, as Europe seeks to become increasingly fortified economically, politically and territorially, it is also becoming more racially and culturally diversified. This is raising further concerns about multiculturalism as a viable policy aim especially as the policy is becoming discredited as 'essentialist, illiberal, less agency-oriented and less concerned with unity' (Meer and Modood 2011:5).

In some academic quarters, the attack on multiculturalism has been in the context of its inability to deal with structural socio-economic inequalities (Barry 2001, Hansen 2006, Sivanandan 2010). Moreover, in the context of 9/11 and 7/7, and the perception of growing Islamic fundamentalism, multiculturalism is regarded as not conducive to social cohesion – a shared collective vision. Thus attempts to achieve social cohesion have led to the introduction of a series of measures designed to instill a sense of loyalty to the nation-state and to prevent the immigration of those who are not proficient in the language of the receiving country and who could hamper social cohesion. These measures include, amongst others, swearing of oaths of allegiance at naturalisation ceremonies, language proficiency requirements for citizenship and marriage to a British citizen, and citizenship education in schools. In some European countries such as France and Belgium, the banning of religious symbols/clothing such as headscarves and the burka (veil) has been introduced in the name of secularism and gender equality and has been conceptualised by some as a retreat from multiculturalism (Joppke 2004, McGee 2008). The perceived failure of multiculturalism which is seen to encourage separate identities is now being replaced with a new concept, namely interculturalism.

Interculturalism

The concept of interculturalism in contemporary European multi-cultural societies is being seen as a useful tool to address marginalisation and achieve social cohesion. However, there is little theoretical development and/or empirical support for this concept. It is important to operationalise this idea to help disentangle the opacity which clouds key notions surrounding this concept.

Culture is generally associated with the shared norms, values, beliefs and traditions of a group of people. Such norms and values are not fixed but dynamic and subject to change depending on location, time, and individual and group experiences and social economic, and political situations. Thus, history, geography, economics and politics are key variables in understanding how culture is understood, how it develops, and how it's transmitted from generation to generation and also how it impacts other groups who may subscribe to a different set of values and traditions. Also, the impact and influence of one's own culture on other cultures is contingent upon the social, economic and political power relations which exist in a given societal and global context.

The concept of interculturalism in Europe is relatively recent and it places it focus upon being a new model and therefore different from previous models in its approach and management of diversity (Gundara and Jacobs 2000, Emerson 2011). Interculturalism is invariably associated with the terms - competence and dialogue. In 2008, the Council of Europe published a white paper entitled ' White

Paper on Intercultural Dialogue "Living Together As Equals in Dignity" (Council of Europe 2008). This document which is intended to serve as a blue print to the 47 European member states, sets out the conceptual framework and the policy approaches necessary to promote intercultural dialogue. The white paper is critical of multiculturalism and argues that such an approach has blurred similarities and sharpened ethnic and cultural differences (Alba 2005). Gender equality is also seen to have suffered within the framework of multiculturalism. The new approach of interculturalism renders previous models of assimilation and multiculturalism as inadequate and insufficient for 21st century Europe; and seeks to build on these for a more creative solution in the management of diversity:

> It [interculturalism] takes from assimilation the focus on the individual; it takes from multiculturalism the recognition of cultural diversity. And it adds the new element, critical to integration and social cohesion, of dialogue on the basis of equal dignity and shared values (Council of Europe:10).

Meer and Modood (2011) report that the concept of interculturalism is now to be found in various European venues ranging from German and Greek education programmes, to Belgian commissions on cultural diversity to Russian teaching on world cultures. However, the extent to which interculturalism is indeed different from other models of cultural diversity is questionable. Indeed, Lentin (2003) has boldly described interculturalism as an 'updated version' of multiculturalism. Bouchard (2011:438) repudiates such claims and argues that 'interculturalism is not a disguised…form of multiculturalism'.

In a carefully thought out piece, Meer and Modood (2011:3) dismantle the four principal claims of interculturalism. These are:

1. That interculturalism is allegedly more geared towards interaction and dialogue than multiculturalism.

2. That interculturalism is conceived as less 'groupist' or more yielding of synthesis than multiculturalism.

3. That interculturalism is something more committed to a stronger case of the whole in terms of social cohesion and national citizenship.

4. That interculturalism is more likely than multiculturalism to lead to criticism of illiberal cultural practices, for example, in the area of gender equality and sexual orientation.

In their critique of what they describe as 'political interculturalism', that is, the ways in which interculturalism is appropriated in the critique of multiculturalism, Meer and Modood (2011:18) conclude that the proclaimed values of interculturalism 'in terms of encouraging communication, recognising dynamic identities, promoting unity and challenging illiberality' are also key features of multiculturalism. Furthermore, they argue that multiculturalism surpasses interculturalism as a political orientation given the focus of the former on individuals and groups in the context of formal and informal power structures, and citizenship (Parekh 2000).

In the context of Quebec, Bouchard (2011) identifies reciprocity, pluralism, reasonable accommodation, rejection of discrimination based on difference, and recognition of a majority/minority duality as the key identifying features of interculturalism. He points to majority culture anxieties about the non-integration of minorities, and the minority group fears about their future in their newly adopted land. It is argued that the tensions between continuity and diversity can be reconciled under the arbitration of the law. He argues that some policies and practices such as the dominance of the language of the majority group, and the predominance of the majority narrative in the form of religious symbolism are acceptable ad hoc precedents. Whilst favouring the general principle of 'ad hocism' within such arbitration of the law, Bouchard (2011:459-460) identifies several examples as an abuse of this principle, for example, 'keeping a cross on the wall of the National assembly and in public courtrooms', and the funding of chaplain or Catholic pastoral care positions in public hospitals with state funds, to the exclusion of other religions'.

In the context of Europe, the body that is doing much to give recognition to the concept of interculturalism states that 'intercultural dialogue cannot be prescribed by law', and that state authorities must take up the open invitation to implement the underlying principles of interculturalism (Council of Europe 2008:2). The Council places its emphasis upon democratic citizenship. It argues that participation should be strengthened; intercultural competences should be taught and learned; spaces for intercultural dialogue should be created and widened; and intercultural dialogue should be taken to the international level. Equally, however, whilst the Council makes mention of human rights, democracy and the law in the framework of the European Court of Human Rights, it is less sanguine about a legal approach to the process of interculturalism.

In writing about the CoE's intercultural cities programme, Barn (2011) highlights the role of individuals who are deemed to be intercultural innovators, that is, they are involved in community development and have a capacity to communicate across boundaries, often requiring them to find commonalties between cultures. This is said to lead to increasing interaction and hybridisation between cultural communities. Modood (2011), however, regards such interlocutors as the very fabric of multiculturalism. He points to paradoxical practices by politicians and governments who on the one hand attack multiculturalism and on the other hand engage in multicultural and ethnic 'group consultations, representation and accommodation' (Modood 2011:15).

It would seem that interculturalism is also invariably associated with the notion of competence (Deardorff 2004). How 'intercultural competence' (ICC) is defined, understood and implemented at differing levels from individual to organisational within the equality and human rights framework for all inhabitants in a municipality remains unclear. Though ICC refers in its origins to the interaction of individuals, and not systems such as corporate or national "cultures", yet every interpersonal encounter takes place within a framework that is defined by the predispositions and norms. Most of the system framework includes hierarchical relationships or demands assimilation in accordance with certain preconceptions of identity. In a "culturally" diverse environment, changing these types of frameworks is a core issue for the municipality (administration) and is also a general socio-political responsibility of all members of society. Thus, the key objective of ICC is said to be not only to teach and train ICC to impact attitudes, knowledge and skills, reflection and interaction, but also to reflect and come to arrangements on policies and structures to lead to notions of identity that include all inhabitants of a society and promote the idea of a "culturally" heterogeneous society. It is argued that such a framework exists when actors involved meet at "eye-level".

It is evident that interculturalism is not only about good communication, it is also about power, inequalities and discrimination. Thus, notions of equity, non-discrimination, anti-racism, intercultural adaptation, inter-creation and inter-action, are crucial in the integration of 'minority' and 'majority' communities. However, the extent to which the communication and dialogue-based approach is achieving racial equality is debatable.

Conclusion

Given the widespread concerns about the pernicious effects of marginalisation and social exclusion of migrant communities and the impact of this on majority and minority communities, this paper contributes to the literature regarding the salience of the concept of interculturalism in modern contemporary European society. The intercultural approach is built on the premise that the concepts of fluidity and multi-dimensionality are crucial in understanding contemporary cultural communities. In other words, ideas of ethnicity and race are conceptualised as too limiting in their imposition of fixed boundaries. Thus, one of the key principles of interculturalism is to involve individuals and groups across the boundaries of ethnicity, faith, gender and generation. The interculturalism approach dismisses both the assimilationist and multicultural models on grounds of irrelevance and inadequacy respectively.

Arguably, in the management of diversity, notions of interculturalism and multiculturalism could be viewed as not mutually exclusive but intertwined concepts. Given its focus on communication, dialogue and interaction in the identity project, notions not dissimilar to multiculturalism, whether interculturalism is an advancement to the notion of multiculturalism is questionable.

The rise of Islamophobia in the West is leading to a perception that multiculturalism as a model of cultural diversity has failed (Fekete 2008). Whether interculturalism can claim to take this ground and replace multiculturalism remains to be seen. Interculturalism's claim that over time, both the majority culture and minority cultures will find themselves changed to varying degrees is indisputable. We know that culture is dynamic, fluid, transformative and transformational. The extent to which interculturalism takes account of globalisation, transnationalism and diasporic links is unclear and requires further attention.

It is increasingly evident that racialised exclusion in socio-economic patterns and structures of society impacts upon retention, and even the development of ethnic ties and solidarity as a form of survival. If the concept of interculturalism can challenge racism and foster inter-collegiality between the dominant group and the minority ethnic groups, then it may well succeed where multiculturalism may have failed.

Arguably, for it to be recognised as a viable model of cultural diversity, the concept of interculturalism needs to be adopted by public administrative organisations at all levels of policy making. Currently, there is limited evidence of policy initiatives with measurable outcomes to support the concept of interculturalism being seen as a fact. In the absence of such evidence of the workings of interculturalism, there is every possibility that the concept cannot be obviated from being dismissed as a fad or fiction.

Bibliography

Alba, R (2005) 'Bright vs. blurred boundaries: second-generation assimilation and exclusion in France, Germany, and the United States', *Ethnic and Racial Studies*, 28(1), 20-49.

Alba, R and Victor, N (2003) *Remaking the American Mainstream*, Cambridge: Harvard University Press.

Barn, G (2011) Making the most of diversity – profile of intercultural innovators, Strasbourg: Council of Europe. URL:http://www.coe.int/t/dg4/cultureheritage/culture/cities/newsletter/newsletter16/innovator_EN.asp

Barn, R (2010) Diversity: Planning, Provision and Progress in Social Services in the UK, In Rene, C and Guidokova, I (eds) *Diversity and community development: An intercultural approach,* Strasbourg: Council of Europe.

Barry, B (2001) *Culture and equality: an egalitarian critique of equality*, London: Polity Press.

Barth, F (1994) 'Enduring and emerging issues in the analysis of ethnicity'. In Vermeulen, Hans and Govers, Cora (eds.), *The Anthropology of Ethnicity. Beyond 'Ethnic Groups and Boundaries'*, 11-32. Amsterdam: Het Spinhuis.

Berry, JW (1980) Acculturation as varieties of adaptation. In A. Padilla (Ed.), *Acculturation: Theory, models and some new findings. (pp.9-25).* Boulder: Westview Press.

Bouchard, G and Taylor, C (2008) *Building the Future, A Time for Reconciliation,* Abridged Report, Quebec: The Consultation Commission on Accommodation Practices Related to Cultural Difference.

Bouchard, G (2011) What is Interculturalism? *McGill Law Journal*, 56(2), 435-468.

Council Of Europe (2008) White Paper on Intercultural Dialogue *"Living Together As Equals in Dignity"*, Strasbourg: Council of Europe.

Deardorff, DK (2004) The identification and assessment of intercultural competence as a student outcome of internationalization at institutions of higher education in the United States, *Unpublished dissertation*, North Carolina State University, Raleigh, NC.

Emerson, M (ed) (2011) Interculturalism: Europe and its Muslims in search of sound societal models, Brussels: centre for European Policy Studies paperbacks.

Fekete, L (2008) Integration, Islamophobia and civil rights in Europe, London: Institute of Race Relations.

Gordon, Milton M (1964) *Assimilation in American Life*, New York: Oxford University Press.

Goulbourne, H and Solomos, J (2003) Families, Ethnicity and Social Capital, *Social Policy and Society,* 2 (4), 2003, p. 329-338.

Gundara, JS and Jacobs, S (eds) (2000) *Intercultural Europe: diversity and social policy*, Aldershot: Ashgate.

Hansen, R (2006) The Danish carton controversy: a defence of liberal freedom, *International migration*, 44(5), 7-16.

Haug, W; Compton, P and Courbage, Y (eds) (2002) The demographic characteristics of immigrant populations, *Population studies*, No. 38, Council of Europe Publishing.

Jenkins, R (1967) 'Racial equality in Britain', in A. Lester (ed.), *Essays and Speeches by Roy Jenkins,* London: Collins.

Joppke, C (2004) The retreat of multiculturalism in the liberal state: theory and policy, *British Journal of Sociology*, 55(2), 237-257.

Kymlicka, W (2003) Multicultural states and intercultural citizens, *Theory and research in education,* 1, 147-169.

Lentin, A (2005) Replacing 'race', historizing the 'culture' in the multiculturalism, *Patterns of prejudice*, 39(4), 379-396.

McGee, D (2008) *The end of multiculturalism? Terrorism, integration and human rights*, maidenhead: Open University Press and McGraw-Hill Education.

Maiz, R and Requejo, F (eds) (2005) *Democracy, Nationalism and Multiculturalism*, London?New York: Routledge.

Meer, N and Modood, T (2011) How does interculturalism contrast with multiculturalism? *Journal of intercultural studies*, 1-22.

Modood, T (2007) *Multiculturalism*, Cambridge: Polity.

Parekh, B (2000) *Rethinking multiculturalism: cultural diversity and political theory*, London: Palgrave.

Park, RE (1914) 'Racial assimilation in secondary groups with particular reference to the negro', *American Journal of Sociology*, 19(5), 606-623.

Phillips, M. (2006) *Londonistan: how Britain created a terror state within*, London: Gibson Square Books.

Powell, E (1968) - Enoch Powell's 'Rivers of Blood' speech, The Telegraph, http://www.telegraph.co.uk/comment/3643826/Enoch-Powells-Rivers-of-Blood-speech.html#disqus_thread (accessed 03.02.12).

Sivanandan, A (2008) Preface in L. Fekete, *Integration, Islamophobia and civil rights in Europe*, London: Institute of Race Relations.

Sprague-Jones, J (2011) Extreme right-wing vote and support for multiculturalism in Europe, *Ethnic and Racial Studies*, 34:4, 535-555.

What is the Role of Scholars in Formulating and Communicating the Concept of Interculturalism?

Yasmin Valli [63]

Introduction

This paper aims to explore the role of scholars in formulating and communicating the concept of interculturalism through 'cultural inclusivity'. This approach allows us to discuss the concept of interculturalism firstly by addressing it within the educational context and then by considering its impact both politically and socially. As our cultural experience is shaped by power differentials, minority status, gender divisions and class divisions, the paper seeks to explore how scholars perceive their role, through engaging with 'cultural inclusivity' in promoting interculturalism to understand how people from different countries and cultures behave, communicate and perceive the world around them. 'Cultural inclusivity' will encompass a range of items including cross-cultural learning, intercultural competence, difference in the social positions of learners, relevance of the curriculum and assessment methods, differences in profiles of cognitive abilities between populations and differences in interactions at academic levels. The ever increasing diversity around us demands that we all need to become more conscious of our own stereotypical beliefs and consequently become more eager to learn the actual differences in what Hofstede (1984 p. 21) refers to as 'the collective programming of mind' which distinguishes the members of one human group from another'. (Note: in this article, the term scholar refers to academics in Higher education. Cross-cultural, multicultural and intercultural terms are used interchangeably.) As the student population is made up of many ethnicities, cultures, languages and

63 Yasmin Valli is a Principal Lecturer and Teacher Fellow at Leeds Metropolitan University, Carnegie Faculty. Before taking up hercurrent position at the University, she was an advisory teacher for Information Technology in Lancashire. She has taught on the undergraduate, postgraduate, MA and in-service training courses and was a Route Leader for the ICT with English Route. In her current role as Principal Lecturer, she is the coordinator for widening participation for the Carnegie Faculty of Sport and Education and Level Leader for the final year students on the teaching programme. She is also involved in a national project, seconded by the DfES, to establish a website http://www.teacherworld.org.uk/. She also carries out OFSTED duties as inspector and AI for independent schools. She was recently awarded a fellowship of the National Teaching Awards Trust. She is a member of the Higher Education Academy and reviews editor for the International Journal of Teacher Development. In 2004 she was involved in a 'Role Model' project with the Royal Society.

religions, and it is constantly evolving through advancement in technology and increased migration, we are faced with the challenge of engaging effectively with issues of diversity and difference within our student population. This places upon us an imperative to promote the concept of interculturalism in order to better connect with the diversity our students bring. This paper explores the notion of 'cultural inclusivity' as an approach, under various headings related mainly to education and examines how 'cultural inclusivity allows academics to encompass and promote the concept of interculturalism through their pedagogy. As educational environments become increasingly multicultural, the need to develop skills to deliver a culturally sensitive and culturally adaptive curriculum has arisen. For scholars whose knowledge is based on their own cultural frameworks and therefore personal and norm-based, this factor could presented a challenge as it may prove difficult for them to discern and divest themselves of those beliefs, hence exacerbating the disconnect (Zeichner, 1993). Furthermore, scholars would perceive that the cultural experiences of the students they aspire to teach may be quite different from their own and feel unprepared to meet the needs of their students (Powell et al. 2000). There is much research that focuses on the cultural mismatch between the academic and the students within the classrooms they teach (Grant & Seceda1990, Clandinin & Connelly 1996, Greeno,1997, Blackridge 2000). This paper also explores the cross-cultural challenges faced by academics as they endeavour to ensure that students, through both the formal and informal curricula, engage in activity that will prepare them to step out into the 21st-century global and multicultural world.

> Everywhere cultural identities are emerging which are not fixed, but poised, in transition, between different positions which draw on different cultural traditions at the same time, and which are the product of those complicated cross-overs and cultural mixes which are increasingly common in a globalised world. (Hall 1992)

Interculturalism and Multiculturalism

Albo (2001) has contributed much to the debate and discussion around interculturalism. He highlights the positive and negative kind of interculturality that arises when people from different cultures meet. According to Albo negative interculturality arises when the encounter leads to destruction or reduction of certain groups and positive interculturality arises when it results in the acceptance and recognition for the culturally different. Albo goes on to assert that one needs to operate beyond mutual respect that is offered by interculturality and multiculturality which equal the descriptive and quantitative use of the concept. One enters into real interculturality when one is seriously considering each person's contributions and values to create something together, making a common loom where everybody recognises their own part and is enriched by the others' contributions (Albó 2001 p. 4).

The debate on interculturalism has also generated a wealth of academic commentary. Parekh's main contribution to this debate is his understanding of pluralism; what he also calls 'interactive multiculturalism' (2007b p. 46). He sees this as a dialogue between communities and individuals where each sees the value of opening up and learning from the other (2007b p. 46-47). However, Parekh concedes that this kind of dialogue requires certain conditions. Participants in the dialogue should enjoy a broad equality 'of self-confidence, economic and political power and access to public space' (2006, p. 337). In this sense interculturalism is dependent upon wider notions of redistribution and is not itself a panacea (2007a).

Another dimension that enters the discussion is that of 'cultural relativism'. Claude Levi-Strauss (1908 - 1999) refers to 'cultural relativism' where cultures can apply their own judgement to their own activities and one culture has no absolute criteria for judging the activities of another culture as 'low' or 'noble'. Thus one should think twice before applying the norms of one person, group or society to another (Hofstede & Hofstede 2005). However, the 'wider notions of redistribution' as expressed by Parekh above have become a reality for some ethnic groups for whom the concept of interculturality appears limited. On a daily basis, some students certainly experience the positive and negative kind of interculturality, as expressed by Albo above, through their learning experience in schools or higher education particularly in situations where academics overlook the importance of embedding interculturalism into the curriculum.

Cross Cultural Learning and (Intercultural Competence)

As classrooms are now increasingly multicultural and multilingual, they are made up of learners with different languages and dialects each with their own educational, social, historical and economic backgrounds adding to the diversity in the classroom. This diversity alone has the potential to transform the perspectives and capabilities of both learners and educators. Because learning is individually constructed, socially supported and culturally mediated, learners in unfamiliar social and cultural environments may experience difficulty in 'hooking' onto new knowledge which could result in 'cognitive dissonance' for some, this could hinder the learning process and result in low self-esteem (Carroll and Ryan 2005).

Diversity also brings with it many challenges and for learners to become interculturally competent, it is essential that all participants in the education system – administrators, learners and educators – become – aware of their own cultural background and how their own beliefs and values influence their interactions with learners of other cultural backgrounds (Lustig and Koester 2006, Bennett and Bennett 2004). Situations such as this call for a better understanding of cultures by educators. Bourdieu (1984) describes the social and cultural knowledge that the students bring with them as their 'cultural capital': that should be used to drive learning. However, some scholars have moved away from a focus on difference and stress instead the need for creating contexts where students can understand their new situation (Biggs 1997) and where teachers and all students can value different ways of thinking and learning. This approach creates an inclusive context for learners from diverse backgrounds and promotes critical and intercultural learning opportunities (Volet and Ang, 1998). Similarly, Hofstede and collaborators argue:

> If we inhabitants of the globe do not acquire an awareness of our mutual differences, knowledge of basic cultural variables, the skills to communicate effectively across boundaries and the will to do so, our world will be the worse for it. We need to communicate effectively with people who were raised in ways utterly unlike our own. (Hofstede et al. 2002p. xviii)

Scholars become more focused on what students learn as more importance is given to learning outcomes and they are less occupied with the process and the content that drives learning. We need to become more open to the reality of the changing classroom as it is clear that the requirements of our students can vary from our own experiences of learning. Scholars in diverse classroom settings need to become aware not just about the subject matter they teach but also see the need to create an environment to facilitate learning in order to promote cross cultural understanding. As Ya-Wen Teng (2005) said, intercultural communication is not only a need, but a requirement for success in today's pluralistic society. This view was earlier recommended by Fox (1992), who argued that intercultural communication provided 'the critical process of making meanings, of shared meanings and of building bridges across those multiple realities and multiple truths' (Fox 1996 p. 298). The Hofstedes (2005 pp. 358-9) discuss learning intercultural communication under three phases: awareness, knowledge and skills. Through awareness one recognises the fact that one carries a particular mental software due to the way they are brought up and that others will have a different mental software for equally good reasons. Through knowledge one can learn about other cultures; even though we may never share their values we need to get an intellectual grasp of where their values differ from ours. Skills are based on awareness and knowledge and are supported through our practice within other cultures in order to appreciate the complexities of life among others. We live in a society where increasingly it is known that ignorance is no longer an option and surely amongst academics there must be an urgent need to address gaps in their understanding about other cultures so that they can add value to their teaching which supports students in the learning process.

Challenges Faced by Academics

Formulating and communicating the concept of interculturalism has presented challenges for academics. Many lecturers faced with unfamiliar student characteristics and needs are unsure about how to respond whilst at the same time meeting what they perceive to be the academic expectations for the institution regarding new developments or income generation. Such situations could present a challenge to academics leading them to constantly 're-invent the wheel' and in some cases rely on their existing assumptions about the expectations of the 'ideal student'. This approach will see them operating within a 'deficit model' (Fox 1996) wanting students to conform as quickly as possible to the academic tradition without placing any onus on themselves to reconsider their approaches to teaching and assessment. Many students come from rapidly changing cultures and those who succeed in life learn to manage these cultural changes skilfully and successfully. This fact is evident in the migrant communities living in Britain over the generations. The challenge here is to avoid stereotyping and help students develop 'meta-cultural' sensitivity in order to assess different cultures as students need to realise how their culture may be shaping their own reactions. It is important for them to see the world from the others' points of view. Academics also face the challenge of designing an inclusive curriculum to provide opportunities for all students to reflect on and express their own sources of cultural influence, as well as to value the knowledge and experience they bring with them to the educational environment (Valli et.al 2009). Furthermore, students potential lack of participation in classroom activities puts constraints on classroom interaction and learning (Ryan 2000, Jones 2005). For example, group dynamics presents a constant challenge for academics as students often form groups with those who they feel most comfortable with, particularly if they happen to speak the same language. Such groupings will do little to promote intercultural awareness. However, if this is observed by academics as a potential barrier, the massive opportunity that it presents to promote intercultural awareness will be missed and there will be no gains for the students. Other factors such as different world views, different values and beliefs, prejudices, different languages, different ways of using and interpreting the non-verbal code, different ways of constructing messages, unequal power, and the failure to allow for individual cultural differences within a group also need to be considered by academics in order to promote a suitable environment that enhances the promotion of interculturalism. Ignoring this could hamper the learning process and lead to intercultural communication difficulties. Globalisation has presented challenges for academics and the need to constantly reassess the suitability of the curriculum is of paramount importance if one is to churn out graduates fit to operate in the globalised world equipped with the necessary skills. More of the same will quickly be realised as unsuitable for the increasingly diverse classrooms that academics are presented with.

Interculturalism - Power Dynamics, Places and Spaces

On a broader front, interculturalism requires that structural inequalities, unequal power relations and discrimination be addressed. Hewstone (2003) stresses that successful intergroup contact depends on a social context that supports equality. He points to the need for places and spaces for different groups to come together, cooperate, build lasting friendships and reduce prejudices. Parekh stresses the importance of spaces for intercultural dialogue (2007a). He also notes that if members of a political community are to engage in society, the conditions must exist whereby they can participate equally. The authors agree that interculturalism requires the redistribution of political and economic power and the eradication of racism and all other forms of discrimination. If people do not have the self-confidence, economic or political power, or if they are discriminated against because of their ethnicity, culture, gender, sexuality or religion, then they are unlikely to be able to participate on equal terms in an intercultural society.

Scholars should transmit this wider knowledge through their teaching, by presenting opportunities to engage in discussion around political issues so that students can forward their perceptions and contribute to the understanding of all. Such an approach could also promote the learners' self-esteem. Establishing true integration amongst members of culturally different groups requires environments in which these people can meet and mix as equals. Academic institutions can assume this role. One must not underestimate the role of language in intercultural encounters. Numerous assumptions are made about students' contextual understanding without any regard given to how this may impact on some learners' understanding. The power dynamic that dominant languages present is in itself a factor to be reckoned with as it quickly opens up a gap between those learners who feel at ease and those who struggle to keep up. Not recognising and addressing situations like these will only add to the anxiety felt by learners and stifle progress towards promoting interculturalism. Intercultural spaces for intercultural dialogue can be both valuable and potentially transformative if the right conditions exist and academics can provide open spaces for interculturalism to flourish. Academic institutions can play a vital role in leading the field to promote interculturalism.

Conclusion

It is clear that there is an ever-increasing need to promote interculturalism within the academic community. Simple understanding that cultures are different is not enough. Students need to have the basic knowledge or tools to deal with intercultural communication or conflict. National cultures differ and one way to understand this according to Hofstede, (1980, 1999) is to examine their values, as relationships between people in a society are affected by values programmed in the minds of these people. Because teaching and learning is heavily dependent on interpersonal relationships, recognition of these different values is crucial to providing an appropriate learning environment for people from diverse backgrounds (Dalglish and Evans 2008). To send students out into a working environment where it is anticipated that most will be working in culturally diverse settings places an imperative upon institutions to provide them with the tools to help them flourish in a diverse environment, hence influencing the programmed mind to take on board new learning. One can see that the challenges towards promoting interculturalism are all around us and the need to face up the challenges is on the increase. Technological developments and global movements have resulted in different cultures living side by side. Schools are now known to have increasing percentage of pupils from diverse backgrounds and although efforts are made to build cultural awareness at school level, progress in this area is patchy and highlights a lack of confidence in some teachers to deal with cultural matters. A similar situation exists at higher education level. Without intercultural understanding these situations will give rise to tensions and indeed we have already seen the results of tensions caused due to cultural misunderstandings. All this has speeded up the urgency of the matter even further alerting scholars to wake up to the call. The concept of interculturalism is rapidly being promoted over multiculturalism which is deemed to be associated by fragmentation and fear of segregation. This was voiced recently by leaders of the western world (Cameron 2011). Furthermore, assimilation is seen to be rejected due to its association with the violation of individual rights. However, it has to be emphasised that these shifts are open to debate and discussion. Currently, interculturalism is favoured as a middle path, as a model of balance and equity that also encompasses the best parts of multiculturalism. Scholars need to locate their thinking at the centre of these shifting paradigms and incorporate such developments in their teachings and daily interactions with students to promote inter cultural dialogue and connect with the reality of the outside world.

Bibliography

Albó, X. (2001) *"Eso que llamamos interculturalidad"* in"La encrucijada cultural. Anuario deCosude" 2001. Ed. Xavier Albó et al., La Paz: Plural Editores.

Bennett, J, M. and Bennett, M. J. (2004). *Developing Intercultural Sensitivity: An Integrative Approach to Global and Domestic Diversity.* In Landis, D., Bennett, J. M., and Bennett, M. J. (Eds) *Handbook of Intercultural Training*, 3rd ed). Thousand Oaks, CA: Sage, 147-165

Biggs, J. (1997) 'Teaching across and within cultures'. *Learning and Teaching in Higher Education: Advancing International Perspectives Proceedings of the HERDSA conference*, Adelaide, South Australia, 8-11 July 1997

Blackridge, A. (2000) *Literacy Power and social justice* (Staffordshire, Trenthem Books).

Bourdieu, P. (1984). Distinction: *A Social Critique of Judgement of Taste*, Cambridge, Masachusetts: Harvard University Press.

Cameron, David (2011) Prime Minister's speech on radicalisation and Islamic extremism at the Munich Security Conference, 5th February 2011. http://www.number10.gov.uk/news/speeches-and-transcripts/2011/02/pms-speech-at-munich-security-conference-60293

Carroll, J. and Ryan, J. (eds) (2005) *Teaching International Students– improving learning for all.* Abingdon: Routledge.

Clandinin, D. & Connely, F. (1996) *Teachers; professional knowledge landscape*: teacher stories – stories of teachers – school stories – stories of schools, Educational Researcher, 25(3), 24-30

Dalglish, C. and Evans, P. (2008) *Teaching in the Global Business Classroom.* Edward Elgar. Fielding, M. (1996). Effective Communication in organizations: Preparing messages that communicate. South Africa: Juta & Co. Ltd.

Fox, C. (1996). *'Listening to the other. Mapping intercultural communication in postcolonial educational consultancies'.* In R. Poulston (ed) Social Cartography. Mapping Ways of Seeing Social and Educational Change (pp 291-306). New York and London: Garland Publishing Inc.

Grant, C. & Seceda, W. (1990) *Preparing teachers for diversity*, in: R. Houston (Ed) handbook of research on teacher education (New York: Macmillan), 403-422

Greeno, C. (1997) *On claims that answer the wrong questions*, Educational Researcher, January/February, 5-17.

Hall, S. (1992) *The Question of Cultural Identity*. In: Hall, S. and McGrew, T. (eds) *Modernity and its Futures*. Cambridge: Polity Press.

Hewstone, M., 2003. Intergroup contact: panacea for prejudice. *The psychologist*, 16 (7), 352-355.

Hofstede, G. (1993). *Cultures and Organizations. Software of the Mind. Intercultural Cooperation and its Importance for Survival.* London:Harper Collins Publishers.

Hofstede, G.J., P.B Pederson and G. Hofstede (2002), *Exploring culture*, Yarnmouth,

ME: Intercultural Press

Hofstede, Geert & Hofstede, Gert, Jan. (2005). *Cultures and Organizations: software of the mind*. McGraw-Hill.

Horton, J (1992) *The politics of diversity in Monterey Park California*, in L, L, Lamphere (Ed.)Structuring diversity: ethnographic perspectives on the new immigration (Chicago, University of Chicago Press), 215-246

Jones, Lisa A. (2005) '*The cultural identity of students: what teachers should know*'. Kappa Delta Record, 41 (4)

Lewis, R. D. (2006). *When cultures collide*: leading across cultures (3rd ed.) Boston: Nicholas Brealey International

Lustig, M. W. and Koester, J. (2006). *Intercultural competence: Interpersonal communication across cultures*. Boston MA: Pearson Education.

Miller, D. (2006) "*Multiculturalism and the welfare state: Theoretical reflections*". In Banting K. and W. Kymlicka *Multiculturalism and The Welfare State: Recognition and redistribution in contemporary democracies*". Oxford: Oxford University Press.

Parekh, B., 2007b. *Multiculturalism. In:* J. Baggini and J. Strangroom, eds. *What more philosophers think*. London: Continuum, 45-56.

Parekh, B., 2007 An. Interview with Bhikhu Parekh. 17th October 2007.

Powell, R, Sobel, D., Verdi, M & Hess, R (2000) The influence of situative cognition on selected rural pre-service teachers' perspectives of teaching in contexts of diversity: an exploratory study. Paper presented at the annual conference of American Educational Research association, New Orleans, April

Ryan, Janette (2000). *A Guide to teaching International students*, Oxford: OCSLD.

Valli. Y., S .Brown., P. Race (2009) '*Cultural Inclusivity*': A Guide for Leeds Met Staff. Leeds Metropolitan University

Volet, S. and Ang, G. (1998). '*Culturally mixed groups on international campuses*: an opportunity for intercultural learning'. Higher Education Research and Development, 17 (1), 5-24

Ya-Wen Teng, L. (2005). *A cross-cultural communication experience at a higher education institution in Taiwan*. Journal of Intercultural Communication. Available: http://www.immi.se/intercultural/nr10/teng.htm

Zeichner, K. (1993) *Educating Teachers for Cultural Diversity*. Paper presented at the annual meeting of the American Education Research Association, Atlanta, April.

Part 3
MULTICULTURALISM, INTER-ETHNIC RELATIONS AND DIALOGUE

Multiculturalism in Britain on the Basis of the Qur'an, Rumi or the Traditionalist Vision

Dr. Tarik Quadir [64]

Religion being integral to major cultural communities of Britain such as the Christian, Islamic, Jewish, and Hindu ones, when we discuss Britain we are speaking of a multi-religious society (Abbas 2007 p. 289). In this connection, at a time of high Islamophobia in Britain, more than ever, Muslims should make every effort to offer a vision that would pave the way for interreligious respect and not just tolerance. This paper is an attempt to do just that in light of the Qur'an, Rumi and the Traditionalist vision of some contemporary Muslims.

Since 1997 the New Labour policies in Britain encouraged intercultural including interreligious dialogues as part of a drive to bring about greater harmony among all the ethnic, cultural or religious groups (Nam-Kook 2011 p. 128). The New Right which governed Britain during the previous two decades largely ignored the need to appreciate the minority cultures including their religious traditions (Nam-Kook 2011 p.127). The New Labour's multiculturalist vision was in part an effort to unite the various ethnic, cultural or religious groups through greater mutual understanding.

---

64 Dr Tarik Masud Quadir is Assistant Professor at Mevlana University, Konya, Turkey. Since September 2011 he has been based at Mevlana (Rumi) Research Centre and the Dept. of English Language at the university. In Spring Semester 2011 Dr Quadir taught a course titled Rumi: His Life and Teachings for the Department of Eastern Languages and Literature, Selcuk University, Konya. Between the years 2008-2009 he taught English preparatory courses (part-time) at the Selcuk University, Konya. Between 1987 – 2002 he worked in New York City as a Financial Analyst at the Chemical Bank, as an Underwriter at the Blue Cross Blue Shield Insurance Company, and in Marketing Research at the Singapore Airlines, respectively. Dr Quadir's research interests include the Teachings of Mawlana Jalaluddin Rumi, Sufism, the Islamic Civilisation and the West, the Enviromental Crisis and the Islamic Response, Islamic Philosophy, History and Philosophy of Islamic Science; Modern Turkish History, World Religions.

However, since 2001 the multicultural project of the New Labour faced major challenges. In 2001, the Northern riots in the UK involving South Asian Muslims followed by the September 11 terrorist attacks in the United States carried out by 19 Arabs living in the West raised questions in the minds of many in the UK on the long term prospects of multicultural project. Suspicions against the effects of multiculturalist policies were further deepened by the London suicide bombings by mostly British born Pakistani Muslims in 2005. Many feared that the multiculturalist policy was an impediment to integration of the minority groups into the dominant culture and thus breed an anti-Western attitude that could eventually manifest as violent acts. However, such a narrative overlooks the effects of the racial, cultural or religious prejudices against minorities as possible factors behind their violent acts.

Indeed, Tariq Modood and Tahir Abbas have cogently argued that multiculturalism had nothing to do with extremism of the sort that caused the terrorist attacks in the US or in the UK (Abbas 2007; Modood 2010a). On the contrary, for them, since 2001, it was the retreat from the multicultural ideal, British support for the global 'war on terror' together with subjecting the local Muslims to ethnic and religious profiling by the police, etc., that were probable causes for the terrorist acts like the London suicide bombings (Abbas 2007 p.292). Modood and Abbas's conclusions are credible because dialogues between cultures or religions which the multiculturalism project of the New Labour sought to promote were anti-extremist by nature; it was largely confined to encouraging positive recognition of other cultures and religions by inclusion of their study in school curriculums and through government support of 'faith schools' (Bowen 2011).

Unfortunately, the relative freedom of religious education allowed in the multiculturalism project had also been misused in the way a tiny but vocal extremist political organisation such as *Hizb ut Tahrir* could preach provocative messages against non-Muslims through easily accessible literature and events organised by the organisation's student members in university campuses (Lewis 2006 pp. 166-169, Husain 2010, Mustafa 2008). While the problems that most British or European Muslims encounter in their daily lives do not have to do directly with theology but with social, economic or cultural issues, when Muslims are involved in violent acts their religion is implicated by many non-Muslims in part because of provocative messages from groups like *Hizb ut Tahrir*. While the vast majority of Muslims do not identify with radical ideologies of the kind preached by such groups, there are many who sympathise with their message without verifying it in light of the traditional Islamic resources (Hussain 2009). On the other hand, extremist groups within each religious tradition exploit a tendency among the majority of adherents of any religion which view all other religions as essentially false or inferior. Indeed, the normative theology in each religion claims itself as the most efficient way, if not the only way, to God, peace, or a truly meaningful life. In the Muslim world this relates especially to the kind of discourse that views Islam as the only true religion and non-Muslims as unbelievers.

Before the worldwide availability of the modern means of mass travel and instant communications in the twentieth century, the appreciation of the religions practiced by others would not be nearly as important as it is now. But in a world where religious element of one's identity or culture remains strong and has been growing over the last three decades even in the secular Western countries, it is imperative that we find ways of living together with greater appreciation of religions of our neighbours and colleagues. Such a vision requires inter-religious *respect* and not just tolerance (Modood 2010b).

Interreligious respect, of course, cannot be decreed. It requires understanding the phenomenon of religious diversity in the world without undermining the integrity of any tradition as understood by its adherents. In this respect, the exclusivist normative theological stances in religions must be seen in broader perspective within each religious tradition which includes not only theologies but also the religion's inner dimension and associated philosophies. I believe if we can broaden Muslim appreciation and respect for the phenomenon of religious pluralism in the world with arguments from within the traditional sources, we will have gone a long way in undermining extremist ideologies which play a role in breeding mistrust of Islam and Muslims on the one hand and help us to appreciate Islam at a deeper level on the other. If Muslims can better appreciate other faiths, similar gestures are most likely to be reciprocated by many non-Muslims who now question Muslim intentions. As Mawlana Rumi (1207 – 1273) said 'Whoever brings respect, receives it' (*Mathnawi* I 1494 in Chittick 1983 p.85).

Perhaps what is most common among religions are most of the moral values they proclaim. These values, along with the argument for the existential need for mutual tolerance, are generally the basis of much of the interfaith dialogues that take place. But beyond finding common grounds in the moral values, religions have many differences among themselves. The challenge of our day is to recognise that the goal of all the traditional religions which the overwhelming majority of the world's population follow, is one, and to accept the differences as alternative approaches to the same goal even if we cannot understand it with our ordinary rational faculty. As the prominent British Muslim intellectual Charles Le Gai Eaton remarked, 'The question as to how the contradictions between the different traditional religions can be reconciled is meaningless. Why should they be reconcilable in terms of our limited, earth-bound ideas of what does or does not make sense? Why should God bow down before our peremptory demand for rationality?' (Gai Eaton 2000 p.151). This is not to say, human beings have no way of making sense of the differences.

But, as we will see, at least from the Islamic point of view, that requires faith in the Qur'an or the realised visions of its saints such as those of Rumi (1207-73) and Ibn Arabi (1161-1240).

An argument can be made that religious exclusivists are more able to peacefully co-exist than those who deny exclusivist claims. The reason given is that exclusivist communities may work together more harmoniously if no demand is made of them to change their fundamental beliefs (Donovan 1993 p. 225). However, the fundamental lack of respect for the religions of our neighbours is likely to seriously disrupt the semblance of such a peace under difficult circumstances. The prospect for peace is even dimmer when the segregated communities base their understanding of the 'other' on violent or provocative messages originating in the other.

It would be far more preferable to find a way that does not deny the claims of the mainstream exclusivists and yet finds logic, grounded in one's own *religious* tradition, for genuine respect for the faiths of others. I believe that such a *religious* approach has already been proposed in modern times by those who are known as Traditionalists including prominent British Muslim intellectuals Martin Lings, Charles Le Gai Eaton, Reza Shah-Kazemi and its most well-known living exponent, the Iranian-American Islamic philosopher Seyyed Hossein Nasr. What's more, this approach is not anything new but an intellectual presentation in contemporary language of what the Qur'an appears to suggest and what immensely influential Muslim sages like Rumi and Ibn Arabi (1161 – 1240) point at.

The Traditionalist Vision of Religious Diversity

The Traditionalist understanding of religious diversity is based on what has been termed the Perennial philosophy. As articulated by Nasr, the Perennial philosophy proclaims three fundamental metaphysical truths: 1) An Absolute indivisible Reality 'beyond all determinations and limitations' which gives rise to the universe (Nasr 1993 p.56). 2) A hierarchic structure of reality from the Absolute Reality at the top down to the material realities on the earthly plane such that each plane of reality is derived from a higher plane of reality above it(Nasr 1993 p.58). Conversely, everything on the material plane has higher levels of reality all the way to divine order. A corollary to this principle is the existence of a hierarchic capacity for awareness of the different levels of reality; a prophet or the founder of a particular religion can access all levels of reality of what we find on earth. 3) Only an authentic religious tradition – based on revelations from the Absolute Truth – and comprised of all its doctrines, rites, and symbols, can help people properly understand the different levels of existence and guide them to higher planes of reality (Nasr 1993, p. 56). Most importantly, the Traditionalists assert that these metaphysical conclusions are not based on speculations but revealed by scriptures and verified by direct perception by the pure hearts of the prophets, saints and sages of the various religious traditions. The full implications of the first of the two metaphysical principles are expounded in the inner dimensions of all the major religious traditions (Smith 2001 p.149). We can cite, for instance, the views of Shankara, Meister Eckhart and Ibn Arabi speaking on behalf of Hinduism, Christianity and Islam, respectively.

The third principle of the Perennial philosophy is also based on the first two principles. According to the Traditionalist position, 1) each religion originates in the divine as an archetype in the sense of possessing certain 'principial possibilities' (Nasr 1993 p.62) ; 2) these potentials are then realised in historical time among the human communities the religion is destined for on the earth below (Ibid). Both of these factors are responsible for differences in doctrines, rites and symbols. The existence of the Absolute Reality and the hierarchic structure of reality necessitate seeing all things on the material plane as symbols of their higher realities in God. Since, in this view, religions are in part based on their celestial archetypes and since only the prophets and saints have access to higher realities, they alone can determine rites and symbols which then can be the most efficacious means of spiritual knowledge or the knowledge of higher realities for others. As such, as elaborated by Ibn Arabi, we cannot ignore the rites and symbols in the name of eliminating religious differences (Ibn Arabi in Chittick 1994 pp. 145-146).

In this manner, the Perennial philosophy provides a common metaphysical framework for the study of all religions irrespective of outer differences. Most importantly, for us, it accepts diversity as a metaphysical necessity and not as an argument against the possibility of the Absolute Truth as postmodernists may argue or as deviations from the one true religion as various religious fundamentalists would insist.

In principle, the Traditionalists do not see any authentic religion to be superior to another but recognise that for each, his/her religion is 'relatively absolute' (Gai Eaton pp. 149-150; Lings 2007 p. 147). For them only God in His essence is Absolute, and only at that level we can speak of an unity of religions (Nasr 1993 p. 60; Schuon 1993); all else beside the Absolute is 'relatively absolute', or 'absolute' from a limited point of view. Likewise, Nasr explains how every religion is 'absolute' within its own worldview,

> Within our solar system our sun is the sun, while seen in the perspective of galactic space, it is one of the many suns. The awareness of other suns made possible by means as abnormal to the natural and normal human state as the 'existential' awareness of several religious universes, does not make our sun cease to be our sun...within each religious universe the laws revealed,

the symbols sanctified, the doctrines hallowed by traditional authorities, the grace which vivifies the religion in question are absolute within the religious world for which they were meant without being absolute as such (Nasr 1993 pp.63-64).

However, as Martin Lings explains, an entity can be 'relatively absolute' without losing its universality, and vice versa. He points at the great religious monuments such as the Taj Mahal, the Chartres Cathedral and the Temple of Hampi belonging to the Islamic, Christian and Hindu tradition respectively, which also convey timeless beauty and grace that cannot be particularised (Lings 1982 pp. 17-19). This sense of universality may be even more palpable in saintly men and women from various religious traditions. In the same way, the Traditionalists suggest that we recognise the universal within each particular religion.

The Qur'an, Rumi and the Traditionalist Vision

I will seek to demonstrate that the Traditionalist vision is akin to Rumi's views as well as to the Quranic statements on the plurality of religious traditions in the world (Nasr 1999a and 1999b). I hope to emphasise two aspects of Quranic position in this regard: 1) God has willed the existence of the diversity of religious phenomena; 2) One's devotion to God, rather than attachment to a particular religious path, is the ultimate criterion by which God judges people and how we ought to judge one another.

The One and the Existence of the Diversity

At the most fundamental level we ought to consider God's relation to His names or attributes. It is the most fundamental relationship that also determines God's relationship to the multiplicity of creations. In Islamic understanding, we can know God by His attributes but unless we possess pure hearts like those of the prophets and saints, we cannot know God in His essence. His attributes are diverse but He is one. He is not separate from His attributes but in His essence He transcends them (Ibn Arabi in Chittick 1989 p. 49 and Chittick 1994 p. 53). Everything in the world of space and time is sign of God in the sense that it reflects His attributes even if we cannot perceive them in their full grandeur (Chittick 1994 p.24). Rumi summarises the whole about God's attributes in the world in these memorable verses:

> Consider the creatures as pure and limpid water
> Within which shine the Attributes of the Almighty.
> Their knowledge, their justice, their kindness ---
> All are stars of heaven reflected in flowing water. (*Mathnawi* VI 3172-73 in
> Chittick 1983 p. 43)

Already, within this worldview we see the first two of the principles of the Perennial philosophy: the existence of an Absolute Reality and levels of His manifestation at the level of his attributes and at the level of creations which reflect His attributes. In fact, the first half of the Muslim profession of faith, 'there is no god but God' can be taken to mean that *only* God and nothing else is Absolutely Real or the only source of being or existence for all. Moreover, the unlimited nature of God and the existence of a diversity of God's attributes prove that first, He cannot be limited to just one mode of expression and second, He reveals Himself in diverse ways. As we will see next, careful reading of the many verses in the Qur'an which touch on the subject of the plurality of religions suggest a universalist thrust in the Qur'an in terms of the source, meaning and the purpose of all traditional religions in spite of its occasional criticisms of other religions.

To begin with, the Qur'an asserts that God has sent His messengers to every nation (10:47) and sent revelations in the language of the various nations (14:4). These are clear statements indicating universality of revelations. Moreover, the Qur'an contains many verses which not only acknowledge a diversity of revelations and religions, but also promise God's rewards for those who may not follow the formal religion of Islam taught by the Prophet Muhammad:

> Verily, those who have attained to faith [in the Qur'an], as well as those who follow the Jewish faith, and the Christians, and the Sabians – all who believe in God and the Last Day – and do righteous deeds shall have their reward with their Sustainer, and no fear need they have, and neither shall they grieve. (*Qur'an* 2:62; also see 5:69)

The exclusivists point to the possibility of abrogation of such verses by citing the verse 2:106: *We abrogate no verse, nor do We cause to be forgotten, but that We bring one better than it or like it.*

However, some of the most influential commentators of the Qur'an, both in the Sunni and Shia communities including the influential Sunni commentator Tabari (d. 310/923), disagree. Tabari holds that the arguments for abrogation cannot apply to verses such as 2:62 or 5:69 where God makes promises of rewards to Jews, Christians, Sabians and to *any who believe in God, the Day of Judgement, and do righteous deeds.* Tabari argues that abrogation applies only to legal rulings and not to reports (Shah-Kazemi 2006 p.168). In the same vein, the Shia commentator Tabarsi (d.548/1153) in his refutation of the abrogation arguments states that they do not apply to God's promises to people but only to legal judgements (Ibid).

The Purpose of the Diversity

The Qur'an states that the diversity among human beings and in creation is divinely willed (3:22) and that the diversity has the purpose of making each know the other (49:13). Here we may recall the *hadith qudsi*, 'I was a hidden treasure, and I loved to be known, so I created the world.' If everything in creation reflects God's attributes, diversity among human beings, or for that matter among creation, just as in the existence of the diversity of divine names or attributes, has the purpose of making God known.

But how does the diversity of created entities become the means for knowledge of God? If each entity reflects divine attributes, each is also a means for making known something of God. Also, each entity is known by contrasting it with what is other than itself. We know what an 'apple' is because nothing else in the world is quite like an apple. By the same token, a thing becomes most apparent when we experience its opposite. As Rumi says,

> The locus of manifestation for a thing is its opposite,
> and each opposite aids its own opposite.
> If you write on a black page with black ink, your script will be hidden.
> (*Diwan* 3761-62 in Chittick 1983 p.50)

The third principle of the Perennial philosophy which upholds the necessity of following doctrines, rituals and symbols of each religion also reflects Quranic acknowledgement of the differences among religious laws and encouragement for their observance by those who profess to believe in the associated paths:

> For each We have appointed a law and a path; And if God had wished
> He would have made you one people. But He hath made you as you are
> That He may put you to test in what He hath given you.
> So vie with one another in good works. Unto God you will all be brought back
> And He will then tell you about those things wherein you differed. (5:48; also see 22:67)

Moreover, the existence of the diversity of religions appears to be a means used by God to preserve the very diversity (Qur'an 22:40):

> If God had not enabled people to defend themselves against one another, monasteries and churches and synagogues – in [all of] which God's name is abundantly extolled – would surely have been destroyed.

We might say that the differences between religions also has the purpose of making it known that God is greater than what any one religion can say of Him. Just as God in His essence transcends the multiplicity of divine attributes, God transcends any religious path even though the religions, like the divine attributes, are diverse modes of knowing Him or drawing near Him. In light of the numerous Quranic declarations suggesting God's will behind the existence of a diversity of religions, Gai Eaton pointed out, 'Reproaching those who regard religions other than their own as necessarily false, Ibn Arabi accused them of showing bad manners towards their Creator. They try to tell Him what He can or cannot do, and that is – to say the least – ill-mannered' (Gai Eaton 2000 p. 151).

The Purpose or the Goal is God

Perhaps it is not difficult to accept that there has been a multiplicity of revelations because most of us are already aware of the existence of religions and revelations other than our own. It is more difficult to understand that there is an essential *unity* in the messages of these revelations (Qur'an 41:43; 4:163-65; 42:13). The unity appears to be with regards to the ultimate purpose or goal of each religion – God: *We never sent any apostle without having revealed to him that there is no deity save Me, [and that,] therefore, you shall worship Me [alone] (21:25).* As Nasr has observed, that perennial 'religion' which is at the heart of all authentic religions consists of the way of *tawhid*, the knowing and acting in accordance with the unity of God who is also referred to in the Qur'an as the only Truth or Reality (Nasr 1999a 132). In relation to that objective all revelations are fundamentally one revelation and all nations are like one community: *Verily, this community of yours is one single community (umma), since I am the Sustainer of you all! Worship then me [alone]* (21:92).

Shah-Kazemi has drawn attention to a most likely universalist interpretation of verses 4:122-123 in light of the verse 2:111 to argue against God's disapproval of religious chauvinism in general (Shah-Kazemi 2006 pp. 186-187). In the verse 2:111 the Qur'an warns against chauvinism of the People of the Book: *They say: none entereth paradise unless he be a Jew or a Christian. These are their vain desires.* In the verse 4:122 the Qur'an speaks of God rewarding believers with paradise, without qualifying them as only the followers of the Prophet Muhammad, and then in the following verse the Qur'an warns that *it will not be according to your desires, nor the desires of the People of the Book (4:123).* To Shah-Kazemi, these verses suggest, once again, to the ultimate importance given by the Qur'an to the quality of one's submission to God irrespective of the religious path one follows.

It is in light of the above discussion that we ought to try to understand the verse, *Truly the religion with God is Islam (3:19).* It is frequently quoted by exclusivist Muslims to argue that Islam, the formal religion with its particular set of doctrines, laws, and rituals is the only religion accepted by God. However, the Qur'an appears to use the term '*islam*' and its verbal form to refer to 'submission to God' or 'to submit to God' which is also the central focus of the formal religion of Islam taught by the Prophet Muhammad. Thus, Abraham and the disciples of Jesus see themselves as *muslims* or those who have submitted to God (3:52; 6:163; 5:3). In this connection, many scholars have pointed out that 'The word *mu'min* (believer, faithful) is used 230 times in all 114 chapters... [whereas] the word *muslim*, in its different forms is used only 42 times. In many cases, *mu'min* is used to refer only to one who believes in God (*man amana bi-Allah*), be he/she a Muslim, a Christian or a Jew (Este'lami 2003 p. 429).' Since the formal religion of Islam is also a means for submission to God and the Qur'an speaks of rewarding non-Muslims (2:62; 5:69), the need to preserve the diversity of faiths (22:40), and against religious chauvinism, it is most reasonable to suppose that the verse 3:19 refers to submission to God in the universal sense.

Rumi on the Multiplicity of Religions in the World

Finally, I will briefly present how Rumi, whose example of respect for non-Islamic traditions is the *raison d'etre* for holding this workshop in Konya, has essentially the same view on religious diversity as we understand the Qur'an has. To begin with, he does not ignore the differences among religions but reminds us that the goal for each is God.

> Every prophet and every saint has a way of religious practice, But, as all those lead us to God, they are one. [*Mathnawi* I .'086 in Chittick 1983 p. 136]

With regards to love and devotion to God, for Rumi, even if the mode of worship chosen is anathema to the religion of Islam, it has a value because God only looks at the quality of one's heart: *Only he will be happy who comes before God with a heart free of evil* (26:89). This point is elaborated in a tale about Moses' encounter with an illiterate shepherd whose conception of God was grossly erroneous in the eyes of the prophet:

> Moses saw a shepherd on the way, who was saying, "O God who choosest (whom thou wilt), Where art thou that I may become Thy servant and sew Thy shoes and comb Thy head? That I may wash Thy clothes and kill Thy lice and bring milk to Thee" (*Mathnawi* II 1720-23 in Nicholson 2008)

Hearing this Moses is enraged and with theological arguments he explains how wrong it is to address God in this manner. The shepherd is confused and unable to continue with his adoration of God as he was used to. God's response in this situation illustrates Rumi's understanding of the whole issue of religious pluralism which essentially echo the verses 5:48, 22:67, 14:4, and 28:89 in the Qur'an.

> How the high God rebuked Moses, on whom be peace, on account of the shepherd.
> A revelation came to Moses from God – "Thou hast parted my servant from Me.

Didst thou come as a prophet to unite, or didst thou come to sever?...
I have bestowed on everyone a special way of acting and to everyone a form
of expression.
In regard to him it is worthy of praise, and in regard to thee poison.
I am independent of all purity and impurity...
I did not ordain (Divine worship) that I might make any profit, nay but that
I might do a kindness to my servants.
In the Hindoos the idiom of Hind is praiseworthy; in the Sindians the idiom
of Sind...
I look not at the tongue and the speech; I look at the heart and the state...
(*Mathnawi* II 1748-59 in Nicholson 2008)

As I have tried to demonstrate the Qur'an's perspective is essentially the same as that
of Rumi who said, 'So long as my life persists, I am the servant of the Qur'an and a
speck of dust on the path of Muhammad, the Chosen' (*Diwan*, Rubaiyyat No: 133
in Hidayetoglu 2011 p.64).

What About the Exclusivist Quranic Verses?

To be sure, there are verses in the Qur'an which criticise some fundamental doctrines
in other religions and condemn their followers as unbelievers. These exclusivist
verses form the strongest argument of those who hold an exclusivist position against
non-Islamic traditions. This situation demands a deeper probing into the possible
rationale for such statements in the Qur'an.

While it can be argued that the apparent meanings of these verses are "context-
specific and cannot be applied as universal principles," (Shah-Kazemi 2006 p.214)
and thus help dissipate exclusivist tendencies, many Muslims would protest that the
apparent meanings also contain some ahistorical value suggesting divine preference
for the religion of Islam taught by the Prophet Muhammad, especially as it appears
to be the message in the verse 4:47.

In any case, we cannot ignore the apparently exclusivist verses. The key, as Shah-
Kazemi points out, is to give priority to inclusivist or universalist verses over the
exclusivist verses (Shah-Kazemi 2006, p. xiv). The particular nature of an entity
cannot be properly appreciated unless we understand its universal nature first. For
instance, my universal reality in the ordinary sense is that I am a human being and
only afterwards does it make sense to speak of how I am different from another
human being. In other words, it is more important to realise the presence of *islam*
in the universal sense of *submission to God* in another religion before we focus on
how that religion differs from the formal religion of Islam taught by the Prophet
Muhammad.

In fact, even the most influential Sufis including Abu Hamid al-Ghazzali (d.1111), Ibn Arabi and Rumi did not ignore the exclusivist verses. They condemned non-Muslims for their failure to recognise the superiority of the religion of Prophet Muhammad. For Rumi, Christians had proved their "bat nature" by failing to recognise the light of the last of the prophets and failed to use their intelligence in believing Jesus as God (*Maktubat* 68: 74/148-149 in Chittick 1983 p. 124; *Discourses* pp. 135-36). However, as we have seen earlier, Rumi recognises that God has ordained different ways for different people and what may be worthy of praise to one could be "poison" for another.

Sufi commentators of the exclusivist verses take a position that does not negate the outer meanings but at the same time highlight the particularly Islamic perspective which condemns the certain Jewish or Christian doctrines that *can be* taken to ignore God's transcendent nature. For instance, Shah-Kazemi brings to light Sufi commentaries on the verse, *They have disbelieved who said: Truly God is the Messiah Son of Mary...(5:17)* which can be a major stumbling point in any Muslim-Christian dialogue (Roberts 2011 pp. 73-74; Burrell 2010 pp. 418-19).

Basing on a number of *hadiths* and *hadith qudsi* and many Quranic verses, the Sufi view that every human being has the potential to realise his/her unity with God without forgetting his/her nothingness before God, many Sufis would concur with Ibn Arbi's comments on the verse in question in his *Fusus al-Hikam*: "The real error and unbelief in the full sense of the word is not in their saying "He is God" nor "the son of Mary," but in their having turned aside from God by enclosing [God within one particular human form]." (Ibn Arabi in Shah-Kazemi 2006 p.221)

The Sufi way of interpretation allows us to understand non-Islamic theology in Islamic terms and at the same time appreciate the exclusivist verses in the Qur'an without rejecting salvific value of other religions. We might say when we take the 'exclusivists' verses under consideration, even the Sufis cannot completely give up the claim of superiority over other traditions. The Traditionalist Islamic scholars like Nasr, Lings and Eaton may see in this superior attitude a manifestation of the principle of 'relatively absolute' we discussed earlier. But as Lings suggests, Islam may claim its relative superiority on the ground that the Qur'an, more than scriptures of other religions, has been explicit in acknowledging the universality of revelations (Lings 1982 pp. 23-24).

In summary, the Muslim need not believe in the Sufi interpretations or give up the notion that Islam was preferable to other religions while at the same time accept the salvific value of other religions. However, the Sufi interpretations of the exclusivist verses can further soften the Muslim exclusivist stances, especially among the contemplatives. And finally, the Traditionalist vision of contemporary

Islamic scholars provides a powerful tool to view the exclusivist and the inclusivist stances as well as the fundamental unity of various religious traditions in proper perspectives. I believe, if these views are widely discussed, the influence of extremist ideologies is bound to dissipate and make way for a more united multicultural society in Britain and elsewhere.

Bibliography

Abbas, T. (2007) 'Muslim Minorities in Britain: Integration, Multiculturalism and Radicalism in the Post-7/7 Period', *Journal of International Studies*, Vol. 28, No. 3, August 2007: 287-300.

Burrell, D. B. (2010) 'Christian Muslim Dialogue in a World Gone Religiously Awry', *The Muslim World,* Vol. 100: 414-423.

Chittick, W.C. Imaginal Worlds: Ibn al-Arabi and the Problem of Religious Diversity. Albany, NY: State University of New York Press, 1994.

Chittick, W.C. (1989) *The Sufi path of knowledge: Ibn al-Arabi's metaphysics of imagination.* New York: State University of New York Press.

Chittick, W.C. (1983) *The Sufi Path of Love: The Spiritual Teachings of Rūmī.* Albany, NY: State University of New York Press, 1983.

Donovan, P. 'The Intolerance of Religious Pluralism', Religious Studies, vol. 29.

Este'lami, M. (2003) 'Rumi and the Universality of his Message', Islam and Christian-Muslim Relations, Vol. 14, N0. 4: 429-434.

Gai Eaton, C.L. (2000) Remembering God: Reflections on Islam, ABC International Group.

Hussain, E. (2010) 'Radical Departure', New Statesman, 15 February, Vol. 139 issue 4988: 28-30.

Hussain, E. (2009) The Islamist, London: Penguin.

Hidayetoglu, S. (2011) 'Rumi and Sufism' in Rumi and His Sufi Path of Love, ed. Fatih Citlak & Huseyin Bingul, New Jersy: Tughra Books: 60-66.

Lewis, P. (2006) 'Only Connect: can the ulema address the crisis in the transmission of Islam to a new generation of South Asians in Britain', Contemporary South Asia 15(2): 165-180.

Lings, M. (1982) What is Sufism? London: Unwin Paperbacks.

Lings, M. Ancient Beliefs and Modern Superstitions, 2nd edition. London: Unwin Paperbacks, 1980.

Lings, M. (2007) "The Past in the Light of the Present." In The Underlying Religion: An Introduction to the Perennial Philosophy, eds. Martin Lings and Clinton Minnaar. Bloomington, IN: World Wisdom, 2007: 35-54.

The Message of the Qur'an (2003) trans. Muhammad Asad, Watsonville, CA: The Book Foundation, 2003.

Modood, T. (2010a) 'Multicultural Citizenship and Muslim Identity Politics', *interventions* Vol. 12(2) 157-170.

Modood, T. (2010b) 'Moderate Secularism, Religion as Identity and Respect for Religion', The Political Quarterly, Vol. 81, No. 1: 4-14.

Mustafa, U. (2010) 'Why I Left', New Statesman, 3 March, Vol. 137 issue 4886: 32-33.

Nam-Kook, K. (2011) 'Deliberative multiculturalism in New Labour's Britain', *Citizenship Studies*, Vol. 15, No. 1: 125-144.

Nasr, S.H. (1993) The Need for a Sacred Science. New York: State University of New York.

Nasr, S.H. (1999a) 'Islam and the Encounter of Religions' in Sufi Essays, 3rd edition. Chicago: ABC International Group: 123-151.

Nasr, S.H. (1999b) Sufism and the Integration of Man, Temenos Academy Papers No. 21, London, UK: The Temenos Academy.

Rumi, Jalaluddin. (2008) *The Mathnawi,*trans. Reynold A. Nicholson, Konya: Konya Metropolitan Municipality Book No: 145.

Roberts, N. (2011) 'Trinity vs. Monotheism: A False Dichotomy', *The Muslim World,* vol 101: 73-93.

Schuon, F. (1993) *The Transcendental Unity of Religions*, Wheaton, IL: Quest Books.

Shah-Kazemi, R. (2006) *The Other in the Light of the One: The Universality of the Qur'an and Interfaith Dialogue*, Cambridge, UK: The Islamic Texts Society.

Smith, H. 'Nasr's Defense of the Perennial Philosophy', in The Philosophy of Seyyed Hossein Nasr, The Library of Living Philosophers, Volume XXVII, eds. Lewis Edwin Hahn, Randall E. Auxier, Lucian W. Stone, Jr. Chicago: Open Court Publishing Company, 2001: 139-158.

Multiculturalism and the Essentialist Trap

John T. S. Madeley [65]

In a rare display of harmonious agreement the leaders of Europe's three principal centre-right parties recently pronounced the death of multiculturalism after a long decline. In October 2010 German chancellor Angela Merkel of the Christian Democratic Union said that her country's attempts to build a multicultural society had 'utterly failed'. Some three months later Prime Minister David Cameron of the Conservative Party declared the United Kingdom's long-standing policy of multiculturalism a failure and called for the better integration of young Muslims to combat home-grown extremism. And less than three weeks later the Gaullist President of France Nicolas Sarkozy echoed the same judgement than multiculturalism had failed in his country and more widely, adding: 'We have been too concerned about the identity of the person who was arriving and not enough about the identity of the country that was receiving him'. Other centre-right politicians in Europe and beyond – the former prime ministers Jose Maria Aznar of Spain and John Howard of Australia, for example – have added their voices to the choral libretto that multiculturalism is now dead. (Daily Telegraph 11 February 2011.)

In this, Europe's centre-right might be seen as doing little more than climbing onto the bandwagon of Europe's far-right who have opposed multiculturalist policies from the start, typically on the grounds that they could not work because of some essential incompatibility between the traditions and values of growing numbers of immigrants from non-European cultures and the Christian traditions and values of Europe's host countries. The recent growth of far-right movements can reasonably be assumed to have encouraged the centre-right to shift further right on this issue as in recent years extreme rightist political parties have won roles in government in Italy, Austria, Bulgaria, Denmark, Hungary, Latvia and Slovakia, as well as in the European Parliament. And, more ominously, even countries which have for long maintained strong profiles of openness and liberal toleration have succumbed to the trend: in Sweden the anti-immigration Sweden Democrats despite being regarded as a pariah by Sweden's established parties won 5.7% of the votes and 20 seats in their breakthrough general election of 2010, while in the Netherlands in

---

65 John T.S. Madeley is Senior Lecturer in Government in the Department of Government, London School of Economics and Political Science. He writes on the government and politics of the Nordic countries and on religion and politics, particularly in Europe. He published the reader Religion and Politics in the Ashgate series, International Library of Politics and Comparative Government (2002).

the same year Geert Wilders' Party for Freedom (PVV) became the country's third largest party with over 15% of the vote after only four years of existence.

This paper discusses one feature of the debates of the last ten years which appear to have encouraged and rationalised the condemnation of multiculturalism in Europe: it attempts to assess the role played in them by accusations and counter-accusations of the intellectual vice of essentialism. Confusingly, essentialist arguments have featured on both sides – on the part of those who espouse multiculturalist policies as well of those who reject them, thus paradoxically providing one of the few points of agreement namely that essentialism is indeed a sociological vice. The risks associated with essentialism are however argued to be asymmetrical relative to the two sides of the debate and the argument is presented that multiculturalists need to dispense with the essentialist assumptions to which they have on occasion resorted , something they can do without undermining their core commitment to mutual respect, dialogue and intercultural understanding – and, indeed, that by abandoning essentialist errors they could strengthen their claim on public attention and support. Their antagonists on both left and right on the other hand stand condemned, in particular by their assumptions about 'the essential nature' of Islam and/or Muslim culture(s), to remain caught in an 'essentialist trap' which prevents them from seeing a way forward from the current circumstance of different cultures coexisting awkwardly in European societies to a possible future condition of intercultural understanding, religious freedom and mutual tolerance.

The Multicultural Circumstance

The recent rightward party-political shift has involved the instrumentalisation of critiques of multiculturalism which have been expressed over at least a decade by prominent media journalists and commentators whose principal target of choice has been Islam and/or Islamism, presented as a generalised threat to Western values as well as the source of quite particular threats to the security and stability of many individual Western countries. Most of these critics qualify their comments with statements to the effect that the great majority of Muslims who now reside in the West are decent, law-abiding citizens. Thus, for example, Melanie Griffiths in the introduction to her book *Londonistan: How Britain is Creating a Terror State Within*, an excoriating attack on British 'appeasement' of radical Islamism – which she presents as 'an evil ideology that hijacked a religion' – states: 'In Britain, hundreds of thousands of Muslims lead law-abiding lives and merely want to prosper and raise their families in peace.'(Phillips 2006 p.17) Christopher Caldwell's more wide-ranging *Reflections on the Revolution in Europe: Immigration, Islam and the West* on the other hand leaves it until the very last page of his long polemic against Muslim immigration into Europe to declare, rather discordantly: 'Islam is a magnificent religion that has also been, at times over the centuries, a glorious and generous culture. But all cant to the contrary, it is in no sense Europe's religion and it is in no sense Europe's culture' (Caldwell 2009 p. 286). Other commentators have dispensed with even these moderate disclaimers – the late Oriana Fallaci, for example, whose *The Rage and the Pride* became the best-selling book in the history of Italy in 2002. And in similarly radical terms the prominent Dutch politician Geert Wilders apparently refuses to allow the crucial distinction between Islam the religion and Islamism the radical political doctrine, or set of doctrines, subscribed to by some Muslims:

> the problem plaguing Western societies is Islam, full stop. Terrorism, tyranny, the subjugation of women — these are not perversions of Islam, as he sees it, but rather its very essence. "The word 'Islamism' suggests that there is a moderate Islam and a non-moderate Islam," he told me during an interview in Toronto on Sunday. "And I believe that this is a distinction that doesn't exist. It's like the Prime Minister of Turkey Erdogan, said 'There is no moderate or immoderate Islam. Islam is Islam, and that's it.' This is the Islam of the Koran. (Kay 2011)

The academic debates about the nature of multiculturalism, its merits and demerits, have been rather more modulated than -- if in many respects equally as fraught and bitterly contested as -- those in journalism and politics. Will Kymlicka's claim in 2001 that multiculturalism then represented a new consensus position in the world's liberal democracies was unfortunately timed. 2001 was also the year of the terrorist assaults of 9/11 in the United States by jihadi Islamists, of serious religious-ethnic conflicts and riots in the north of England and, coincidentally, the year that Brian Barry's coruscating book *Culture and Equality: An Egalitarian Critique of Multiculturalism* appeared. Barry claimed rather dismissively in the introduction to his book that, far from achieving consensus support beyond the sub-group of theorists who followed Kymlicka, Charles Taylor and others, 'there is something approaching a consensus among whose who do not write about it that the literature of multiculturalism is not worth wasting powder and shot on' (Barry 2001 p.6). Rather than let the multiculturalist case win by default however he then went on over 400 pages to develop a critique which argued that multiculturalism was subversive of liberal Enlightenment commitments to equal citizenship and the social democratic politics of distributive justice which underlay Europe's welfare state regimes. This academic assault from the egalitarian left was then echoed from the right a year later when from a completely different set of premises the conservative political philosopher Roger Scruton observed: 'The official view in most Western countries is that we are multicultural societies, and that cultures should be allowed complete freedom to develop in our territory, regardless of whether they conform to the root standards of behaviour that prevail here. As a result, the "multicultural" idea has become a form of apartheid' (Scruton 2002 pp.62-3). To the surprise of many, these arguments and observations appeared to be endorsed by Trevor Phillips in September 2005 – two months after the 7/7 bombings in London – when, acting as an important public official in his capacity of chairman of the Commission for Racial Equality, he warned that Britain could indeed be described as 'sleepwalking [its] way to segregation. We are becoming strangers to each other' (http://news.bbc.co.uk/1/hi/uk/4270010.stm).

One of the problems in discussing multiculturalism is, as Jonathan Chaplin has pointed out, that the term can be used to refer to at least six different things only some of which are implicated in the term's fall from grace. (Chaplin 2011 p. 32). Its semantic decay into the virtual status of a 'boo word' for many, alongside, for example, the tendentious term 'political correctness' actually only relates to some of these. The term has, he explained, been variously used to identify:

1. a *fact* of cultural diversity;
2. a *fact* of religious diversity;
3. a *doctrine* of multi-faithism;
4. an *assumption* of cultural relativism;
5. a *principle* of public policy towards minorities;
6. a *cause* of segregation.

As to the facts of contemporary multiculturalism – the extent of cultural and religious diversity, which Paul Kelly refers to as 'the circumstances of multiculturalism' – these remain matters of widespread public knowledge, although as will be seen, projections of likely future developments remain deeply controversial (Kelly 2002 p.3). The doctrine of multi-faithism and the postmodern scenario of cultural relativism have also been vigorously contested amongst theologians and philosophers, while their relevance to multicultural public policies affecting minorities remain open. Finally, multiculturalism as a cause of segregation or apartheid, for example in the manner claimed by Barry, Scruton and Trevor Phillips – is perhaps better seen in the context of the social-scientific analysis of the dynamics which have produced or sustained multiculturalism as fact. The concern here is to evaluate the implications for an understanding of both the nature and the importance of the facts, the relevance of the associated doctrines and assumptions, and the likely success or otherwise of multiculturalist public policies, of what can be called 'the essentialist trap'.

But first it is useful to review the relevance of the so-called multiculturalism of 'facts'. The Table gives figures – some estimated, others based on more robust data sources such as censuses – for all Muslim sections of the population in European countries as of 2012. It shows that, except in the area of the former Ottoman territories of South-Eastern Europe, where they represent large historically-settled populations, Muslims in fact represent only small sections of the resident populations in most countries, the largest in Western Europe being France with an estimated 5-10%. The modesty – indeed marginality – of this proportion is all the more remarkable when compared to the overwhelming size of the population with a Christian identity. To take the case of France again: despite its reputation for a dogmatic attachment to secularism (*laïcité*), those identified as in some sense Catholic are shown to account for between 83 and 85% of the population. As the Table indicates, the existence of very large single-confession Christian majorities is in fact typical of most European countries, 30 of the 40 predominantly Christian countries listed being shown as having more-than-two-thirds majorities identified with a single Christian confession (Catholic, Protestant or Orthodox). This feature of contemporary Europe is of course a legacy of the era of the confessional state when the enjoyment of full citizenship rights (however conceived) was typically restricted to those belonging to the officially established religion (Madeley 2003, 2009). Nowadays when citizenship rights are no longer conditional on religious tests and religious freedom is, in principle at least, the almost universal rule, the figures for single-confession majorities cannot be said to represent – if they ever did – corresponding levels of orthodox religious belief, practice or even of membership. Both 'belonging without believing' and 'believing without belonging' are common in different parts of Europe and levels of religious observance have declined or are declining to historically low levels with very few exceptions (Davie 2000). Even those, such as Pope John Paul II or his biographer, George Weigel, for whom European civilisation is to regarded as essentially Christian recognise these – for them, melancholy – facts, while insisting that the drafters of the European Constitution (now the Lisbon Treaty) should have acknowledged the foundational contribution of Christianity to the making of European civilisation (Weigel 2005).

The figures in the Table (see Appendix) which reflect the numerical marginality of Muslim minorities in most of Europe as proportions of the total resident population are insufficient to persuade some critics of multiculturalism that the presence of Muslims does not nonetheless present a distinct threat to the identity and security of Europe's nominally Christian host societies. Thus, authors such as Bat Ye'or, Bruce Brawer, Oriana Fallaci, Niall Ferguson and Melanie Phillips with their talk of 'Eurabia' and 'Londonistan' remain unpersuaded and undeterred and typically point to the concentration of some immigrant groups – particularly those of Muslim origin and identity – in some urban environments. Christopher Caldwell in addressing the question 'Can Europe be the same with different people in it?' implicitly de-emphasises the issue of numbers and opts instead for an impressionistic measure of intensity: 'If you measure Islam by the intensity of its followers' convictions, by its importance in political debates, by the privileges it enjoys under the laws of many

European countries, or by its capacity to intimidate potential detractors, then Islam is not the second religion of Europe but the first' (Caldwell 2009 p.142). It is the contrast between what might be called Euro-Christian weakness and loss of faith or what Weigel identifies even as Europe's century-long 'civilisational crisis' on the one hand and the seeming strength of Islamic identification on the other that persuades him to conclude: 'When an insecure, malleable, relativistic culture meets a culture that is anchored, confident, and strengthened by common doctrines, it is generally the former that changes to suit the latter.' (ibid. p.286) Eric Kaufmann meanwhile argues that, while Bernard Lewis and George Weigel's predictions that by the end of the twenty-first century Europe will have a Muslim majority are almost certainly exaggerated, demographic trends nevertheless suggest very significant changes by 2100 – according to calculations he reports Austria's Muslim population, for example, can be expected to grow from the current 4.2% to 36% (Kaufmann 2010 p.182). Less controversial surely is Kaufmann's conclusion that the principal reason for the growth of extreme rightwing movements and parties is not fear of, or disagreement with, certain religious doctrines or practices but the rapid growth of 'an ethnic minority which is deemed to be unmeltable' (ibid. p.185). Jenkins meanwhile questions the extent to which the designation 'Muslim' can be taken in the case of many young second-generation immigrants to reflect anything more than a loose cultural recognition of their parental origins (Jenkins 2007 p.18). And it is here that unavoidably the problem(s) of essentialism arise.

The Problem(s) of Essentialism

Essentialism is often used to describe a particular identity – ethnic, cultural, gendered, religious etc. – as a given, based on some 'essence' or set of core features shared by all members of a particular collectivity and distinguishing it from others. The contention is that by defining groups of actors by reference to certain essential characteristics, 'those things without which X would not be X' (Phillips 2007 p.30) one is using an inflexible lexical device to obscure the universal fact that in human affairs identities are constructed under particular circumstances by diverse human agents and are, at least potentially, always open to change or renegotiation. The essentialist trap, which can be shown to inhibit mutual understanding and dialogue on the part of those who fall into or get caught in it, leads to a constriction or occlusion of vision which inhibits awareness of the constructed nature of identities. The unwitting distortion of perspective on the part of anti-multiculturalists needs, then, to be exposed for the fallacy it is and the dangers which it presents. Unfortunately the associated dangers are all the greater because of the existence of so-called 'fundamentalists' in minority as well as majority population groups for whom the prejudiced stereotyping of religious, ethnic or cultural 'others' is either politically or socially useful – or both.

Some critics of multiculturalist theorising insist that it is itself vulnerable to the charge of essentialism. Thus Barry appears to endorse the criticisms made of Iris Marion Young's proposals for group representation that 'it seems to require an essentialized and naturalized conception of groups as internally homogeneous, clearly bounded, mutually exclusive, and maintaining specific determinate interests', adding that it all fitted nicely with 'the essentialism of the Counter-Enlightenment'. (Barry 2001 p.11) Tariq Modood summarises this particular critique as the claim that 'cultures' or 'groups' do not exist in the ways presupposed by multiculturalism:

> It is said that the positing of minority or immigrant cultures, which need to be respected, defended, publicly supported and so on, appeals to the view that cultures are discrete, frozen in time, impervious to external influences, homogeneous and without internal dissent....group membership falsely implies the existence of some shared essential characteristics, an essence. (Modood 2007 p.89)

He also cites Steven Vertovec's claim that multiculturalist theory itself assumes 'a picture of society as a "mosaic" of several bounded, nameable, individually homogeneous and unmeltable minority uni-cultures which are pinned onto the backdrop of a similarly characterised majority uni-culture' (Vertovec 1996 p.5). And it can be added, the evidence of the Table supports the impression of historical Christian mono-confessionalism in much of Europe.

It is in the context of earlier debates within feminism that accusations and counter-accusations of the intellectual sin of essentialism have been most commonly laid and most bitterly contested. In 1989 Diane Fuss targeted feminist essentialism as 'a belief in a true essence – that which is most irreducible, unchanging, and therefore constitutive of a given person and thing' while also arguing that 'there is no sure way to bracket off and to contain essentialist manoeuvres in anti-essentialist arguments' (Fuss1989 pp.2,4) And ten years later in discussing the question whether or not essentialism is at all avoidable Jane Wong pleaded rather despairingly that if it were possible to avoid it at all, then the critiques offered by anti-essentialists should certainly not themselves fall prey to essentialism as they so often seemed to do (Wong 1999). Judith Squires on the other hand has argued that essentialism is in fact considerably more prevalent in – and maybe constitutes a necessary and central feature of– arguments deployed in support of what she calls 'identity politics' in contradistinction to 'diversity politics': 'It is a common mistake to confuse essentialist identity politics with constructivist diversity politics which rejects ideas of essential unity, integrity, discreteness and fixity.' She then points out that 'it is politically significant that advocates of diversity politics aspire to distance themselves from essentialism wherever possible, whilst advocates of identity politics consciously invoke it.' (Squires 2005 pp.115-6)

The so-called essentialist trap can be said to consist of two errors in combination: the first lies in the assumption that some 'essential' feature or quality of a group (or culture) – that without which it would not qualify as a separate group (or culture) – is common to all its members virtually be definition; the second lies in the actual identification of which feature, or combination of features, is posited as 'essential' and why. In the case of groups or cultures identified by a religious label – Muslim, Christian, Hindu or whatever – the first is open to the challenge that by assuming homogeneity across the group and fixity across time it fails to acknowledge the existence and importance of intra-group differences, the presence of which are often registered among the members themselves by the use of 'sectarian', ethnic, or linguistic labels. In the case of religion, furthermore, these differences are frequently associated quite precisely with historic disagreements about what actually constitutes the 'essence' of the religion – in terms of, for example, doctrine or practice or ethical requirements. To take the extreme case of Wilders quoted earlier his claim that 'Islam is Islam' and that there is no distinction to be made between moderate and non-moderate forms – let alone between Sunni and Shi'a, or Moroccan and Moluccan etc – encapsulates the projection of homogeneity, discreteness and fixity onto the object of his dislike (or hatred). But it is the connection made with his second claim about 'terrorism, tyranny, the subjugation of women' as not perversions but the 'very essence of Islam' which compounds the first essentialist error and probably justifies the Muslim Council of Britain calling him 'an open and relentless preacher of hate'.

Since the time of Aristotle philosophers have made a distinction between the 'essential', and what are called the 'accidental', properties of a thing. 'Accidents' in this meaning of the term are the contingent, associated properties without which the thing would still be essentially the same. The second error of essentialism can therefore be said in short form to consist in counting as essence something which should be recognised as accident. And not merely in the case of Wilders but very widely in the West it has been common for Islam to be associated in the minds of Europe's autochthonous majorities more with the 'accidents' of its many cultural forms and traditions than with some supposed essence. Given the historic unfamiliarity of Europe's host societies with Islam and the emergence in recent years of intercultural tensions on the back of the co-called 'war on terror', the proliferation of essentialist prejudices especially directed towards Islam can readily be understood. Any commitment to dialogue and mutual understanding however has to address this additional source of mutual incomprehension. Nor is it simply a matter of confronting and deconstructing 'Orientalism' as Edward Said famously called it. In his book of that title and elsewhere Said pointed to 'a series of crude, essentialised caricatures of the Islamic world' which were common in the West. What particularly concerned him was 'not that it is a misrepresentation of some

Oriental essence — in which I do not for a moment believe — but that it operates as representations usually do, for a purpose, according to a tendency, in a specific historical, intellectual, and even economic setting' (Said 1985 p.273). Others have since appeared to confirm the prevalence of essentialism with its associated political agendas by pointing to the existence in some Muslim quarters of the opposite but equally essentialist error of Occidentalism. Thus in a book of under that title Ian Buruma and Avishai Margalit trace its incidence across many non-Western societies and cultures and argue: 'The view of the West in Occidentalism is like the worst aspects of its counterpart, Orientalism, which strips its human targets of their humanity…To diminish an entire society or civilization to a mass of soulless, decadent, money-grubbing, rootless, faithless, unfeeling parasites is a form of intellectual destruction' (Buruma and Margalit 2005 pp.10-11).

Olivier Roy makes the interesting argument that for Muslims in the West who find themselves 'deterritorialised' – uprooted from the traditional surroundings of the countries from which they or their parents emigrated – there is a tendency, particularly among the youth of the second generation, to reconstruct 'a universal religious identity that transcends the notion of culture' (Roy 2002). This speaks to the possibility of the emergence of an active distinction between religion and culture which, potentially at least, can undercut the essentialist assumptions that glue them together in the minds of their less friendly non-Muslim neighbours. He argues that whereas the essentialist assumptions which lie behind what he calls 'the culturalist approach' conceive of Islam 'as a discrete entity, a coherent and closed set of beliefs, values and anthropological patterns embodied in a common society, history and territory' (ibid. p.9), the lived reality for many young Muslims living in the West encourages a distinction between a core or essence of religion and the accidentals of their inherited culture. Roy's conclusions are not particularly optimistic with regard to future prospects arising from this development however: he suggests that one corollary is the emergence among Muslim youth in the West of what he calls neo-fundamentalism, adding: 'Even if only a small minority is involved, the phenomenon feeds new forms of radicalisation, among them support for Al Qaeda, but also a new sectarian communitarian discourse, advocating *multiculturalism as a means of rejecting integration into Western society*.' (Roy 2002 p.2, emphasis added) The rationale of this form of rejection can be identified as feeding off Occidentalist essentialist assumptions. If Roy is to be believed the development of neo-fundamentalism among young Muslims in the West would seem to indicate that avoiding the second error of essentialism (mis-identifying cultural accident as religious essence) does not guarantee the correction of the first (assuming an essential homogeneity, discreteness and fixity) and without that, dialogue between groups of different religious persuasion are unlikely to be fruitful.

Conclusion: For 'Soft Religion' and Dialogue

Johan Galtung, the Norwegian peace campaigner and analyst, suggests a more positive approach to understanding inter-religious tensions which is relevant to a distinction between what he regards as the essential core of religion as such and its peripheral accidentals. He describes what he calls a really-existing global 'religio-scape' mapped by concentric circles, at the 'warm' centre of which is to be found

> the maximum of intensity of *re-ligio,* of the mystic union, with all life, all humans, with the Almighty, regardless of religious discourse, beyond any language and culture and tradition, just one-ness, the oneness that is the *mysterium tremendum et fascinans.* In this oneness not only violence but even contradiction become meaningless, impossible, contrary to the idea of oneness. (Galtung 1997-8)

This he calls 'soft religion' – 'compassionate, reaching out horizontally to everybody, to all life, to the whole world without ifs and buts, reservations and exceptions' – but beyond it, away from the centre there can be found what he calls by contrast 'hard religion':

> The demarcation lines between faiths and subfaiths become ever-more clear-cut, sharp, stark. And as we move still further out the temperature falls dramatically. Hearts get frozen, love can no longer come forth; all people see is what divides, not what unites, includes others, all others. Exclusiveness is built into their minds through axiomatic, watertight dogma, and into their behavior through vertical religious organizations. (ibid.)

And it is in the outer field of 'hard religion' that different fault lines of division associated with hierachical power relations are particularly prominent:

- humans above the rest of nature (speciesism)
- men above women (sexism)
- adults against children (ageism)
- whites against nonwhites (racism)
- upper classes against lower classes (classism)
- own nation against other nations (nationalism)
- own country against other countries (patriotism)

Moving from the analytical to the practical mode, Galtung argues that there are ways of strengthening the softer, more irenic aspects of religion at its core. Clearly, and aside from the organisational and theological challenges presented by such an aim, 'cooperation among those who identify themselves with the soft, non-dividing aspects of religion and belittle or de-emphasize the harder aspects' holds out the prospect of better outcomes. Like Roy he observes that the existence of contemporary trends towards fundamentalism (whether paleo- or neo-) are less than hopeful but concludes that 'there is no alternative to dialogue without self-righteousness, between soft and hard, between women and men transforming hardened conflicts together' (ibid.).

In this perhaps Galtung, the north European writing at the end of the 20th century of the Common Era, can be seen to mirror some of the intuitions of the great Islamic poet and professor of theology in Konya, Jalal al-Din Rumi, who wrote some seven hundred years earlier. The translator and critic Reynold Nicholson described Rumi as a pantheist, a monist and a mystic and identified the following propositions in the body of his work:

> that all being is in essence One; that this essence is manifested continuously, not in a single act of creation; that God is absolute, immanent and transcendent; that His essence is unknowable except obliquely through names and attributes of the phenomenal world; that the purpose of creation is for God to know Himself; and that the Sufi or Perfect Man – as exemplified in Mohammed and the line of prophets to which he belongs – comes nearest to the realization of divine self-knowledge in human life. (Washington 2006 p.12)

But this is an essentialism beyond all accidentals which bespeaks more a vision of mystical harmony and release than the predicament of an existential trap.

Appendix

Europe: principle religions, size of Muslim groups and state-society-religion regime-types

Countries	Popn (m) 2011 est	Principal religions and size of Muslim population	State-society-religion regime type	SRAS score
Albania	3.0	**M: 70**/ O: 20/ C:10	Accommodationist	7.69
Armenia	3.0	O: 97.7	Official Religion	40.36
Austria	8.2	C: 73.6/ P:4.7/ **M: 4.2**	Cooperationist	24.25
Azerbaijan	0.8	**M:93.4**/ O: 4.8	Separationist	31.65
Belarus	9.6	O: 80	Endorsed Religion	35.66
Belgium	10.4	C: 75/ Other 25 inc **M: 4**	Cooperationist	25.50
Bosnia – Herz	4.6	**M: 40**/ O:31/ C: 15	Cooperationist	16.33
Bulgaria	7.1	O: 82.6/ **M: 12.2**	Endorsed Religion	36.72
Croatia	4.5	C: 87.8/ O: 4.4/ **M: 1.3**	Endorsed Religion	22.42
[Gk] Cyprus	1.1	O: 78	Cooperationist	16.13
[N. Cyprus]		**M: 99**	Cooperationist	16.96
Czech R	10.2	C: 26.8/ P:2.1	Cooperationist	18.19
Denmark	5.5	P: 95/ **M: 2**	Official Religion	26.04
Estonia	1.3	P: 13.6/ O:12.8	Accommodationist	3.52
Finland	5.3	P: 82.5/ O:1.1	Official Religion(s)	32.88
France	66.3	C: 83-88/ **M: 5-10**/ P: 2	Separationist	22.92
Georgia	8.2	O: 83.9/ **M: 9.9**	Endorsed Religion	32.83
Germany	81.5	P: 34/ C: 34/ **M: 3.7**	Cooperationist	19.88
Greece	10.8	O: 98/ **M: 1.3**	Official Religion	33.31
Hungary	10.0	C: 51.9/ P: 18.9/ O: 2.6	Cooperationist	22.79
Iceland	0.3	P: 84/ C: 2.5	Official Religion	29.79
Ireland	4.7	87.4/ P: 4.8	Endorsed Religion	15.75
Italy	61.0	C: 90	Cooperationist	13.00
Kosovo	1.8	**M: 90**/ O: 0.7	?	n.d.
Latvia	2.3	P: 19.6/ O: 15.3/	Cooperationist	17.56
Lithuania	3.5	C: 79/ O: 4.1/ P: 1.9	Cooperationist	17.58
Luxembourg	0.5	C: 87	Cooperationist	10.50

Macedonia	2.1	O: 64.7/ **M: 33.3**	Endorsed Religion	27.17
Moldova	4.3	O: 98	Endorsed Religion	32.34
Malta	0.4	C: 98	Official Religion	25.63
Montenegro	0.7	O: 74.2/ **M: 17.7**/ C: 3.5	Cooperationist?	n.d.
Netherlands	16.9	C: 30/ P: 20/ **M: 5.8**	Accommodationist	1.25
Norway	4.7	P: 86.7/ **M: 1.8**	Official Religion	25.83
Poland	33.4	C: 89.8/ O: 1.3	Endorsed Religion	22.21
Portugal	10.8	C: 84.5	Endorsed Religion	21.94
Romania	21.9	O: 86.8/ P: 7.5/ C: 4.5	Endorsed Religion	22.50
Russia	138.7	O: 15-20/ **M: 10-15**/ P: 2	Endorsed Religion	30.48
Serbia	7.3	O: 85/ C: 5.5/ **M: 3.2**	Cooperationist?	16.75?
Slovakia	5.5	C: 68.9/ P: 10.8/ O: 4.1	Cooperationist	19.88
Slovenia	2.0	C: 57.8/ **M: 2.4**/ O: 2.3	Cooperationist	11.96
Spain	46.8	C: 94	Official Religion	28.46
Sweden	9.1	P: 87	Cooperationist	12.17
Switzerland	7.6	C: 41.8/ P: 35.3/ O: 1.8	Cooperationist	20,50
Turkey	78.8	**M: 98.8**	Official Religion	
Ukraine	43.1	O: 76.5/ C: 2/ P: 2	Cooperationist	19.99
United Kingdom	62.7	P: 55 / C: 10 / **M: 2.7**	Official Religion(s)	26.67

Codes: C = Catholic; P = Protestant; O = Orthodox; M = Muslim

Sources: CIA The World Factbook https://www.cia.gov/library/publications/the-world-factbook/geos/bk.html (accessed 30.01.12) supplemented by information from Fox, 2008 and Barrett et al, 2001.

Note: Fox's SRAS index scores represent an overall measure of Separation of Religion and State (where 0 = full separation). The State-Religious Regime Type labels are a combination of those used by Fox and by Cole Durham (1996, pp. 20-22) The latter's Endorsed Religion is preferred to Fox's Civil Religion, while Fox's Official Religion is preferred to Cole Durham's Established Church(es).

Bibliography

Barrett, Barrett, D., Kurian, G.T. and Johnson, T.D.(eds) (2001). *World Christian Encylopaedia: a comparative study of churches and religions in the modern world* 2nd edn: New York: Oxford University Press.

Barry, Brian (2001) *Culture and Equality: An Egalitarian Critique of Multiculturalism* Cambridge: Polity Press.

Buruma, Ian and Margalit, Avishai (2005) *Occidentalism: A Short History of Anti-Westernism* London: Atlantic Books

Caldwell, Christopher (2009) *Reflections on the Revolution in Europe: Immigration, Islam and the West* London: Allen Lane

Chaplin, Jonathan (2011) *Multiculturalism: a Christian Retrieval* London: Theos.

Davie, Grace (2000) *Religion in Modern Europe: A Memory Mutates* Oxford: Oxford University Press

Durham, Cole (1996) 'Perspectives in Religious Liberty: A Comparative Framework' in J.D. van der Vyver and J. Witte (eds), *Religious Human Rights in Global Perspective* The Hague: Martinus Nijhoff Publishers pp.1-44

Fox, Jonathan (2008) *A World Survey of Religion and the State* Cambridge: Cambridge University Press

Galtung Johan (1997-8) 'Religions Hard and Soft' in *Cross Currents* 47:4 http://www.crosscurrents.org/galtung.html

Jenkins, Philip (2007) *God's Continent: Christianity, Islam and Europe's Religious Crisis* Oxford: Oxford University Press.

Kaufmann, Eric (2010) *Shall the Religious Inherit the Earth?* London: Profile Books

Kay, Jonathan (2011) 'Geert Wilders' Problem with Islam.' *Full Comment: National Post* http://www.nationalpost.com/index.html

Kelly, Paul (2002) 'Introduction: Between Culture and Equality' in Kelly, Paul (ed) *Multiculturalism Reconsidered. Culture and Equality and its Critics* Cambridge: Polity Press.

Kymlicka, Will (2001) Politics in the Vernacular: Nationalism, Multiculturalism and Citizenship Oxford: Oxford University Press.

Madeley, John (2003) 'A Framework for the Comparative Analysis of Church-state Relations in Europe' in Madeley, John T.S. and Enyedi, Zsolt (eds), *Church and State in Contemporary Europe: The Chimera of Neutrality*. London: Frank Cass.

Madeley, John (2009) 'Religion and the State' in Haynes, Jeffrey (ed) *Routledge Handbook or Religion and Politics* London: Routledge

Modood, Tariq. (2007) *Multiculturalism: A Civic Idea* Cambridge: Polity Press.

Phillips, Anne (2007) *Multiculturalism without Culture* Princeton: Princeton University Press.

Roy, Olivier (2002) *Globalised Islam: The Search for the New Ummah* London: Hurst

Said, Edward (1985), *Orientalism* Harmondsworth: Penguin

Scruton, Roger (2002) *The West and the Rest: Globalization and the Terrorist Threat* London: Continuum Books.

Squires, Judith (2007) 'Culture, Equality and Diversity' in Kelly, Paul (ed) (2002) *Multiculturalism Reconsidered.* Culture and Equality *and its Critics* Cambridge: Polity Press.

Vertovec, Steven (1996) 'Multiculturalism, Culturalism and Public Incorporation' in *Ethnic and Racial Studies* 19: 49-69

Washington, Peter (ed) (2006) *Rumi Poems* London: Knopf

Weigel, George (2005) *The Cube and the Cathedral: Europe, America, and Politics Without God* New York: Basic Books

Wong, Jane (1999) 'The Anti-Essentialism v. Essentialism Debate in Feminist Legal Theory: The Debate and Beyond' in 5 *William & Mary Journal.* Women & L. 273

Multiculturalism in Turkey: Possible Solutions to the Kurdish Issue From *Risale-i Nur*

Hakan Gok [66]

Introduction

For every person who has lived in or has had connections with Turkey over the last thirty years, one problem has persistently presented itself on almost every aspect of daily life: the Kurdish issue. Sometimes it took the form of dismay, sometimes hatred and sometimes extreme violence and murder.

Over the years, successive governments have put the military in charge of dealing with the matter in their own way, i.e. using force against force. Many academic researches also have been conducted on the possible sources and the solutions to the problem (Gunter 1988). In this paper, I shall focus on Said Nursi's suggestions for the possible solution to the Kurdish problem in Turkey.

Early Historical Background

Kurds, some 25 million people inhabiting mainly the southeast of Turkey, Northwest of Iran and North of Iraq, are one of the largest stateless ethnic groups in the world. The largest section of this population lives in Turkey. According to 2010 CIA estimates, there are about 14 million Kurds living in Turkey. This constitutes more than half of the entire Kurdish population of the world.

Kurds have always lived in and around the region of Asia Minor in Mesopotamia and came into contact with Muslim Arabs for the first time in the 7th century (CE) as the Islamic empire expanded its borders to the north. This is the beginning of

---

66 Hakan Gok is currently undertaking PhD research at Durham University. His PhD thesis is on 'Philosophy of Religion: Atheism and Theism, Said Nursi's philosophy and *Risale-i Nur*'. Hakan Gok graduated from Middle East Technical University in Ankara in 1995 as a science teacher. He taught science at high school level in various countries including the UK. He completed his Masters Degree in Leadership and Management in Education in the UK in 2005. His interest in Said Nursi's writings led him to studying PhD in Philosophy at Durham University. Hakan is currently living in the UK and working on his book on 'The Arguments for the Existence of God'. His research interests include, but are not restricted to the philosophical and sociological arguments in the *Risale-i Nur*, scientific and social aspects of the Qur'an and questions relating to God-morality-politics and space-time-causality and substance.

most Kurds converting into Islam from their original religion of Zoroastrianism.

From the 9th century, there have been small Kurdish autonomous principalities. The 12th century Ayyubid era was probably the brightest Kurdish age. With the rise of the Ottoman Empire and the fall of the Safavids, Kurdistan was annexed to the Ottoman Empire in the 16th century.

The first Kurdish riot was recorded in 1640 when the Ottoman forces attacked the Yazidi Kurds of Mount *Sinjar* (Saçlı Dağı). According to Evliya Çelebi, some 3,060 Kurds were killed by some 40,000 Ottoman soldiers in a 7-hour battle. Many Yazidi villages were burnt down and hundreds of Yazidis fled to the mountains (Çelebi 1991).

In 1655, due to a dispute between the Ottoman governor of Van and the Kurdish ruler of Bitlis, Kurds revolted again. This rebellion resulted in the death of hundreds (Reid 2000).

After the 1834 Kurdish independence attempt from the Ottoman Empire, the central Ottoman government increased its grip on Kurdistan, heavily garrisoning the Kurdish towns and villages.

The modernisation efforts of Mahmud II antagonised some Kurdish feudal leaders, leading them into revolt again. Since the Ottoman army was fighting Egyptians moving towards Syria, the Kurdish revolt had gone unsuppressed. Consequently, the Kurdish leader, *Bedr Khan* of Botan established a Kurdish principality and declared himself king upon the death of his brother. He raided peaceful Assyrian Christians (Nestorians) in the Hakkari region, killing some 50,000. Bedr Khan's nephew never accepted the authority of his uncle. With the deception of the Ottomans, he gathered forces and fought against his uncle. He defeated his uncle, Bedr Khan, yet he was executed by the Ottomans rather than being made the king (Meiselas & Bruinessen 1997).

In the late 19th century, sultan Abdul Hamid II formed a strong and mobile Kurdish armed cavalry to defend The Empire from Russian and Armenian attacks from the northeast. These Hamidieh soldiers were very successful in defending eastern Anatolia. Their success, therefore, was rewarded by a further integration of Kurds and by a higher position in the government for some of them.

According to Laçiner et al, The Ottomans integrated the Kurds successfully, without forced assimilation (Laciner & Bal 2007). Despite occasional revolts, the Kurdish existence within the Ottoman Empire had been fairly peaceful.

In the 20th Century

The Ottoman Empire collapsed in the early 20th century as a result of the World War I defeat. Kurds, like many other ethnic minorities within the empire were seen as usable elements against the Ottomans by the invading Western forces. Therefore, some of these ethnic groups, including the Kurds, were promised an independent state of their own in return for their cooperation with the invading forces. Some of these promises actually materialised in the form of the creation of independent states out of the collapsed Ottoman Empire. However, the Kurds had their first disappointment after the rejection of their rights as stated in the Sèvres Treaty.

Since the establishment of the secular Republic of Turkey in 1923, there have been four major revolts against the central government. These were partly motivated by nationalist feelings and partly by religious feelings.

1. Sheikh Said Revolt of 1925 was the first Kurdish revolt in modern Turkey. Some 15,000 Kurds revolted against the secular government of Ankara on the grounds that it banned the manifestation of all Kurdish identity. The revolt was crushed swiftly, and resulted in the execution of Sheikh Said and many Kurds.

2. Ararat Revolt: the Kurds from the region of Ağrı declared The State of Ararat in 1927. This new state failed to gain any support or recognition by any other states. The Turkish army mobilised some 66,000 troops and 100 aircraft to oppress and destroy this newly declared state (Olson 2001). The Turkish state gained full control of the region by 1931 (Abdulla 2007).

3. Dersim Revolt (1937-1938): the Dersim rebellion is one of the most remembered events in the history of modern Turkey. The chain of events developed from the late 19th century when the Ottoman Empire tried to relocate thousands of Armenians since they cooperated with the Russians against the Ottoman Empire. The tribes of the Dersim region, today Tunceli, helped some of the Armenians to take refuge in the Dersim region and refused to extradite them to the central government (Caglayangil 2007). After the declaration of the Republic of Turkey, the Ankara government repeatedly failed to gain full control of the Dersim region. Eventually, the army crushed the rebellion in 1937 with an aerial bombardment of pockets of resistance. The rebellion resulted in the death of 13,000 civilians, 199 troops and the relocation of 12,000 inhabitants of Dersim.

4. Kurdish Nationalism and the PKK: the 1970s marked the beginning of the reorganisation of Kurdish nationalism and resistance. The Marxist Kurdistan Workers Party, PKK, was set up by Abdullah Ocalan to demand independent Kurdish state in 1977 (Pike 2004). The 1980 military coup of General Kenan Evren made the PKK turn to guerrilla warfare, attacking military and police installations. This was the result of severe oppression of the Kurds. According to Burkay, the Kurds chose the armed struggle since the political route was closed down by the army (Burkay 2012). All three military juntas of 1960, 1971 and the 1980 military coup banned the use of the Kurdish language in an attempt to assimilate the Kurdish population (Hassanpour 1992).

Both political and military wings of the Kurdish movement are still active in Turkey. According to the ministry of defence, there have been around 28,000 PKK, 4,828 civilians and 7,946 security forces casualties since the armed resistance started in 1984 (Calislar 2009).

Said Nursi's Diagnosis

Said Nursi was one of the best-known Kurdish scholars that Ottoman Kurdistan has ever produced. He was born and studied in Eastern Turkey. He travelled through the region, and joined intellectual debates with the well-known scholars of the time. He was nicknamed by his teachers as 'Bediuzzaman' (the wonder of the times), due to his extraordinary intelligence. Said Nursi splits his life into two. The period from his birth in 1877 to the collapse of the Ottoman Empire in 1920 is what he calls 'The Old Said Era' where he was actively involved in politics and social matters. The second period of his life, from 1920 onward is called 'The New Said Era' where he abstained from politics and social affairs. He purely dedicated himself to the interpretation of Qur'an, to make it understood by the ordinary people. This naturally involved a fight against the materialist and naturalist philosophical thoughts embraced by the new, secular Republic.

After his visits to the Eastern provinces, Nursi understood that education ought to have top priority to revive the dying empire. He arrived in Istanbul, the capital of The Ottoman Empire, in 1907 in search of a support for his new education project. He presented his ideas to Sultan Abdulhamid II that the major problem in the Kurdish towns and villages was the lack of schools where the locals can learn the requirement of the time from teachers they can communicate with. We understand that the teachers appointed by the central government did not speak the local languages; hence there was lack of communication which had an adverse effect on education.

The barrier of language added an extra burden on the education system. For non Turkish speaking Kurds, accessing to education is extremely difficult.

Medresetü'z- Zehra (1907)

Nursi's life overlaps with the immense world evolution of the late 19th and 20 the centuries. 1776 French Revolution started showing its devastating effects on the old Ottoman Empire which consisted of many different nations. The idea of nationalism was rampant and every small nation wanted to have their own independent state. In part, this happened at a cost of the collapse of empires.

The education system, according to Nursi, was in dire need of reform. Nursi saw that the positive sciences and religious studies are taught independent from each other in different schools. Therefore, people who study modern sciences lack metaphysical awareness, and people who studied religious sciences lacked the knowledge of modern science and technology.

In order to address all of these issues, Nursi came up with a university project, that he called 'Medresetü'z Zehra', which translates into English as The University of Zehra Flower. Nursi provisioned this university as a female partner of Al-Azhar University of Cairo. This university, Nursi explained, ought to be female, a mother in a sense, to be productive, to give birth and to reproduce.

The structure of Nursi's University project addressed all the issues surrounding the Eastern World. This university should have all three languages spoken in the region. The Arabic language, which is the language of Qur'an and the religious sciences has to be the main language. The Turkish language has to be the language of the modern science and the Kurdish language has to be the permitted daily communication language of those who wish to use it.

Court-Marshall (1909)

The declaration of Second Ottoman Constitution in 1908 (2. Meşrutiyet) created yet another anarchic condition in Istanbul. Nursi always openly declared himself as a republican. He gave public speeches in support of democratic constitutionalism. Nursi published his supporting views in a newspaper. He was arrested and tried in the Court-Marshall for his involvement with the Muhammedan Unity Party (*Ittihad-i Muhammedi*) which was accused of being the cause of the 31 March revolt in 1909. After a brief incarceration, he was acquitted. His defence in the Court Marshall later published in 1911 under the title of '*Divan-ı Harb-i Örfi*' where he describes three enemies as [1] ignorance, [2] poverty, and [3] internal conflict. He said: 'We should combat (*jihad*) these enemies with [1] education, [2] industry and, [3] unity (Nursi 2004, p. 1921)

Damascus Sermon (1911)

Another of Nursi's systematic diagnoses of the problems faced by the people of the Muslim world and Ottoman Kurdistan in particular appeared in his 1911 Damascus Sermon. Nursi travelled to Damascus, Syria in the spring of 1911, and gave a speech to some 3,000 people of which 100 were the top scholars of the

Muslim world. Nursi, aged 34, explained to the crowd in the Umayyad Mosque that there are six diseases causing all the troubles of the region. He said:

> In the conditions of the present time in these lands, I have learnt a lesson in the school of mankind's social life and I have realized that what has allowed Europeans to fly towards the future on progress while it arrested us and kept us, in respect of material development, in the Middle Ages are six dire sicknesses. The sicknesses are these:
> Firstly: the coming to life and rise of despair and hopelessness in social life.
> Secondly: the death of truthfulness in social and political life.
> Thirdly: love of enmity.
> Fourthly: not knowing the luminous bonds that bind the believers to one another.
> Fifthly: despotism, which spreads like various contagious diseases.
> And sixthly: restricting endeavour to what is personally beneficial (Nursi 2004, pp.1961-63)

Three elements in Nursi's speeches and writings stand out. The first and foremost is his emphasis on democracy and freedom. Nursi believes that despotism is one of the main sources of hatred. When he was seen feeding some ants from his own food, he replied to his students: 'These ants are republican creatures, I feed them to reward their positive behaviour'.

The second theme in Nursi's works is the emphasis on education. Nursi systematically worked towards modernising the education system which was meant to recognise the Kurdish language along with Arabic and Turkish. This also would make education more accessible to every Kurdish speaking citizen of the Eastern provinces.

The natural consequence of good education is creation of a well-educated, knowledgeable society, which ought to be more creative, more productive and generate its own wealth. Nursi places a great emphasis on the eradication of poverty. It is a well-established fact that unemployment creates purposelessness in life, hence forcing individuals into criminality. The role of poverty and unemployment in the Kurdish insurgence is also acknowledged by the government as well.

Nursi stressed the cultural tendency of eastern people towards the love of conflict and hostility. He prescribed unity and brotherhood as a cure to this disease. He advised his followers to see the positive aspects of events rather than focusing on the negative aspects which might fuel the hatred further. He emphasises the sources of possible unity. He writes in his Brotherhood Treatise (*Uhuvvet Risalesi*) that

> (Among the Turkish and Kurdish believers) you have got the same God,

same prophet, same book, same *qibla*, same village, same country and so forth... All of these things held in common dictate oneness and unity, union and concord, love and brotherhood, and indeed the cosmos and the planets are similarly interlinked by unseen chains. If, despite all this, you prefer things worthless and transient as a spider's web that give rise to dispute and discord, to rancour and enmity, and engage in true enmity towards a believer, then you will understand - unless your heart is dead and your intelligence extinguished - how great is your disrespect for that bond of unity, your slight to that relation of love, your transgression against that tie of brotherhood (Nursi 2004, p.470)

Nursi highlights the dangers of what he calls 'the negative nationalism'. This is praising one's nation in excess to the limits of racism. The food of negative nationalism, according to Nursi, is the hatred and destruction of other nations (Nursi 2004). He calls people to tolerance and fraternity and collaboration. The Qur'anic verse of 49:13 is Nursi's point of support which reads:

O mankind, indeed We have created you from male and female and made you peoples and tribes that you may know one another. Indeed, the most noble of you in the sight of Allah is the most righteous of you. Indeed, Allah is Knowing and Acquainted.

Positive nationalism, Nursi argues, should serve and help Islam, not to replace it. Nursi tacitly criticises the new secular, nationalist Ankara government who aimed to set up a nation state of Turks at a high cost of alienating and rejecting the existence of other nations.

Conclusion

The historical pattern of Kurdish rebellions shows us that they are caused by [1] religious reasons, like Sheikh Said Revolt, [2] political reasons, like Dersim Revolts and [3] nationalist reasons, like the PKK insurgence. Almost all these events indicate that ignorance as in the sense of lack of proper education, poverty, and lack of freedom fuelled the problem.

Therefore, Nursi's suggestions to the solution of the Kurdish problem could be divided into two groups. The first set of recommendations is to the government and the second set of recommendations is to the ordinary members of the public.

Nursi's Advice to the Government

Nursi clearly disagreed with some of the foundational principals of Turkey, such as, secularism and nationalism. He argues that more freedom and better democracy is the first key. This could be achieved through equality of every different nation and tribe. Recognition of each culture, religion and language is essential. The government has to ensure this democratic equality and recognition is achieved.

His second piece of advice is accessible education for all. It is government's responsibility to ensure that the citizens, no matter what language they speak, should receive equal and fair education. One possible formula for this is multilingual universities such as *Medresetü'z Zehra*.

Thirdly, his advice to the government is the eradication of poverty. This could be achieved with more education, and more investment. Nursi believes that poverty is the source of most evils, and poor people are always open to abuse. The recent PKK phenomena showed that it is mainly uneducated and economically disadvantaged individuals that fell into the hands of PKK and are forced to conduct a guerrilla fight against a regular army.

Nursi also criticised the secularist ideology of Turkey which is more of a form of curtailment of religious freedom than the Western version of state having equal distance to every faith. He believed that religion has to play a greater role in the development and governance of eastern societies.

Nursi's Advice to Individuals

Nursi argues that winning over civilised people could be achieved only by convincing them. He explains that the real *jihad* is that of knowledge and industry, not swords and guns. On his advice to the Kurdish porters, he said: 'you should make your swords from science, art, and collaboration' (Nursi 2004, p.1925).

Love of enmity should be replaced with love of love and hatred to enmity. Nursi was well aware of the previous tensions between the different nations within the Ottoman Empire especially that of the Kurds. He clearly prescribed peace and tolerance as opposed to struggle and hatred. He explained that if there were nine murderers and one innocent person on a boat, it is not acceptable to sink that boat. His message in this analogy is that, although there are nasty elements of Turks and Kurds, it is not acceptable to hate entire nations. He built his argument of peace and love around the verses of Qur'an which read:

> The believers are but brothers, so make settlement between your brothers. And fear Allah that you may receive mercy.
>
> And not equal are the good deed and the bad. Repel [evil] by that [deed] which is better; and thereupon the one whom between you and him is enmity [will become] as though he was a devoted friend.

He explains that defeating one's own anger, and forgiving others is more virtuous than punishing them.

Nursi consistently and systematically promoted Qur'anic fraternity and brotherhood between the Kurds and Turks. He tirelessly worked towards convincing the people that the internal conflict between the Kurds and Turks would weaken the remaining Muslim community in Anatolia. He openly opposed Sheik Said and explained to him that although his motivation of revolt is for the sake of Islam, he would not point guns at the children of a nation who had been the servants of Islam for many centuries. Although he was Kurdish himself, he describes his nation as nation of Islam; he did not favour an ordinary Kurdish to a pious Turkish. He argued that the virtue is not in the ethnicity but in the fear and respect to God and His commandments.

Bibliography

Abdulla, Mufid (2007-10-26). "The Kurdish issue in Turkey need political solution". *Kurdish Media.*

Burkay, Kemal. Zaman Newspaper, retrieved 20 January 2012

Çaglayangil, İhsan Sabri (2007) "*Çağlayangil'in Anıları / Kader Bizi Una Değil, Üne İtti*", , Bilgi Yayınevi

Çalislar, Oral (2009) "En çok 'şehit' Şırnak'tan", Radikal Newspaper

Çelebi, Evliya (1991) *The Intimate Life of an Ottoman Statesman: Melek Ahmed Pasha (1588–1662)*, Translated by Robert Dankoff, SUNY Press

Gunter, Michael M. (1988) The Kurdish Problem in Turkey, *Middle East Journal,* Vol. 42,

Hassanpour, Amir (1992). "Kurdish Language Policy in Turkey". *Nationalism and Language in Kurdistan 1918-1985.* Edwin Mellon Press.

Laciner, Sedat. & BAL, Ihsan. "The Ideological And Historical Roots Of Kurdist Movements In Turkey: Ethnicity Demography, Politics".*Nationalism and Ethnic Politics* 10 (3)

504.doi:10.1080/13537110490518282. Retrieved 19 October 2007.

Meiselas, Susan, & Bruinessen, Martin van. (1997). *Kurdistan: In the shadow of history.* New York: Random House.

Nursi, Said (2004) '*Divan-i Harb-i Örfi*', Risale-i Nur Külliyati, Istanbul: Nesil

Nursi, Said (2004) '*Damascus Sermon*', Risale-i Nur Külliyati, Istanbul: Nesil

Nursi, Said (2004) 'The Letters', Risale-i Nur Külliyati, Istanbul: Nesil

Olson, Robert William. (2001). *Turkey's relations with Iran, Syria, Israel, and Russia, 1991-2000: The Kurdish and Islamist questions.* Costa Mesa, Calif: Mazda Publishers.

Pike, John (2004-05-21). "Kurdistan Workers' Party (PKK)". Federation of American Scientists.

Reid, James J. (2000) *Batak 1876: a massacre and its significance*, Journal of Genocide Research, 2(3)

Strengths and Weaknesses of Multiculturalism

Hengameh Ashraf Emami [67]

This paper explores different aspects and concepts of culture, cultural assimilation and multiculturalism, through the weaving together of academic points of view and those of people in the community. To achieve this purpose, the chosen methodology has consisted of looking at various academic reviews and conducting a series of interviews with people from the host society, and also conducting interviews with a range of immigrants to the North East of England. From this variety of sources, suggestions have been derived to assist those policy-makers whose remit is to create and promote a society where people can live in peace and harmony.

The History of Immigration in the United Kingdom

Immigration has always been an important aspect of human history, involving enormous challenges and cultural transitions. It is a topic which has become increasingly controversial, and which has sparked an interest across many disciplines, including history, sociology, politics, anthropology and religious studies.

Migration may occur in the form of a permanent or semi-permanent variation of residency. Everett S. Lee (1996 p. 285) points out four major factors which help to determine a pattern of immigration: the area of origin, the area of destination, intervening obstacles, and personal factors. The history of immigrants to the UK, including Muslims, can be traced by at least one of these factors to varying degrees in different time periods. The late 1950s to 1962 could be called the 'golden age' for immigrants into the UK, as there were not many obstacles to migration; in fact, the great requirement for low-cost labour encouraged immigrants from ex-colonies (Gardner 2002).

---

67 Hengameh is a part-time PhD student at the University of Sunderland. Her research explores culture and identities of two generations of Muslim women in Newcastle upon Tyne and Glasgow. Her research interests include culture and belonging, identity, race, racism, immigration, assimilation and gender. Ms Emami has also translated the book *al-Luma' fi al-Tassawwuf* ed. R.A. Nicholson (Luzac& Co., London, 1914) from English to Farsi (2002) as a Semnan University publication. Hengameh Ashraf Emami has extensive experience in research, teaching adults, and higher education. Her Professional background includes team management, project coordination, mentoring, and liaising with other agencies in the education and community sectors. Hengameh has worked in various communities and academia including Islamic Heritage where she presented three well received exhibitions in the North East of England funded by the Lottery Heritage Fund, contributed to talks and seminars at various occasions, and has been involved in Inter-religious relations in the North East of England.

The media's attention and general debate regarding race and immigration reached a peak after the Second World War. Racial conflict hit its highest point throughout the UK following Enoch Powell's *'rivers of blood'* speech in 1968 (Panayi 1996 p. 196). Racism was not a new phenomenon in the UK; as Anoop Nayak (2003 p. 40) states, 'the roots of racism in the region [the North of England] are longstanding'. Race hatred was increasing, not because of the number of immigrants, but because of the attitude of politicians and the views expressed by the media which provoked prejudice (Gordon and Rosenberg 1989 p. 23). History was witness to a series of racially-motivated murders which took place in Essex, Southall, West London and Leamington Spa (Gordon 1990 p. 8).

The Commonwealth Immigration Act of 1962 was a turning point for the growing Muslim population in the UK. Several Muslim generations of Muslims were already established in cities such as Liverpool, Cardiff and London by 1962 the ones who arrived in the 1960s were mainly from South Asia. Muslims in Britain since 1800 were Yemenis and Somalis on British ships in the early of century 20th. Yemenis who actually remained for a long period, some of whom eventually married English women and settled permanently in the UK. Another series of migrations originated from East African countries. The Commonwealth Immigration Act of 1962 lead to significant growth in the Muslim population of Britain. This was followed by the Race Relations Act of 1968, prior to the arrival of South Asian immigrants from Kenya, Uganda and Tanganyika who had obtained their right of British Citizenship because of the racism they had experienced from the new African governments in East Africa. It took eighteen months to implement the Immigration Act, and this gave the immigrants a chance to decide whether to stay or return to their original homeland. In 1964, new legislation came into force that prevented unskilled workers from working in Britain. The second group of immigrants was from East Africa, comprising huge numbers of Asians who had British passports and were determined to enter Britain.

In 1976 another Race Relations Act was implemented. This was seen as progress for immigrant communities; however, Muslims as a 'faith community' did not fit a specific racial definition. This put them in an awkward position, as they could not easily prove that they were subject to religious discrimination. To do so, they first had to prove that they had been discriminated against due to them being part of a racial group dominated by their religion. As Abbas and Akhtar (2005 p. 131) point out, 'In terms of anti-discrimination legislation, British state policy toward Muslims has been inconsistent at best and patchy at worst'. Muslims are also becoming increasingly over-represented in prisons compared with the percentage of the population that they represent. On the whole, Muslims from South Asia have come to be regarded as making a minimal contribution to the socio-economic and socio-political milieu of British society.

Culture

Muslim culture in Britain is not a recent phenomenon; different cultural aspects originating from Muslims, from spices in food to manners, arts and sciences, have penetrated Britain since the Crusades of the 14th century. To explore and reflect on cultural shifts, it is necessary to analyse the immigration process, as 'a key consequence of international migration and of an ever more interconnected world is that ethno-cultural diversity has increased in most nations, leading to simultaneous processes of both globalization and localization' (Rodríguez-García 2010 p. 252). Cultural modification is not a comfortable process as it may create a striking transformation in whole parts of life (Benish-Weisman and Horenczyk 2009 p. 1). In addition, some of the issues related to localisation, cultural barriers to communication and a sense of 'otherness', implicit in ethno-cultural diversity, may create a complicated environment. Arriving in a new society can result in immigrants losing some of their cultural beliefs and belongings, including values, traditions and language (Henry *et al.* 2009 p. 258). This is significant as values, norms, feelings and beliefs are considered to be part of cultural identity (Freidman1990).

Immigrants face the dilemma of having a cultural identity that imposes an element of alienation on local citizens, while at the same time being unknown to people from the same cultural or ethnic background that they are from. Thus, some immigrants especially the younger generation feel too much pressures from the host society and peer pressure have no choice but to leave behind their original identities and immerse themselves in the host culture, while others maintain the culture and identity of their home country as an essential part of their life. Nevertheless, cultural traditions are kept alive by the 'organizing medium of collective memory' (Giddens 1994 p. 64); thus, cultural transformation will not occur suddenly, but as a gradual process (Lull 2007 p. 115). The level of acceptance by some immigrants of some of the more recent developments in the host culture and the drift away from the culture of origin might be linked, and relevant, to the degree of difference between the host society and the native culture, and also to the situations of individual immigrants (Henry *et al.*2009 p. 259).

Scholars have expressed a variety of views on cultural identification and assimilation. Regarding new cultures, attitudes of immigrants may fit into one of four categories: integration, separation, marginalisation, and assimilation (Berry1990). Yet some scholars prefer to 'conceptualize the four options as distinct immigrants' identity orientations, each representing a possible combination of old and new identities' (Benish-Weisman and Horenczyk 2009 p. 2). Assimilation can be regarded as the idealisation of the host country from both immigrants and host country, with full acceptance of whatever the dominant culture believes, requiring immigrants to devalue their own culture (Henry *et al.* 2009 p. 258). Thus, assimilation requires that immigrants submerge one culture in favour of the host culture, and this either proceeds through a gradual adaptation process or is forced by the dominant culture. The host society anticipates, therefore, that immigrants will throw away their unique language and culture and embrace its own core values. Monoculturalism suggests the notion of full adoption of the dominant culture in such a way that immigrants are not recognised by people who come from the same cultural background, historically (Rodríguez-García 2010 p. 254).

Thus, the assimilation approach emphasises rejection of the culture of minorities in order to achieve the approval of the majority culture. However, this cultural rejection and adaptation does not have to be an inevitable part of assimilation (Ward *et al.* 2001 pp. 28-29, 196; Benish-Weisman and Horenczyk 2009 p. 2).

Multiculturalism

'Solidarity' in a society indicates the concept of 'care' for people working on common ground, as well as demonstrating the courage of people in opposing matters and challenging different points of views (Mercer 1990).

Mercer (1990 p. 21) says that according to Hegel, European colonial powers received a dual advantage from colonialism in the early 19th century: both the expansion of territory and obtaining raw materials and markets for themselves. Furthermore, it increased the labour supply, including that from the slave trade, from Asia and Africa to America. Waltzer (1992 p. 29) argues that critical multiculturalism is not simply a 'product of...greater social and economic equality', but that it represents more basically 'a program for greater equality'.

People in a diaspora are more likely to suffer a loss of their identities, as they are branded with a different label from the one they had in their homeland (Grants 2001 p. 7). For example, some people from the Middle East would have been considered 'white' in their homeland, but after immigrating to Western countries such as the UK they discover that they are perceived and categorised as 'black'.

The points of view of ordinary people in a community offer a profound reading on multiculturalism to evaluate and assess serious and challenging issues on assimilation, domination, shared values, and equality and equal opportunities for all. Some may disagree with multiculturalism because they perceive national identity as a main factor in the national ethos and they may believe that the latter cannot be simply established through legislation (Sleeter and McLaren 1995). Conservative multiculturalism has been shaped ever since colonisation was established as a normal practice; the dominating power was not concerned about the native language and culture of the colonised people.

The term 'diversity' has been abused and used as a means to disguise the framework of assimilation as an ideology. 'Ethnic groups are reduced to 'add-ons' to the dominant culture, so a consensual view of culture must first be adopted' (McLaren 1948 p. 37). In addition, it seems that conservative multiculturalism assumed whiteness as the norm; consequently, other ethnicities had to be judged by it. The main criteria for establishing whether someone was white or black were decided by the dominant culture. In contrast, liberal multiculturalism was founded on the idea of equality for all as a norm, thus it was derived from 'intellectual sameness between all races' (McLaren 1995 pp 39-40).

Parekh (2000) report on multiculturalism in the UK opened a new window to diversity and equality for all.

> Multiculturalism is not about a different identity per se but about those that are embedded in and sustained by culture that is a body of beliefs and practices in terms of which a group of people understand the world and organize their individual and collective lives. Unlike differences that spring from individual choices, culturally-derived differences carry a measure of authority and are patterned and structured by the virtues of being embedded in a shared and historically inherited system of meaning and significance. (Parekh, 2000 p. 2)

Parekh (2000) believes that cultural diversity is one of the main points of multiculturalism, and names sub-cultural diversity, perspective diversity and communal diversity as three forms of cultural diversity. Humiliating a culture can lead to cultural oppression. Thus, 'Multiculturalism is about the proper terms of relationship between different cultural communities. The norms governing their respective claims, including the principles of justice, cannot be derived from one culture alone but through an open and equal dialogue between them' (Parekh 2000 p.13). Parekh argues that modern economics cannot survive in isolation. Moreover, democratic views and political equal rights require societies to be more aware of the values that multiculturalism can imbue in society. National culture and cultural unification is not feasible or advantageous due to globalisation and the nation state. Thus, it is vital to recognise that equal citizenship will improve through a distinct relationship between culture and politics, with the promotion of respect and recognition between one another, well-being, cultural and economic rights, to create a society in which social justice can perform effectively.

Methodology

Mills states (1959 p. 105), 'Social science deals with problems of biography, of history, and of their intersections within social structures … these three, biography, history, society, are the co-ordinate points of the proper study of man.'

A literature review has been undertaken covering different aspects of immigration, the history of immigration and legislation, and culture and multiculturalism. This research applies a 'grounded theory' approach (Straus and Glaser 1967). Data has been obtained through qualitative research methods, including fifteen semi-structured interviews, participation, observation, and in-depth ethnography. The data have been coded and analysed to provide a theoretical model of the relationship between ethnicity, narrative and identity within the British Muslim communities studied. Gathering qualitative information about human life is highly contextualised and personalised (Atkinson 2001 p. 125). Oral history is believed to mediate the relationship between the individual and the public (Portelli 2004).

Qualitative methods were used to obtain the data required. Questionnaires with open-ended questions were used to investigate the opinions of 'white British' people living in the North East on multiculturalism, assimilation, Monoculturalism, the events of 9/11 and 7/7, and their perspectives on the wearing of veils (both hijab and niqab) in Western society. The questionnaires included questions such as 'Do you think immigrants have to assimilate into the host society?' Discussions led to the discovery of their views on the meaning of multiculturalism and their perspectives on the subject. Some data were used from the author's study Muslim Oral History in the North East, which was funded by the Heritage Lottery Fund (2009-2011). The author interviewed a diverse sample of intergenerational Muslims who had lived in the North East for more than a decade. Their life experiences, cultural and religious issues, emotions and feelings, racist experiences, education and barriers were all discussed through semi-structured interviews.

Six interviews on multiculturalism from professionals (white and non-white) were conducted and recorded. Questionnaires were also used with interfaith group (all white) to ascertain some of the views and opinions of the host community on multiculturalism, assimilation, Islamophobia and possible suggestions for policy makers. The selected groups included people with managerial positions, interfaith group members, film-maker, a councillor, equality and diversity officer, revert Muslim and community worker. Culture was discussed as a changing phenomenon, as culture change when migration takes place happens as a result of the movement of people from all ethnicities who do not intend to stay in one corner of the globe for their whole life. Some may believe that this has led to people being deprived of a position of equal power.

Findings

One of the interviewees stated: 'The Europeans changed African cultures as they moved there to make a profit from whatever they found. American advertisements convince everyone all over the world that without a brown, sticky drink overloaded with sugar to rot their teeth and livers, life is not worth living'. Another interviewee argued: 'Why should we see it as a bad thing if European countries are enriched with some cultures of other countries?' Multiculturalism was perceived by all the research participants as a mechanism that allows anyone from any background who lives in Britain to practice their own religion and live by their own cultural norms, as well as have their cultural heritage recognised and valued.

The fear of indigenous white citizens that their culture may be diluted by welcoming people from other cultures was also addressed. All of the interviewees believed that culture and religion should not be forced on anyone in a society. One of the interviewees discussed how, subsequent to the First World War, some political leaders used the results of conflict to justify National Socialism in Germany and apartheid in South Africa. Later, Irish, Scottish and foreign migrants were considered second-class citizens in Britain one of the interviewees believed. It was also discussed that when people have less contact with other groups, fear may grow between them. Martin Luther King Jr., a leader of the civil rights movement in America, said in 1958: 'Men often hate each other because they fear each other; they fear each other because they don't know each other; they don't know each other because they cannot communicate; they cannot communicate because they are separated.' Although racism in the UK is not as a result of contact, yet it could be said they have been separated mentally as they have not being aware of reality of immigrants and ethnic minority's cultures and beliefs truly. It is the harsh and racist tabloids that are mainly imposing wrong perceptions about immigrants by misrepresenting and stereotyping of the immigrants, thus, we can say lifting up the physical and environmental barriers cannot put an end to the main issues of misunderstanding and misrepresenting of various ethnic groups.

There is an argument that multiculturalism is a valuable means of remaking public identities 'in order to achieve an equality of citizenship that is neither merely individualistic nor premised on assimilation' (Modood 2005 p. 5). With regard to assimilation, more or less all of the interviewees believed there was no reason for immigrants to lose their cultures; however, it was agreed by all that they should obey the laws of the country and learn the dominant language in order to be able to communicate and integrate well. Moreover, the ability to speak the language will give them a platform to express and share their beliefs and values with the wider society. One white British interviewee said that she had refused to go to America because she believed they were not allowed to have a black president. All participants believed that every individual has the right to be themselves; however, Tina the film-maker expressed her disagreement with wearing the Hijab-niqab both, and proposed that there should be a debate with those women who choose to appear in a Western country covered up in accordance with this type of Islamic belief as she perceived hijab- as strange as a person with purple hair. While most of interviewees believed that if both head scarf and niqab is based on personal chose they would not oppose it. Daniel believed head scarf was used to be a British norm in 1950s, therefore wearing it by Muslim women is rejuvenating British culture, and thus it could not be distinguished as a cultural threat to British identity. David Faulkner, the councillor of Newcastle-upon-Tyne and the chair of Newcastle for peace pointed out the negative perception of wearing head scarf in Western society by referring to a dram called "scarf" by Farah Khan couple of years ago. In that play Farah appeared on the stage wearing a silk colourful scarf around her neck, facing to the audience, and asked their opinions on it, which all admired the beautiful scarf, then she turned her back and put it on her head, faced to the audience again and said "now I have a new identity, I am a dangerous person! A weak woman oppressed by a barbaric religion, I am a terrorist." The play exposes the fact that simply a piece of fabric, a scarf makes Muslim women suitable target for abuse and even physical attack. This powerful play reflects the real lives of Muslim women live in the West, either they are originally British/ White or if they are British as a result of migration. It demonstrates the negative stereotyping of Muslim. Freedom of the individual was believed to be a vital part of British values, yet striking a balance between the rights of the individual and the customs of the wider community some said to be crucial.

Interviewees disagreed with a recent comment about the failure of multiculturalism, and could not see any grounds for it. It seems that some people were not sure about the meaning of the word 'multiculturalism' and some avoided using the term; the word 'diversity' was felt to be safer than the former, as it was thought that the term 'multiculturalism' may cause conflict or resentment from the white population. For this reason, a new multicultural centre in Gateshead was renamed a 'community centre'. The British film maker Tina, one of the interviewees, identified herself as having multiple identities: 'Iranian by birth and culture, American by misfortune'. Other interviewees said that the word 'multiculturalism' describes a society in which differences are less obvious and expressed diversity as a sign of success since there is a greater combination of differences and colours exist, afterwards differences are highlighted just about when one rummage around for division. Although it was believed there were both successes and failures, the story of Stephen Lawrence was used as an example of a failure of our values. The story of the Yemenis of South Shields was also seen as a story of challenges. The host society felt threatened from outside. It was bizarre, argued one interviewee, as even invaders had an effect on human struggle, forming Western civilisation and making it a dominant culture; to some extent assimilation was seen as a natural process. However, the level of assimilation varies between different cultures and generations. Dominant cultures cannot lose their identity because of a minority, another interview stated. Fear of

Sharia law is irrational fear caused by the media, stated one interviewee, and as we live in a democracy this fear is not valid.

Some of the people from Muslim backgrounds had not discovered their Muslim identity until 9/11, as one interviewee stated: 'It was then forced on me after 9/11, though I do not feel easy'. With the extreme reaction to this event, always tension between I and we, what is the correlation, many feel to be a part of society. One of the interviewees believed that we are all individuals with an individual identity, but at the same time we have to negotiate a shared identity. Individual freedom is the greatest aspect of Western society, allowing people to differ from the norm, and also allowing them to be Muslim. However, at the same time some have found that Western society is not tolerant of their choices, which is illogical.

None of the interviewees would prefer to have a monoculture. Daniel the British revert Muslim perceives monoculturalism as a boring society and believed it would be a disaster if it happened and he felt he would not feel comfortable with it, he then gave example of Sunderland and East of London, which both cities have been dominated by one particular culture, the former by white and the latter by Bengalis cultures therefore both cases are undesirable to live in. Daniel pointed out that monoculturalism might lead to what Nazis in Germany has done in the World War. Tina criticised English schools as being very monoculture, with one dimension and a lack of free thinkers. She also thought that there was a lack of positive, radical, open and intelligent minds among British academia based at universities: 'they might all have gone to the Sorbonne in France'. She believes that societies in both the West and the East are going through dark times and enlightenment is going out the window. Most interviewees emphasised the common fact that we are all different but can work together, and so there is no need to be divided. The best policy would be to appreciate that all men are created equal, and so society should support and implement equal opportunities for all. To defend real British values, it was said, society has to combat the EDL. 'There was an incident on the train where they were chanting against Muslims ("kill Muslims"). I was defending British values, [so] I reported it to the police and was arrested; perhaps they were thinking the same!' Tina said. As Ansari states (2004 p. 116), 'Muslims in Britain found themselves forming a broader multicultural identity, which coexisted with and sometimes transcended religion.' One interviewee believed that national unity was used to support the dominant culture in the UK. It was noted that extremism exists in all societies where there are minority groups, and politicians who fear losing votes may express opinions close to those of the EDL (English Defence League) and the BNP (British National Party) in order to attract more votes, especially at a time of economic hardship. It was pointed out that immigrants may convey positive values to British society, such as the importance of education, and also that professional migrants contribute valuable skills.

The effect of 9/11 on Muslims living in Britain has been explored through many interviews, both with men and women. One interviewee, who had arrived early in September 2001, said 'I arrived in Newcastle on 5th September 2001. My first day of university was 9/11. The terrible news was announced. It was a little bit hard that time, children, the teens sometimes shout at us "oh Osama Bin laden".' He then added his belief in Islam as a peaceful religion, however it has been used by some people propagate it in an extreme dangerous way. Thus 'Islamophobia has been shaped since then and affected most immigrants, especially Muslims' background and appearance.' Thus, the impact of those events on Muslim identity became clear; many Muslims who had not previously been thought of or perceived as Muslim started to see it as their identity.

Conclusion

In terms of cultural identity and multicultural life, one interviewee, Dr Adel, considers himself as having a multi-identity, declaring:

> 'I am pleased to tell you that my friends are a very wide mixture of Egyptians and Pakistanis and English and Indian and all manner of Turkish and Tunisians and Persians. It's very important not to limit your acquaintances to one specific circle of people, otherwise you will not grow, and you will not create the understanding between people that the Qur'an talks to us about'.

Then he maintained that immigration gives everyone the chance to explore other dimensions and lives, to know how other people live, and compare it, therefore to be capable to enrich and enhance their own history, so then make up their own profile and make up their own mosaic. Modood (2006 p. 55) highlights the fact that Bosnian Muslims were 'ethnically cleansed' by people who were phenotypically, linguistically, and culturally the same as themselves because they came to be identified as an 'ethnic' or 'racial' group. He argues that multiculturalism is a valuable means to remake public identities 'in order to achieve an equality of citizenship that is neither merely individualistic nor premised on assimilation' (Modood 2005 p. 5). Nitin Shulka the Diversity officer believes it is not sufficient to have good policy makers and policy to tackle discrimination and racism but it is also essential to make sure to implement the law. David Faulkner mentioned three strands in British society for promoting multiculturalism: Education, challenge, debate and dialogue and celebrated the different cultures.

Bibliography

Abbas, T. and Akhtar, P. (2005) *The experience of British South Asian Muslims in the post-September 11 climate,* in Henke, H. (2005) *Crossing over: Comparing recent migration in the United States and Europe,* The Rowman & Littlefield Publishing Group, Inc.

Ansari, H. (2004) *The Infidel Within: Muslims in Britain Since 1800,* London: Hurst and Co. Ltd.

Ashraf Emami, H. (2010) *The Songs of Swallows* (unpublished work), Islamic Heritage Project (funded by Heritage Lottery Fund).

Atkinson, R. (2001) *The Life Story Interview,* in Gubrium, J. F. and Holstein, J. A. (eds.) (2001) *Handbook of Interview Research: Context and Method.*

Benish-Weisman, M. and Horenczyk, G. (2009) Cultural Identity and Perceived Success among Israeli Immigrants: An Emic Approach. *International Journal of Intercultural Relations.* Doi: 10.1016/j.ijintrel. 2009. 11.010.

Berry, J. W. (1990) *Acculturation and adaptation: A general framework. Mental health of immigrants and refugees.*

Evertt, S. Lee (1969) *A theory of Migration,* in J. A. Jackson (ed.), *Migration,* UK: Cambridge University Press.

Feteke, L. (2008) *Integration, Islamophobia and Civil Rights in Europe.* London: Institute of Race Relations.

Freidman, B. (1990) Literacy and cultural identity, *Harvard Educational Review,* 60 (2), pp. 181-204.

Gardner, K. (2002) Age, narrative and migration: the life course and life histories of Bengali Elders in London, Oxford: International Publication Ltd.

Giddens, A. (1994) *Living in a Post-Traditional Society,* in Beck, A. Giddens and S. Lash, *Reflexive Modernization,* Cambridge: Polity Press.

Gorden, P. and Rosenbery, D. (1989) *Daily Racism: The Press and Black people in Britain,* London: Runnymede Trust.

Grants, H. and Cornwell, Eve Walsh (2001) *Global Multiculturalism: Comparative Perspectives on Ethnicity, Race and Nation,* Oxford England: Rowman & Littlefield Publisher, Inc.

Gunaratnam, Y. (2003) *Researching 'Race' and Ethnicity: Methods, Knowledge and Power,* London: Sage.

Hall, S. (1993) *New ethnicities,* in Donald, James and Rattansi, Ali (eds.), *Identity: Community, Culture, Difference,* London: Sage-Open University Press.

Henry, H. M.; Stiles, W. B.; Biran , M. W.; Mosher , J. K.; Birnegar, M. G.; Banerjee , P. (2009). Immigrants' Continuing Bonds with their Native Culture: Assimilation Analysis of Three Interviews. *Transcultural Psychiatry.* 46(2): 257-281.

Lull, J. (2007) *Culture-on-demand: communication in a crisis world,* Oxford:

Blackwell. Sleeter.C.E. and Maclaren, P. (1995) *Multicultural education, critical pedagogy, and the politics of difference,* Albany, United States of America: University of New York Press.

Mercer, K. (1990) *Welcome to the jungle: Identity and diversity in postmodern politics,* in Rutherford, J (ed.) *Identify: community, culture, difference,* London: Lawrence and Wishart.

Mills, C. (1959) *The sociological imagination,* New York: Oxford University Press.

Modood, T. (2007b) Multiculturalism's civic future: a response. *Open democracy,* 20th June.

Modood, T. (1992) *Not easy being British: colour, culture and citizenship.* London: Runnymede Trust.

Modood, T. (2005) *Multicultural politics.* Edinburgh: Edinburgh University Press.

Modood, T. (2006) The Liberal Dilemma: Integration or Vilification? *International Migration,* 44 (5).

Modood, T. (2007a) *Multiculturalism, a civic idea.* London: Polity Press.

Nayak, A. (2003) *Race, place and globalization: youth cultures in a changing world,* Oxford.

Panayi, P. (1996) *Racial Violence in Britain in the Nineteen and Twentieth Centuries,* Leicester University Press.

Parekh, B. (2000) *Rethinking Multiculturalism,* New York: Harvard University Press.

Parekh, B. (2000) *The future of multi-ethnic Britain: the Parekh Report.* London: Profile Books.

Portelli, A. (1998) *Oral history as genre,* in Chamberlain, M. and Thompson, P. (eds.) *Narrative and Genre,* London: Routledge.

Rodriguez-Garcia, D. (2010) Beyond assimilation and multiculturalism: A critical review of the debate on managing diversity. *Journal of International Migration and Integration,* 11 (3), pp. 251-271.

Struss, A. and Glaser, B. (1967) *The discovery of grounded theory: Strategies for qualitative research.* Chicago: Aldine Books.

Waltzer, M. (1992) *Multiculturalism and individualism,* p.191.cf. Andrew hacker, *Two Nations: Black and white, separate, Hostile, Unequal* (New York: Charles Scribner, esp. ch.3 "Being Black in America" pp.31-49

Ward, C., Bochner,S & Furnham. A. (2001) *The psychology of culture shock.* Hove: Routledge.

http://www.opendemocracy.net/faith_ideas/Europe_islam/multiculturalism_future (accessed 19.06.11).

Stride Toward Freedom: The Montgomery Story (1958). Available at: http://progressivescholar.wordpress.com/2010/01/18/reverend-doctor-martin-luther-king-jr (accessed 02.01.12).

http://www.tv.com/people/martin-luther-king/trivia/

Part 4

MULTICULTURALISM AND COMMUNITY COHESION: POLICIES, EFFECTIVENESS AND PRACTICE

Turkish Youth in the UK: an Analysis of Their Identity Formation, Belonging and Perceptions of Europe

Dr. Sibel Safi [68]

"Where I belong" is certainly a question that is posed by and for many people who have undergone migration or translocations of different types, whether of national movement or class movement, and is especially true for the children of such people. It is represented in inter subjective relations by that question so many visible 'outsiders' face (visible either through skin, colour, language, accent or name) about 'where are you really from' and 'where do you really belong'. (Floya-Anthias 2009 p.45)

This chapter is about how these Turkish-speaking young people feel about their parent's country of origin, about their own belonging, identity, culture and above all what it means to be British. This research interviewed the young people on their attitudes towards citizenship, nationality, exclusion, cultural values, faith, relationships, social cohesion about their Turkish-British identity and about their European identity. In this chapter, the research draws mainly on the qualitative data from Turkish speaking immigrants with a special reference to young people between the ages of 15 and 24. Eighty-four respondents agreed to give interviews

68 Dr. Sibel Safi (LLB, MA, LLM, Ph.D) is a senior research fellow in the field of International Law. She is an associate member at the University of East London, the Centre for Migration, Refugees and Belonging. She also works as an academic coordinator at the London Centre for Social Studies. She has numerous journal articles focusing on gender-persecution, honour killing in Refugee Law, Cultural Identity of immigrant Turks, Women's human Rights and Multiculturalism. She was involved in extensive teaching in European Union law lectures at the Academy of Sciences of Economy and she is the author of the 'Evaluation of Human Rights; Turkey case', 2010. She fluently speaks English, Romanian, and Turkish.

(53 females and 31 males). The sample consisted of forty-eight Turkish, twenty-three Turkish-Kurds and thirteen Turkish-Cypriots.

It is important to differentiate belonging and the politics of belonging. Belonging is about emotional or even ontological attachment, about feeling at home. As Hage (1997 p.41) points out, however 'home is an on-going project entailing a sense of hope for the future (Taylor 2009). Part of this feeling of hope relates to home as a safe space (Ignatieff 2001 p.62). In the daily reality of the early twenty-first century, in so many places on the globe, this emphasis on safety acquires a new poignancy. At the same time it is important to emphasise that feeling 'at home' does not necessarily only generate positive and warm feelings. (Hesse 2000 p.17)

Belonging tends to be naturalised and to be part of everyday practise (Fenster 2000 p.403). It becomes articulated, formally structured and politicised only when it is threatened in some way. The politics of belonging comprise specific political projects aimed at constructing belonging to particular collectivities which are themselves being constructed in these projects in very specific ways and within very specific boundaries (i.e. whether or not, according to specific political projects of belonging, Jews can be considered to be German, for example, or abortion advocates can be considered Catholic). (Yuval-Davis 2011 p.36) As Antonsich (2010 p.644) points out, however these boundaries are often spatial and relate to a specific locality/territoriality and not just to constructions of social collectivities. According to Doreen Massey (2005 p.221), space in itself is but an embodiment of social networks. As Ulf Hannerz (2002 p.575) claims, home is essentially a contrastive concept, linked to some notion of what it means to be away from home. It can involve a sense of rootedness in a socio-geographic site or be constructed as an intensely imagined affiliation with a distant locale where self-realisation can occur.

Belonging has been one of the major themes around which both classic psychology and sociology emerged. Countless psychological and even more psychoanalytical, works have been dedicated to writings about the fears of separation of babies and children from the womb, from the mother, from the familiar, as well as the devastating effects on them when they cannot take belonging for granted (Rank 1973 p.34; Bowlby 1969 p.46). Similarly, much of social psychology literature has been dedicated to people's need to conform to the groups they belong to for fear of exclusion and inferiorisation and the ways people's interpersonal relationships are deeply affected by their membership or lack of membership of particular groups as well as their positions in these groups (Lewin 1948 p.28; Billig 1976 p.20; Tajfel 1982 p.39).

People can belong in many different ways and to many different objects of attachment. These can vary from a particular person to the whole of humanity, in a concrete or abstract way, by self or other identification, in a stable, contested or transient way. (Yuval-Davis 2011 p.162) Belonging is usually multi-layered and to use geographical jargon-multi scale (Antonish 2010 p.644) or multi-territorial (Hannerz 2002 p.575).

To clarify our understanding of the notion of social and political belonging, it would be useful to differentiate between three major analytical facets in which belonging is constructed.(Yuval-Davis 2011 p.162-163) The first facet concerns social locations; the second relates to people's identifications and emotional attachments to various collectivities and groupings; the third relates to ethical and political value systems with which people judge their own and other's belonging. These different facets are interrelated, but cannot be reduced to each other.

Social Locations

When it is said that people belong to a particular sex, race, class or nation, that they belong to a particular age group, kinship group or a certain profession, we are talking about people's social and economic locations, which at each historical moment would tend to carry with them particular weights or grids of power relations operating in their society. Being a woman or a man, black or white, working class or middle class, a member of a European or an African nation, has a different social meaning in each case. People are not just different categories of social location, with different contextual meanings, they also tend to have certain positionalities along axes of power that are higher or lower than other such categories.

Such positionalities, however , would tend to be different in different historical contexts and are also often fluid and contested. Sometimes, however, as Sandra Harding (1991 p.382-91) and Nancy Fraser (1998 p.309-36) have commented, certain differences would not necessarily have differential power positionings but are only the markers for different locations. According to this study, some of the young Turkish speaking interviewees emphasised that they did not feel like they belonged anywhere; their home is where they currently live and will change if they move again.

Identifications and Emotional Attachments

Identities are narratives, stories that people tell themselves and others about who they are and who they are not (Martin 1995 p.5-16; Kaptani & Yuval-Davis 2008 p.8-10). Not all of these stories are about belonging to particular groupings and collectivities-they can be, for instance, about individual attributes, body images, vocational aspirations or sexual powers. However, even these stories will often relate directly or indirectly, to self and/or others' perceptions of what being a member of such grouping or collectivity (ethnic, racial, national, cultural, religious) might mean. Identity narratives can be individual or they can be collective, with the latter often acting as a resource for the former. Although they can be reproduced from generation to generation, it is always in a selective way; they can shift and change, be contested and multiple. These identity narratives can relate to the past, to a myth of origin; they can be aimed to explain the present and probably; above all, they function as a projection of future trajectory. Margaret Wetherell (2006 p.38-55) argues that identity narratives provide people with a sense of 'personal order'. Some of the Turkish-speaking interviewees emphasised that they can relate to and identify with many great British thinkers and writers, and believe that these intellectuals have shaped their identity, interests and personality. They also have very good command of the language. As they described when they walk around, they enjoy hearing the musicians' on the underground, seeing the artists along the river, and exploring theatres and musicals all around the country. So it's not just about the tea or stiff upper lip people mention. According to my research the Turkish-speaking young generation seemed to have developed hybrid identities and although the discussions show that they, too, privilege their Turkishness as well by saying "We have great tea in Turkey too.

Ethical and Political Values

Belonging, is not just about social locations and constructions of individual and collective identities and attachments, it is also concerned with the ways these are assessed and valued by the self and others, and this can be done in many different ways by people with similar social locations who might identify themselves as belonging to the same community or grouping. These can vary not only in how important these locations and collectivities seem to be in one's life and that of others, but also in whether they consider this to be a good or a bad thing. Closely related to this are specific attitudes and ideologies concerning where and how identity and categorical boundaries are being/should be drawn, in more or less permeable ways, as different ideological perspectives and discourses construct them as more or less inclusive. It is in the arena of the contestations around these issues where we move from the realm of belonging into that of the politics of belonging. Some of the young interviewees of Turkish origin have stated that they feel stronger when they know that they belong to a large community, like Turkish Community in London. However other young Turkish people have claimed that they prefer being left out of that Turkish community so that they are not labelled accordingly. A few of the Turkish-speaking interviewees described their cultural belonging in terms of beliefs, religion, language, literature, music, arts, food etc. And they emphasised that if these are the things they are assessing culture in terms of, then yes, they would say that they belong to English culture. They also described their reasons for feeling that they belong to this culture because it is open-minded, progressive and liberal. Their rights as an ethnic minority have been protected; and they have had equal opportunity and have never felt the need or pressure to confirm to a particular way of thinking. Some of the Turkish-speaking interviewees claimed that they belong to Turkish culture and they expressed it that they don't think it's something to do with them, because they are very different culturally. That's why they never feel themselves a part of this country. And they described that with a British passport, they can have a right to live in this country, that's all. One of the young Turkish-speaking girl described her belonging to the community as she would say she feels she belongs to both Turkey and England. But when there is war, when there is a football match, and if England is playing against France or something she would have support England but if England is playing against Turkey she would support Turkey and she describes the reason of that emotion as it is her race.

Nationalism and Belonging

'What is a nation and how does one belong to it? Who is a member of the nation and how does one become a member?'
The answer to these questions depends on particular political projects of belonging and how they define the pathways to membership of particular nations. Enoch Powell, as a minister in the Conservative government in Britain from 1960 to 1963, argued that 'the West Indian does not by being born in England, become an Englishman.'(Gilroy 1987 p.46) For Norman Tebbit, a minister in a later Conservative British government, the test was not the ethnic/racial origin but loyalty to the English cricket team, he deemed those who applauded the other team as not belonging to the English nation(constructed as being equivalent to British in this discourse), even if they were born in Britain and had British citizenship and a British education. The essential characteristics of membership in the British nation as defined by David Blunkett (2002 p.20-67), a British Home Secretary, were knowledge of the English language as well as a belief in the values of the Human Rights Act.

Exclusionary national boundaries, therefore, even within the same nation, can be constructed and imagined in different ways and according to different organising and categorical principles (i.e. biological origin for Powell, emotional attachment and identification for Tebbit, shared culture and value for Blunkett).

What does it mean, then for national boundaries to be imagined? According to Benedict Anderson (1991 p.58-74), nations are imagined communities 'because the members of even the smallest nation will never know most of their fellow-members, meet them, or even hear of them, yet in the minds of each lives the image of their communion'. Poole (1999 p.1-14), comments that the real difference between what constitutes imagined communities and a nation is that as 'society' is whether or not imagining themselves as a community informs the way people live and relate to each other.

Understanding nations as 'imagined communities' can also explain why people who are differentially located within and outside the collectivity would view the boundaries of the nation in different ways- as more or less exclusionary, as more or less permeable. For example e.g. many Jews imagined themselves as members of the German nation while German Nazis saw them as not belonging. The question of whether or not 'there is Black in the Union Jack' (Gilroy 1987 p.35-46) has been the subject of major political contestation in Britain and the recent rise of the British National Party in the UK as well as similar political parties in many other western countries presents similar contestations in regard to the inclusion of Muslims.

Young Turkish-Speaking People in the UK and Their Perceptions of Europe

According to the 2001 Census, 45 per cent of Britain's minority ethnic people live in London, where they comprise 29 per cent of all residents (www.statistics.gov.uk). In this sense, Britain's capital could be referred as a multicultural city at the centre of a new nexus of global movements. London's Turkish speakers are concentrated particularly in the boroughs of Hackney and Haringey, which exist in the North London. This community is itself fragmented, comprising of three main groups; Cypriot Turks, mainland Turks and Kurdish refugees. The presence of Turkish Cypriots is an important feature of the British story because they have not settled in such numbers in any other European country. Turkish Cypriots formed the first of the UK Turkish speaking communities and unlike other Turkish-speaking migrants, they had a colonial connection with Britain. They first migrated to Britain in significant numbers between 1945 and 1955 due to these colonial links, conflict and high levels of employment here in the post-war years. Migration slowed following the UK Immigration Act of 1962 and subsequent Turkish Cypriot immigrants arrived either through family reunification or as refugees following the 1974 war in Cyprus. Turkish migration from mainland Turkey to the UK did not start until the late 1960s and was largely a consequence of limited employment opportunities in Turkey. In contrast to migration to other European countries, migration from both Turkey and Cyprus to Britain was neither organised nor regulated by the government. As a result, migration routes were not chosen by Turkish government policy, as was the case with migration to other European countries. Instead, they were largely determined by individual initiatives and chain migration by using social networks. Ethnic Kurds began to enter in larger numbers during the late 1980s and early 1990s, often with refugee and asylum seeker status, and at a time when the economic circumstances in the UK were far less favourable. Anecdotal evidence from the community suggests that this increase was due to Britain's recognition of the plight of the Kurds, which led to many people claiming asylum in Britain from Turkey because of the perception that the political conditions were more favourable for their claims (Engin 2011).

However there is a degree of inter-marriage between these groups and also with majority ethnic groups. The Turkish, Turkish-Kurds and Turkish-Cypriot communities are working and living in the same areas of London (Mehmet Ali 2001 p.19-23). A young Kurdish taxi driver described his feelings as; in his opinion, North London was not a part of Britain; he felt himself 'in Britain' only when he left North London and visited other places. In North London, he believed that Turkish people have everything they might expect to find in Turkey, apart from some family members (Kucukcan and Gungor 2009 p.243-258). In fact, the Turkish-speaking community is probably one of the most self-sufficient communities in London with half dozen local community-based newspapers, together with Turkish television channels and countless digital radio channels. Community members can provide any service within community ranging from mortgages to a quit-smoking help line, driving instructions to massage parlours. It could be christened 'Little Turkey' (Enneli & Modood 2005 p.142-159).

However, there are the negative effects of the families' economic conditions on the young people's employment experiences and the employment patterns change due to various needs of the families. The Turkish-speaking families do not have many opportunities in offer to the next generation, so the working condition in ethnic enclave gives no promising signs for an easy transition and for a possible upward mobility. Turkish-speaking young people experience that strong ethnic inclusion in the current labour market is pushing them to make choice; whether to accept the jobs which their parents already do or attempt to improve their future life-chances. The transition to adulthood would be no doubt an uneasy one for these young people. And it would be not so wrong to say that the ethnic economy might not serve the majority of these young people for an upward mobility, though with these coming from relatively advantaged backgrounds could use the ethnic enclave to jump up to broader labour market (Kucukcan and Gungor 2006 p.243-258).

In England where multicultural agendas are strong and the concept of Europe is marginalised in political and educational discourses, it seems unlikely that middle-class Turkish youth have the same emotional access to Europe. There is little reason why the country should reconceptualise her national identity in European terms and the processes of European integration have not seriously affected policymakers. The Europeanisation of British national identity is undercut by Britain's special relationship with the United States; the geographical detachment from continental Europe; and England's post-war role in the Commonwealth (Geddes 1999 p.23-32). Europe did not appear amongst the cross-curricular themes of the 1988 National Curriculum. The Department of Education and Science responded to the 1988 Resolution of the Council of Ministers of Education on the European dimension in education, stating that the government's policies were aimed at 'promoting a sense of European identity; encouraging interest in and improving competence in other European languages; and helping students to acquire a view of Europe as a multicultural, multilingual community which includes the UK. (The Department of Education and Science 1991) However, advice and curriculum guidance on precisely what content and form the European dimension should assume has not matched official British concerns with multicultural issues.

In 1988, multicultural education (unlike European education) became one of the dimensions of the English National Curriculum and the integrationist approach attempted to recognise albeit to a limited extent, cultural and ethnic differences within the concept of Britishness (Geddes 1999 p.111-124).

The notion of being European did not sit comfortably with some of the Turkish interviewees, the concept of Europe as a political identity did not easily fit with those Turkish national identities. However some of them felt themselves familiar with the impact the EU has on their life, and recent economic instability within the Eurozone is a timely reminder of how connected they are with the continent. They told that they travel to Europe quite often for business and holiday purposes and have a great deal of friends with continental roots as well.

The Religious Question: the Sacred, the Cultural and the Political

Both Durkheim (1968 p.249-69) and Weber (1905 p.221-45) saw religion as being central to social life. Weber expanded in his 'Protestant Ethics' thesis, the argument that particular forms of religious ideologies and practices had originally facilitated and energised the rise of modern capitalism.

It is important to note that two contradictory elements co-exist in the operation of cultures. On the one hand, there is a tendency towards stabilisation and continuity, and on the other hand, perpetual resistance and change. Both of these tendencies grow out of the close relationship between power relations and cultural practice. (Bourdieu and Nice p.331-52 1977; Asad, 1986 p.117-31; Bottomley 1992 p.42). As Friedman (1994 p.89) points out cultures are not just an arbitrary collection of values, artefacts and modes of behaviour. They acquire, to a greater or lesser extent, 'stabilising properties' which are inherent in the practices of their social reproduction. Cultural homogeneity in this view would be a result of hegemonisation and it would always be limited and more noticeable in the centre rather than in the social margins, being affected by the social positioning of its carriers (Yuval-Davis, 2011 p.113-134).

Cultural models become resonant with subjective as well as collective experience.

They become the intersectional ways in which individuals experience themselves, their collectivities and the world, and thus often occupy central spaces in identity narratives. In all of these ways the religious domain bears a close relationship to that culture, although the two cannot be reduced to each other. Religion relates to the sphere of the sacred, of the ultimate meaning (Tillich 1957 p.19-24; Beyer 1994 p.95; Armstrong 2007 p.143-53). Moreover, religious discourses supply the individual, within specific social and historic contexts, with explicit or implicit answers to the three basic existential questions people have to grapple with- what is the meaning/ purpose of one's life?; what happens to us when we die?; and what is good and evil? The relations between the world of everyday life and the sacred religious domain are usually indirect, although in most religions there will be specific times and places which will be dedicated to the realm of the sacred. Spatially, places such as churches, mosques, synagogues and temples are designated places of worship, while specific holy-dates like the Muslim month of Ramadan, the weekly Jewish Sabbath or Christian church services, or praying at several times of day in different religions play a part. So these times and places are sharply differentiated from the secular by specific performative religious acts , such as praying or fasting or lighting special candles. As Karen Armstrong (2009 p.143-53) argues; religions are more about performativity- i.e. regular repetitive practices that gain their internal as well as social authority with repetition (Butler, 1990 p.1-23) – than about implicit beliefs, although this differs even formally between religions. For example, Christianity is generally much more about specific beliefs than Judaism. Saba Mahmoud (2005 p.26-44) also argues strongly that the conceptual relationship between the body, self and moral agency differs in the ways in which these are constituted within different ethical-moral (cultural and religious) traditions. Armstrong also points out that people differ in their talents and ability to immerse themselves in religious spirituality, as is the case with people's differential artistic and poetic capabilities.

However, once these transcendent super-ordinated and integrated structures of meaning are socially 'objectivated', to use Luckman's terminology (1967 p.35-78), i.e. a personal spirituality becomes a religious institution, a paradoxical situation often develops. Because of their ultimate meaning, religious practices and beliefs can become some of the most intractable and inflexible symbolic border guards for belonging to specific collectivity boundaries and cultural traditions.

An estimated 23 million Muslims live in Europe (Vertovec & Peach 1997 p.3-47) and the presence of Muslims in Europe is not a new phenomenon. The growth of western-educated young generations and the rise of global/transnational Islamic movements are important sources of motivation for Muslims in Europe to express their identity in western public spheres (Kucukcan 2009 p.79-103). For example, in recent years, Muslims in Europe become more concerned with the religious education of their children. Turkish Muslims are part of the larger Muslim community in the UK and religion is one of the significant markers of Turkish collective sense of belonging. Therefore the first generation of the Turkish community established Islamic Institutions as soon as they acquired sufficient resources. These institutions were meant to facilitate the transmission of religious values to young Turkish-speaking people. However, attitudes of young people towards religion are variable; research clearly shows that young Turks know very little about Islam. A symbolical religiosity, (practising but not feeling the meaning), is developing among the Turkish youth in the UK who seems to be increasingly feeling the tension generated by the continuity of traditional values and changes in social and cultural environment (Kucukcan 2009 p.79-103).

Some of them feel at ease as an Atheist in this country and are free to express their beliefs without fear of taboo or estrangement and they only feel this infringed upon within the Turkish-speaking community. Some of them complain about their fathers who try to make them to go to the Mosque when it is Eid.

Some of the interviewees describe their religion as Islam, but they do not feel comfortable in their celebrating festivities because of they are not widely recognised in the host country. They say that, the ambiance of the religious festivities do not have the same feelings as it does in Turkey.

Some of the interviewees responded the question by saying that even though they are completely allowed to express their religious beliefs, they suggest it that it still did not give the same taste as it were compared to exercising their religion in Turkey.

Conclusion

It must be pointed out that, crucially, people cannot be simply defined, in most situations, as either belonging or not belonging. Emotions, from feeling comfortable, safe or entitled to various rights and resources are endemic to belonging, but different people who belong to the same collectivity would feel different degrees and kinds of attachment, the same people would feel different in different times, locations and situations and some people would feel that they belong to a particular collectivity while others would construct them as being outside those collectivity boundaries and vice versa (Yuval-Davis, 2011 p.113-134).

This chapter deals with the kind of identity and sense of belonging expressed by the young people. The focus was on what was said about British, religious and ethnic identities as forms of self-identification. It was clear from research on ethnic minorities that many groups have a strong, albeit varying, sense of one or more minority identity; and that, increasingly, this does not prevent them from also having a sense of other identities, such as being. The young people were asked in the survey to pick one or more identities from several options, which included Turk, Kurd, Turkish Kurd, British Turk, British Kurd, Cypriot, Turkish Cypriot, Middle Eastern, Muslim, Christian, British, Atheist and, finally, Alevi.

According to the research the Turkish-speaking young generation seemed to have developed hybrid identities and had few cross-ethnic friendships and formed an ethnic solidarity group on the basis of common religion, language, culture and physical appearance. The identity formation is deeply affected by their ethnic experiences.

This chapter suggests that in my sample the Turkish-speaking young people in London, there is no singular identity position but employed hybrid ethno-national, ethno-local and national-European identities as a result of their national location and especially, schooling and social class positioning rather than their families' migration histories. The evaluation shows that the young generations in the UK live a minority culture at home and British culture in the schools, and as a result they have a third hybrid culture.

There was a strong relationship between being born in this country and choosing British as an identity. The research shows that 80 per cent of the young people who were not born in this country did not think of themselves as British. Rather, during the interviews, it became clear that there was a narrow and a wide meaning of 'British' being used. For some, 'British' meant the possession of a passport. An extension of this narrow meaning is that people are British if they live in Britain, which also introduces a wider, cultural or ethnic meaning of British.

On the other hand, not having British as a self-identity does not mean that the young people chose only Turkish as an identity. Indeed, nearly 70 per cent of the young people chose multiple identities for themselves. In fact, only 20 per cent of the males and 10 per cent of the females chose only Turkish as a self-description. Religious identity does not seem to be central. Less than 5 per cent chose religion as their only identity. 72 per cent did not subscribe to a religious identity at all.

The failure to choose Muslim as an identity may partly be because, for some of these Turkish-speaking young people, being Turkish or Kurdish or Turkish Cypriot already included a sense of religious belonging. Being Muslim was indeed seen by some as a cultural identity rather than as a religion. As Ceylan, a Turkish-Kurd who did not pick Muslim as an identity, explained: "I'm an atheist and the only negative side to my life in England comes from the pressure of my family puts me under to hide my religious beliefs from the Turkish community here. In British culture everyone tends to keep themselves to themselves and there's something of a taboo towards being intolerant or unaccommodating. I feel at ease as an Atheist in this country and am free to express my beliefs without fear of taboo or estrangement. I only feel this infringed upon within the Turkish-speaking community."

In relation to the young people's attitudes towards religion, the research also discussed Islamophobia, the fear of, and hostility towards, Islam and Muslims. In general, Islamophobia did not seem to be a big problem for the young people. In fact, this term was not a familiar concept for them. Almost all of them needed further explanation of the term. Although they did not think that being Muslim was a reason for being discriminated against personally.

In conclusion, the research found that the young people usually choose multiple ethnic identities, but, in the majority of the cases, the term 'British' was not (yet) part of that plurality. This is complicated by the fact that the majority of Kurds refused to self-identify as Turks. Finally, the young people's relationship with religion is not straightforward. They do not consider themselves as part of a Muslim community, but rather, for some, their religious identity is a natural extension of their ethnic identity.

Bibliography

Anderson, B.(1991) Imagined Communities; Reflections on the Origins and Spread of Nationalism. London, Verso

Antonsich,M. (2010). Searching for Belonging- An Analytical Framework, Geography Compass.

Asad, T. (1986) The Idea of an Anthropology of Islam. Washington, DC, Centre For Contemporary Arab Studies

Beyer, P. (1994). Religion and Globalization. London, Sage

Billig, M. (1976). Social Psyhology and Intergroup Relations. New York Academic Press

Blunkett, D. (2002) Secure Borders, Safe Haven (White Paper). London, Home Office

Bottomley, G.(1992) From Another Place: Migration and the Politics of Culture. Cambridge, Cambridge University Press.

Bourdieu, P.and R.Nice.(1992) Outline of a Theory of Practice. Cambridge, Cambridge University Press.

Bowlby, J.(1969). Attachment. Vol.1 of Attachment and Loss. London, Hogarth Press, and New York, Basic Books.

Butler, J. (1990). Gender Trouble; Feminism and the Subversion of the Identity. New York, Routledge.

Durkheim, E. (1968). The Elementary Forms of Religious Life. New York, Free Press.

Engin, Z. (2011) A Complexity Approach to Analysis the Social Integration of the Turkish Speaking Community in Britain, Conference paper.

Enneli, P.; Modood, T., (2005) Young Turks and Kurds; A Setof Invisible Disadvantaged Groups, York; Joseph Rowntree Foundation.

Fenster, T.(2004) The Global City and the Holy City; Narratives of Planning in Israel, Social and Cultural Geoghraphy, 5;403-417

Fraser, N. and A. Honneth (1998). Redistribution or Recognition? A Philosophical Exchange, London, Verso.

Friedman, J.(1994). Cultural Identity and Global Process. London, Sage.

Geddes, A.(1999) Britain in The European Union, Tisbury; Baseline Book Company.

Geertz, C. (1966). Religion as a Cultural System, in M. Bainton, Anthropological Approaches to the Study of Religion. London, Tavistock.

Gilroy,P.(1987). There Ain't No Black in the Union Jack; The Cultural Politics of Race and Nation. London, Hutchinson.

Hage, G.(1997). At Hoem in the Entrailsof the West Multiculturalism, Ethnic Food and Migrant Home Building. Western Sydney, Pluto Press.

Hannerz, U.(2002) 'Where are we and Who We Want to Be' in U. Hedetoft and M. Hjort (Eds), The Post National Self; Belonging and Identity. Minneapolis,

MN, and London, University of Minnesota Press.

Harding, S.(1991) Whose Science? Whose Knowledge? Ithaca, NY, Cornell University Press.

Hesse, B.(2000) Un/Settled Multiculturalism; Diaspora,Entanglement and Transruptions. London,Zed Books.

Ignatieff, M.(2001). Human Rights as Politicsand Idolatry, Princeton, NJ, Princeton University Press.

Kaptani, E. and N. Yuval-Davis (2008). Participatory Theatre as a Research Methodology, Sociological Research Online 13/5 ,http//www.socreson-line.org. uk/13/5/2.

Kucukcan, T. (2009) Turks in Europe, Culture, Identity, Integration, Turkevi Research Centre, Amsterdam.

Kucukcan,T &Gungor, Y.(2006) Euroturks and Turkey-EU Relations- Amsterdam, Turkevi Research Institute.

Lewin, K.(1948). Resolving Social Conflicts; Selected Paperson Group Dynamics, New York, Harper and Row.

Luckman, T.(1967). The Invisible Religion. London, Macmillan.

Mahmoud, S.(2005). Politics of Piety; The Islamic Revival and the Feminist Subject. Princeton, NJ, Princeton University Press.

Massey, D. (2005) For Space, London Sage.

Poole, R. (1999). Nation and Identity. London, Routledge.

Rank, O.(1973) The Trauma of Birth. London, Routledge

Rowe, A.C.(2005). Be Longing; Towards a Feminist Politics of Peace. London, The Women's Press.

Tajfel, H.(1982). Social Psychology of Intergroup Relations. Annual Review of Psychology 33; 1-39

Taylor, H. (2009)Landscapes of Belonging; The Meaning of Home for Cypriot Refugees in London, Ph.D thesis, School of Humanities and Social Sciences, University of East London.

Tillich, P.(1957). The Dynamics of Faith. New York, Harper and Row.

Vertovec, S. and Peach, C. (1997) Islam in Europe and the Politics of Religion and Community, Basingstoke, Macmillan.

Weber, M. (1905). The Protestant Ethic and the Spirit of Capitalism. London and New York, Penguin.

Wetherell, M.(2006) Introduction of the Day; Identity and Social Action, residential conference, ESRC programme, University of Aston, Birmingham, July.

Yuval-Davis, N. (2011) The Politics of Belonging, Intersectional Contestations, Sage. Los Angeles, London, New York, Singapore, Washington DC.

Yuval-Davis, N.(2011). Citizenship, Autochthony and the Question of Forced Migration, paper presented at the seminar series, Conceptual Issues in Forced Migration, organised by the CMRB (Centre for Research on Migration, Refugees and Belonging) and Oxford Refugee Studies Centre, Oxford, February.

From Multiculturalism to Monoculturalism? The Socio-Political Demonisation of Muslimness in the Age of Terror

Stefano Bonino [69]

Introduction

This paper aims to explore various interconnected themes related to the post-9/11 state and social demonisation of Muslims within a security, legislative, political and social framework. Initially, the all-encompassing British counter-terrorism approach and normalisation of exceptional measures will be broadly explored. The 'Prevent' strand of the CONTEST strategy, in particular, will be considered in light of the pervasive, negative and burdening effects that it has on Muslim communities within a superimposed monocultural framework. The emergence of the Leviathan and the state of hyper-control will be briefly analysed, as it represents a crucial point in understanding the state construction of an exclusive society and the shaping of a Muslim suspect community within an Islamophobic institutional and social framework. The concept of the suspect community will be set against the precedent with the Irish community. Unlike Irish communities, however, the discrimination against many Muslims operates on a prima facie level: therefore, the related hampered interaction with non-Muslims and problematisation of socio-ethnic integration will be discussed. Finally, three tentative recommendations will be postulated in order to move beyond the current hyper-securitisation and demonisation of Muslimness operating at both state and social levels: 1) the promotion of community self-policing capacities and police partnership; 2) the fostering of a better understanding of Islam within civic society and the related clearing of grounds on which media can operationalise Muslim scapegoating; 3) a better reflection on the meanings of difference and diversity and their roles in the shaping of a pluralistic, multiethnic society.

---

69 Stefano has been undertaking PhD research at the University of Edinburgh since 2010. His research broadly aims at exploring how Scottish Muslims play out their 'Muslimness' within the global framework of a Western society. Qualitative fieldwork has been underway in Edinburgh since September 2011. He previously conducted research on the sociology of the Japanese terrorist sect called Aum Shinrikyō; and, more recently has been researching the British counter-terrorism strategies for combating terrorism and their impact on Muslims communities.

The British 'Muscular' Liberalism and Hyper-Pervasive Domestic War on Terror

The socio-political consequences of 9/11 (and subsequent terrorist attacks in Madrid, London and Glasgow) have conflated with the symbolic and ideological meanings of the 'war on terror' and coexisted with us for over ten years now. The British state response to a perceived high risk of an Islamist terrorist attack has taken the form of an all-encompassing counter-terrorism strategy called CONTEST that aims to 'Pursue', 'Prevent', 'Protect' and 'Prepare' the country for a potential terrorist attack (Home Office 2009). The most significant threats that CONTEST aims to tackle are deemed to spring from al-Qaeda groups, affiliates and inspired sources (Home Office 2010 p. 6), while less significant, and yet nevertheless recognised threats originate from Ireland-related and extreme right wing terrorism and other terrorist groups (Home Office 2011).

The political and legal direction taken by British counter-terrorism has steered away from the perimeter of temporary action in response to an exceptional state of emergency (Zedner 2008). Instead, it has embodied a permanent nature (Hickman, Thomas, Silvestri and Nickels 2011) that normalises fears of terrorism through the manipulation of symbols and meanings of personal and collective security within the perimeter of a post-modern world characterised by social fragmentation, insecurity and uncertainty (Bauman 2007). Despite being ideologically considered as a last option, dealing purely with a clear, real, imminent and grave threat, intrusive measures have been employed in the ordinary policing of Muslim communities (Zedner 2008). Indiscriminate stops and searches, heavy-handed tactics, the political demonisation of British Muslims (Cameron 2011) and the rhetorical exploitation of the Huntingtonian clash of civilisations (Huntington 1993) have alienated, marginalised and discriminated against large Muslim communities (Hewitt 2008 pp. 107-118).

Ignoring internal reports (Home Office and Foreign Office 2004) and far from pursuing a macro socio-political strategy aimed at winning 'hearts and minds' (De Vries 2006, Hewitt 2008), the British government has overtly deployed massive anti-terrorist legislation, surveillance and control measures (Spalek 2008) that are 'disproportionately experienced by people in the Muslim community' (House of Commons 2005 p. 46). The liberties and activities of terrorist suspects can be legally restrained, for example, by means of control orders as indicated by the Prevention of Terrorism Act 2005 (Hewitt 2008 pp. 29-55). The sanctioning of praise and glorification of terrorism under the Terrorism Act 2006 risks endangering individuals' freedom of speech and can easily fall into political manipulation, given the problematic univocal definition of what 'praise' and 'glorification' precisely means (Thiel 2009). Some pieces of legislation, such as Section 44 of the Terrorism

Act 2000 (allowing authorities to stop and search people in any location without needing any reasonable suspicion) or Part 4 of the British Anti-Terrorism, Crime and Security Act 2001 (authorising the indefinite internment of foreign nationals suspected of terrorism), were even ruled illegal, in the former case by the European Court of Human Rights, in the latter case by the House of Lords. Against such a heated political and legal framework, this paper will now move its focus onto the widely discussed and highly debated 'Prevent' strand of CONTEST and the ways in which it has impacted the lives of Muslim communities in Britain.

'Prevent[ing]' Terrorism, 'Prevent[ing]' Otherness, 'Prevent[ing]' Muslimness?

A few contextual clarifications are needed at this stage. 'Prevent' comes into existence with the enforcement of CONTEST, which itself has evolved as follows: a first unpublished classified version (2003-2006); a second partly declassified version (2006-2009); and a third almost fully declassified version (Gregory 2009). The 'Prevent' strategy was reviewed and updated by the Home Office (2011) in June 2011. The revised 'Prevent' fosters a state reinvigoration of British values, ideologically following the mono-cultural 'muscular liberalism' promoted by Cameron (2011) in his notorious Munich speech. It subliminally reiterates a culture of control (Garland 2001) typical of post-modern Western states that shape docile bodies (Foucault 1977) out of 'ontologically insecure individual[s]' (Giddens 1991 p. 53) who need to counterbalance identity uncertainties with superimposed perceptions of stability (Bonino 2011). The revised 'Prevent' sets three main objectives: 1) responding to terrorist ideological challenges; 2) preventing individuals from becoming terrorists by cutting funding from extremist groups and supporting early intervention programmes such as 'Channel', which is a 'multi-agency programme [aimed] to identify and provide support to people at risk of radicalisation' (Home Office 2011 p. 8); and 3) working in partnership with those key institutions and sectors, such as education, faith, healthcare, criminal justice system and charities, where radicalisation is considered to take place.

The first academic reactions to the revised 'Prevent' strategy have been quite critical towards what is considered an outright top-down approach, disguised as a democratic bottom-up approach (Spalek 2011a) that has been constructed within a value-based framework that risks endangering the open discussion of controversial issues, promoting a unique political viewpoint that controls malleable bodies (Foucault 1977) instead of creating active and engaged citizens (Jackson 2011). Furthermore, the state attempt to categorise British values is opposed as it neglects the changing, volatile and political nature of values and identities and might end up stigmatising and otherising those who hold different viewpoints, values and beliefs (Jarvis 2011). Clearly enough, in the current socio-political securitised state of affairs there seems to be little space for 'dialogised polyphony and heteroglossia', that is the inclusion of informal, marginal or even subversive discourses and discursive modalities in order to mould a pluralistic, democratically organised and 'dialogised' society (Campbell 2011). Melossi's (1990) powerful argument that democratic states exert a strong social-controlling, unitary (this being sometimes too hastily labelled as 'socially cohesive') and disciplinary action through the monopolistic mass production of meanings, processes of subjectification and exclusive control over the limits of legitimate opinion fits extremely well within critical discourses aimed at understanding the social pervasiveness and political reconceptualisation of the post-9/11 nation state.

Although pieces of literature, evaluations and case-studies focusing on the socio-political implications of the revised 'Prevent' are still scarce due to its very recent update, the above-mentioned initial criticisms have reinforced a strong climate of negativity that has surrounded 'Prevent' since its first public edition. Thomas, for example, points the finger at the state apparatus as a carrier of a programme of social engineering through the employment of a value-based approach (as opposed to a means-based approach) 'that has had a negative impact by reinforcing the otherness of Muslim communities' (Thomas 2010 p. 445). The author (Thomas 2010) further maintains that such an approach has clearly aimed at moulding religious practices and promoting (read also: funding) specific organisations (e.g. the Quilliam Foundation, the Sufi Muslim Council and the Radical Middle Way) at the expense of others, the most notable example being the Muslim Council of Britain that was originally set up in the 1990s under the auspices of both the Conservative and the Labour parties.

While counter-terrorism policies and the new terrorism context in general shape a low trust environment that engenders fear and suspicion within Muslim communities, the particularity of 'Prevent' is that it may problematise Islamic religious identities (Spalek 2011b) and produce a bitter sense of racial and religious discrimination and ethnic profiling that is experienced by some Muslims in their daily lives. The disproportionate employment of Schedule 7 (Terrorism Act 2000) giving authorities the power to carry out stops and searches at airports without any reasonable suspicion (Choudhury and Fenwick 2011) gives a clear example of the potential criminalisation of Muslim communities at the hand of the state. Furthermore, figures clearly show that stops and searches in the UK have disproportionately targeted and criminalised Asian communities (Cowan 2004, Dodd 2005), as they follow a logic of ethnic profiling that, it must be noted, has thus far produced in Europe 'few charges on terrorism offenses and no terrorism convictions to date' (Neild 2009 p. 11). As a matter of interest, it should be noted that full acquittal was granted to 56% (n=819) of those arrested for terrorism (n=1471) in the UK (Northern Ireland excluded) between September 2001 and March 2008 (Neild p. 2009). Among many others, the controversy over the deployment of more than two hundred CCTVs in two predominantly Asian neighbourhoods in Birmingham (Lewis p. 2010) has reiterated the view that Muslims are nowadays a suspect, mostly unduly surveilled and highly discriminated against population. A recent study (Choudhury and Fenwick 2011) shows that counter-terrorism practices have negatively impacted on Muslims by contributing towards a feeling of being a 'suspect community' and deepening their sense of alienation, isolation, anxiety and vulnerability.

Pantazis and Pemberton (2009) are particularly critical of the pre-emptive set of measures that has shaped a 'terror of prevention' in the form of 'day-to-day harassment of Muslims through stop and search to high-profile police raid [that] has had a corrosive effect on the relations between Muslim communities and the police' (Pantazis and Pemberton 2009 p. 662). If we add here the consideration that Muslim communities are usually concentrated within specific neighbourhoods in a few large urban areas – i.e. London, the West Midlands Metropolitan County, Greater Manchester and the West Yorkshire Metropolitan County (Peach 2005) – we can understand that the pervasiveness of police action can become unbearable for communities and severely undermine Muslims' confidence and trust in the law enforcement agency and the state. The totalising nature of the current security mantra leading to wrong arrests and reaching those places of education (such as schools, universities and mosques) that should guarantee free expression adds to young Muslims' deep sense of mistrust, vulnerability and anxiety (Choudhury and Fenwick 2011). Arguably, serving the public interest and protecting national security must be top state priorities. However, 'Prevent' seems to have gone far beyond its intended scope and has eventually alienated Muslims, targeted the wrong people, jeopardised some initiatives that could have promoted community cohesion and furthered intercommunity tensions (Bartlett and Birdwell 2010).

The Emergence of the Leviathan in the Securitisation of the Suspect Muslim

It should be clear by now that the post-9/11 socio-political framework has been characterised by a visible display of state power which builds on a reinforced state sovereignty (Foucault 1977) and embodies the normalisation of a 'state of permanent exception' in which the securitisation mantra penetrates the social fabrics (Hallsworth and Lea 2011) and individual rights are superseded in favour of enhanced state authority (Agamben 2003). While it is important to recognise that balancing the tension between serving the public good and respecting civil liberties is a highly problematic effort (Manningam-Buller 2005), it is still clear that the post-9/11 British state of security has gone far beyond the mutual obligatory relationship set by the social contract (Rousseau 1968), and has steered instead towards the re-embodiment of the Leviathan (Hobbes 1914). The British Leviathan has arguably mishandled those civic sacrifices that, according to Allen (2006), certain people and communities are always requested to endure more than others but that should be carefully negotiated in order to create an environment of social trust, democratic citizenship and political friendship. In her brilliant essay *The Cultural Politics of Justice: Bakhtin, Stand-Up Comedy and Post-9/11 Securitization*, Campbell (2011) notes 'a sea change in the nature of political deliberation about security in insecure times [...] and the fact that the policy response to risk, danger, threat and uncertainty is primarily based on the resurgence of sovereign and authoritarian forms of rule' (Campbell 2011 pp. 161-162). The oppressive state presence has burdened on the overall social domain made up by 'majority ordinary citizens' and 'minority citizens in a limbo'; the latter category includes Muslim communities who live in fear of, if they are not already feeling it, being placed outside social structures and, following Aristotle (2007 pp. 1-4), then becoming no longer part of the state. The state presence has particularly steered towards the securitisation of Muslim communities in the form of 'the application of a security discourse to domains of social and political life in ways that convert them into domains of security policy' (Brown 2008 p. 476).

State and police targeting of a whole community is not a novelty in Britain. In the 1974-1991 period examined by Hillyard (1993), more than 7000 individuals were arrested in relation to Northern Ireland matters under the Prevention of Terrorism Acts (PTA). Over 85% of those arrested were released without any charge after detention (from a few hours up to seven days) in the police station. Hillyard maintains that the exceptional measures and draconian legislation – he bluntly describes the PTA as 'an example of institutional racism' (Hillyard 1993 p. 33) – led to a widespread infringement of civil liberties and shaped imaginaries of the Irish people as 'a problem population, a dangerous class which needed regulation, discipline and control' (Hillyard 1993 p. 3). According to Hillyard (1993 pp. 1-12), Irish became synonymous with inferior race in the common English perception. Arguably, the process of shaping an Irish suspect community through a combined political and legislative set of (normalised) exceptional and emergency measures and hostile social perceptions set a precedent for the otherisation and inferiorisation of Muslim communities in post-9/11 'Prevent' oriented Britain, since 'the reactions and responses to political violence in 1974 clearly had embedded within them the principles, and gave rise to, the prevention measures that have been practised on an even more systematic scale throughout the 2000s' (Hickman, Thomas, Silvestri and Nickels 2011 p. 5). Similarly, the shaping of the Irish suspect community and, even more so, the Muslim suspect community took place within socio-political discourses massively advertising the concept of a 'society under attack' and constantly promoting a polarised rhetorical construction of 'us' against 'them' that revolves around the meanings of a mono-cultural, white Britishness (Hickman, Thomas, Silvestri and Nickels 2011).

Muslims' Demonisation at First Sight

The ruling out of non-Britishness from the social sphere and the problematisation of Muslim identities after 9/11 could be more broadly connected to both the European progressive shift to the far right and those socio-political discourses that promote widespread Islamophobia by understanding Muslim presence in Europe as a cultural, social, economic and security threat (Savage 2004). Meer (2010 pp. 179-197) notes that there is a distorted perception that Muslims are anti-modern and Islam is unfavourable to democracy and human rights. More generally, Meer argues that Britishness is usually considered a product of Western cultural sensitivities and 'presented as a take-it or leave-it affiliation with little room for contestation nor revision' (Meer 2010 p. 194). In a recent study into national identity recognition, it appears that some politicians and journalists fail to recognise Muslims' British identity, as they are considered a political and cultural threat (here the rhetoric applied to the veil and women's submission is exploited by some to prove an irremediable clash between Islamic and British values and sensibilities) and their national belonging is allegedly problematised by economic deprivation and the un-Islamic state of Britain (Uberoi, Meer, Modood and Dwyer 2011). Although recent polls reveal that two-thirds of non-Muslim Britons have a generally favourable view of British Muslims (Field 2007), such a socially quite diffuse positive attitude could be undermined by the harassment and violence that a minority of non-Muslims carry out against Muslims (Lambert and Githens-Mazer 2011). According to a quantitative study conducted by Field (2011), despite being quite content with their life in Britain, a majority of Muslims 'express anger at attacks on Islam and feel vulnerable in the face of worsening Islamophobia' (Field 2011 p. 170). It must be noted that some authors, such as Joppke (2009) and Malik (2005), have been critical of the notion of Islamophobia as it allegedly conflates two different concepts: criticism of Islam and discrimination against Muslims. However, after having explored state and police targeting of Muslims and Muslimness, the allegations of institutional Islamophobia (Commission on British Muslims and Islamophobia 2004) cannot be dismissed too hastily. State Islamophobia is doubly dangerous, since it not only impacts directly on Muslim communities but also penetrates the social fabric and reinforces the public demonisation of Muslims. As a passing note, it should be remembered that broader issues of endemic Islamophobia in the form of 'discrimination against [...] and exclusion of Muslims from mainstream political and social affairs' (Spalek 2002 p. 20) has operated within a legal framework that only recently protected Muslims against religious discrimination with the enactment of the Equality Act 2010.

Building up on a 'process of creating a "demonized Other"' (Hellyer 2007 p. 237) that dates as far back as the English Renaissance, Islamophobia became a matter of public concern in the 1980s, following the Honeyford Affair and the Rushdie Affair (Hellyer 2007). Nowadays, Islamophobia usually takes the form of political demonisation (Hewitt, 2008 pp. 107-118) and media otherisation (Jaspal and Cinnirella 2010). In particular, the media has played a very important role in the negative stereotyping and criminalisation of Muslims (Frost 2008). The demonisation of Muslims in the popular imaginaries could construct what Cohen (2002) would call 'folk devils' or suitable enemies in a postmodern realm where British society at large personifies that suitable victim whose ideological Britishness, which is grounded on monocultural whiteness and identity securitisation from the threat of the social other, is to be preserved. The emergence of widespread moral panics (Goode and Ben-Yehuda 1994) risk shaping a collective conscience grounded on absolutist ontological boundaries that perpetuate Islamophobia and further mould fifth column discourses around Muslim communities (Hellyer 2007).

While, in the case of the Irish, the discrimination against and the making of a suspect community worked at the communicative interactional level, many Muslims are alienated and targeted on a prima facie level. To understand how this mechanism works, it is necessary to draw on Goffman's theory of interaction order and note that for many Muslims their distinctive body markers and signs (e.g.: skin colour, beard, hijab) endanger the employment of front stage techniques (Goffman 1990a) that would help negotiate their identities and interactions on a socially more equal level. Thus, many Muslims' position in social situations is situated a priori, to the extent that discrimination and stigma can be attached on the basis of visual contact as a socially constructed way to classify them as 'discredited' individuals (Goffman 1990b) and inform mass social behaviours. State discrimination in the form of police targeting and ethnic profiling has already been mentioned. The post-9/11 securitised political climate has shaped social attitudes and daily encounters between Muslims and non-Muslims too. To substantiate theory with evidence, Hopkins (2004), for example, found that visible markers of Muslimness increase the likelihood of suffering from racism, marginalisation, and employment difficulties (Hopkins 2004). In other studies, visible display of Muslim features was connected to increased chances of experiencing daily discrimination in the form of verbal violence (Choudhury, Aziz, Izzidien, Khreeji and Hussain 2006), harassment and physical abuse (Spalek 2002). Yet clearly enough, negative experiences and exclusion from the socio-political sphere are a product of a more complex interconnected set of variables that complement being non-white and wearing a beard or a hijab. It will suffice to note that a deeper understanding of the fluid boundaries between inclusion and exclusion reveals that the maintenance or adoption of foreign ethnic/Muslim norms and mannerisms also play an important role in reinforcing exclusionary processes on a cultural and social basis (Kyriakides, Virdee and Modood 2009).

Strained Interaction, Strained Integration

The social consequences of a prima facie negative categorisation are potentially negative for processes of socio-ethnic integration, as they could undermine the ground for fruitful interactions between Muslims and non-Muslims. Low quality contacts between Muslims and non-Muslims seem to further non-positive behavioural intentions towards Muslims (Hutchison and Rosenthal 2011). In a study conducted by Hopkins, Greenwood and Birchall (2007), it appears that most Muslims would welcome increased contact with non-Muslim communities, however it needs to be ensured that people interacting with them do not misrecognise their identities or disrespect them under the influence of socially widespread prejudices and stereotypes. Needless to say, the endangerment of Muslims and non-Muslims' interactions at its very core – reciprocal trust, openness and willingness to engage – problematise the successful shaping of a truly culturally and ethnically diverse society in which plural identities can be played out and negotiated on an equal basis within the public sphere.

McDonald (2011) reiterates the arguments presented so far and maintains that Muslims' fear and mistrust arise from both counter-terrorism practices and broader issues of media-driven Islamophobia, strained interactions with ordinary citizens, anger over British foreign policies and widespread feelings of being part of a suspect community. Interestingly, a recent tentative study carried out by LSE researchers and *The Guardian* into the riots that happened in England in August 2011 showed that those Muslims who took part in the disorder were partly motivated by the politically formative experiences of 9/11 and the subsequent wars in Afghanistan and Iraq, and were mainly responding to diffuse police targeting and discriminatory attitudes in the form of stops and searches, racism and Islamophobic behaviour (Malik 2011).

It should be clear by now that the state political and legislative reaction to the symbolic understanding of 9/11 has not reduced itself to an all-encompassing counter-terrorism policy, whose 'Prevent' strand has been particularly pervasive within Muslim communities. In addition, it has employed such a policy for a broader game of social engineering that has added uncertainty to instability, mixophobia (Bauman 2007) to fear of otherness, alienation to exclusion, and discrimination to inferiorisation. 'Prevent' and the broader counter-terrorism measures have shaped and have been shaped by superimposing macro-structural forces, which are mostly driven by the re-embodied Leviathan, and become visible at the meso- and micro-level where Muslim communities and individuals are placed. Muslims have to at worst accept and at best negotiate the social, political, ideological and symbolical reconfiguration of their identities, their experiences and the meanings that they attach to their daily lives. The shaping of a collective conscience that understands Muslims as a suspect community, a post-modern evil that should be controlled – if not outright purged – then feeds into, informs and reinforces those same macro-structural processes of state Islamophobia in a vicious circle that spins almost out of control.

The Way Forward?

After having explored the post-9/11 securitisation of Muslimness and the relationship between state action (operating mainly within a pre-emptive counter-terrorism political and legal framework), social dispositions (informed by and informing state action) and the experiences of Muslims (working in interplay and merging with the former two), three tentative recommendations will be provided to try to move beyond the status quo and shape a state and collective conscience more disposed towards a self-empowering, plural and critical understanding of society.

1. Enhancing Community's Self-Policing Capacities and Encouraging Police Partnerships

Preventative measures aimed at fighting Islamist terrorism should lay on a more socially accepted and participative ground and improve the capacity of communities to develop self-policing strategies and engage in community partnership. Notwithstanding the well-documented problems related to intergenerational changes and fragmentations (Kabir 2010, Lewis 2007), it is undeniable that there are some patterns of intergenerational continuity within Muslim communities that still place the family at the core of people's development and lives, promote cultural enclosure and reiterate a sense of self-sufficiency that altogether could provide an important avenue for informal social control (Smith 2005). By sustaining self-empowerment, the potential of the Muslim *Gemeinschaft* (i.e. 'community' in the sense of an organic and strong association that binds people through blood affiliation, kinship, language and shared mores (Tönnies 1974)) would be enhanced. Strengthened networks of informal social control are a vital basis for the development of self-policing practices, although this needs to be backed up with processes of better integration and identity building of young Muslims whose socio-cultural gaps with their parents have widened, resulting in looser ties and a general sense of confusion (Bolognani 2009, Lowe and Innes 2008).

As said in another paper (Bonino forthcoming 2012), counter-terrorism strategies need to engage with communities not only in promoting self-policing but also in sustaining policing partnership. Such a soft approach would add up to community self-policing and reduce the oppressive state presence in Muslims' lives. This would address the primary source of Islamophobia and racialisation through the scaling down of the Leviathan towards a more democratic, participative and networked ideological and actualised notion of the state. Although his public credentials have been problematised by revelations of his ethically dubious undercover infiltration of political groups during his initial service at Special Branch (Evans and Lewis 2011), Bob Lambert's experience as head of the Muslim Contact Unit seems to have shown that the police can successfully partner with Muslim groups (Lambert 2008 and 2011) in sustaining de-radicalisation programmes and fighting terrorism. A strategy that promotes an engaging, trust building policing by consent – generally built on broad ideological and operational notions of community policing (Innes 2004, Skogan 2006 pp. 101-137) and bottom-up approaches – can thus be a starting point to restore Muslims' confidence (Jackson 2008) and move beyond the current hyper-securitised status quo.

2. Promoting a Better Understanding of Islam Within Broader Society

A better understanding of Islam should be promoted within mainstream society, through appropriate social channels. Polls (Field 2007) reveal that between one in five and one in four Britons either dislike or are prejudiced against Muslims and Islam – interestingly, Scotland seemingly scores less in Islamophobia than England (Hussain and Miller 2006). Those holding negative views of Muslims are mainly low skilled male workers, pensioners, elders and Conservatives. As previously indicated, contact plays an important role in negotiating reciprocal views since 'the greater the familiarity, the lower the level of prejudice, and vice versa' (Field 2007 p. 465). It is then important to promote inter-community engagement activities that increase interactions between Muslims and non-Muslims and educate society at large. The activity of inter-faith organisations, charities, Muslim associations, schools and academic bodies aimed at fostering a better understanding of Islam within public society have been remarkable but need to be maintained and reinforced through policies that normalise Muslimness in a socially gradual way, in order to ensure that recognition is spontaneously nurtured in collective consciences within the understanding that plurality should discriminate against no groups but also favour no groups.

The media, laden with racist content and hate speeches (Winkler 2006), has criminalised Muslim communities and spread moral panics (Frost 2008), based on the strengthening of societal boundaries and collective conscience (Goode and Ben-Yehuda 1994). The social understanding of Muslimness as a qualitatively 'equal difference' in a context of ethnic pluralism and the related reduced Islamophobic attitudes will hopefully remove the grounds for the media shaping of Muslims as the postmodern evil. However, it would be simplistic to believe that a new scapegoat will not substitute Muslims in the public and media imaginaries. Whether the Jews during the Nazi period, communists in post-WWII America, gays in the 1980s or Muslims in the current post-9/11 world, scapegoats will continuously be evoked throughout history to 'unite a faltering civic society by invoking a common threat [...] and deflect attention away from the genuine causes of insecurity' (Vaughan 2002 p. 205). It is clearly beyond the scope of this paper to argue for a change in social understandings or for the shaping of a utopian society of equals. It will suffice to have indicated a tentative way to move beyond the demonisation of the current scapegoats, i.e. Muslims.

3. Making Sense of Difference and Diversity in a Pluralistic, Multiethnic Society

The philosophical idea of difference and diversity should be reflected on by academics and society in general, in order to try and understand how multiethnic communities can coexist within post-modern, global societies. It will be useful here to borrow Eriksen's definitions of diversity and difference. According to the author, diversity has been understood as 'largely aesthetic, politically and morally neutral expressions of cultural difference' (Eriksen 2006 p. 14), while difference is usually regarded as 'morally objectionable or at least questionable notions and practices in a minority group or category, that is to say notions and practices which are held to (i) create conflicts through direct contact with majorities who hold other notions, (ii) weaken social solidarity in the country and thereby the legitimacy of the political and welfare systems, and (iii) lead to unacceptable violations of human rights within the minority groups' (Eriksen 2006 pp. 14-15). Eriksen maintains that, while diversity is supported within the public sphere, difference is considered a main cause of social problems that are usually connected to immigrants and their descendants. From this the author makes the logical argument that the demarcation between the acceptable and the unacceptable cultural differences could instead hide broader and deeper political and class conflicts, a position that is somewhat close to the ideas of Sartori (2000).

Keeping this in mind, the focus needs to quickly move to the potential that difference has for the individual and the society. Difference is arguably the substratum of individual identity (Jenkins 2008 pp. 37-48) as who and what we are can be discerned through the understanding of who and what we are not (Cesareo 2000 pp. 39-90). Difference then plays a key role in individual identification, thus in one's processes of self-understanding, self-realisation and construction of reality. Combining this important theoretical understanding of difference with more pragmatic discourses, the kind of equality that should be promoted within a pluralistic society is one that includes 'the right to have one's 'difference' (minority ethnicity, etc.) recognised and supported in both the public and the private spheres' (Modood, 2003 p. 105).

In toning down the racial vilification of the 'other' and counterbalancing powerful political processes that shape public imaginaries revolving around the symbolic construction of an hyper-solidaristic, exclusive, monocultural sense of community (Jenkins 2008 pp. 16-27), a politics of democratic recognition should then not only valorise difference, but also actualise full legitimate participation of Muslims within the social and political realms (Noble 2005) of a pluralistic, multiethnic society.

Conclusion

Over ten years have passed since 9/11, but its symbolic cry still resonates in the Western world. Arguably, the British counter-terrorism domestic approach has been unsatisfactory. Muslim communities have been targeted, demonised and alienated from the socio-political sphere. The scapegoating of Muslim communities has been operationalised at the interplay between state action and social behaviour where Muslims' daily experiences, lives and identity negotiations have been trapped in a vicious circle that keeps spinning and reproducing itself. Under the current culture of control and security that promotes feelings of being a suspect community, the socio-ethnic integration of many Muslims becomes highly problematised: a potential retreat within ethnic, cultural and religious comfort zones would be understandable if we considered the perspective of the 'other' by trying to see reality through her eyes. The making of a pluralist society that is grounded on equal recognition must then start by the restructuring of those state policies that have targeted and overly criminalised an entire community, have shaped negative social attitudes and dispositions and have provided fertile grounds on which the media can sow the seeds of the folk devils on call. It would then try to look through those 'other' eyes that might not always represent the majority's viewpoint but are equally important and real in the construction of everyday Britain. This is a process that involves all of those engaged in the making of a democratic society, from the state to members of civic society. It involves academics too. The urge to academics is to make use of the powerful position within which they can operate to gradually shape a collective conscience that moves beyond past and present mistakes and makes an effort to shape a truly participative, pluralistic and multiethnic Britain which Muslims, as anybody else, can comfortably call home.

Bibliography

Agamben, Giorgio (2003) *Lo Stato di Eccezione*, Torino: Bollati Boringhieri.

Allen, Danielle (2006) *Talking to Strangers: Anxieties of Citizenship Since Brown v. Board of Education*, Chicago: University of Chicago Press.

Aristotle (2007) *Aristotle: Politics* [online], translated by Benjamin Jowett, Forgotten Books, 1-4, available: http://www.forgottenbooks.org/read.php?a=1605063371 (accessed 21.12.11).

Bartlett, Jamie and Birdwell, Jonathan (2010) *From Suspects to Citizens: Preventing Violent Extremism in a Big Society*, London: Demos.

Bauman, Zygmunt (2007) *Liquid Times: Living in an Age of Uncertainty*, Cambridge: Polity Press.

Bolognani, Marta (2009) *Crime and Muslim Britain: Race, Culture and the Politics of Criminology Among British Pakistanis*, London: Tauris Academic Studies.

Bonino, Stefano (2011) 'On Post-Modern Consumerist Societies, Crime and Violence', *Rivista di Criminologia, Vittimologia e Sicurezza*, 5 (3), pp. 113-126.

Bonino, Stefano (forthcoming 2012) 'Policing Strategies against Islamic Terrorism in the UK after 9/11: The Socio-Political Realities for British Muslims', *Journal of Muslim Minority Affairs*, 32 (1).

Brown, Katherine (2008) 'The Promise and Perils of Women's Participation in UK Mosques: The Impact of Securitisation Agendas on Identity, Gender and Community', *The British Journal of Politics and International Relations*, 10 (3), pp. 472–491.

Cameron, David (2011) *PM's Speech at Munich Security Conference* [online], Speech delivered at Munich Security Conference, Munich, 5 February 2011, available: http://www.number10.gov.uk/news/speeches-and-transcripts/2011/02/pms-speech-at-munich-security-conference-60293 (accessed 19.12.11).

Campbell, Elaine (2011) 'The Cultural Politics of Justice: Bakhtin, Stand-Up Comedy and Post-9/11 Securitization', *Theoretical Criminology*, 15 (2), pp. 159-177.

Cesareo, Vincenzo (2000) *Società Multietniche e Multiculturalismi*, Milano: Vita e Pensiero.

Choudhury, Tufyal, Aziz, Mohammed, Izzidien, Duaa, Khreeji, Intissar and Hussain, Dilwar (2006) *Perceptions of Discrimination and Islamophobia: Voices from Members of Muslim Communities in the European Union*, Vienna: European Monitoring Centre on Racism and Xenophobia.

Choudhury, Tufyal and Fenwick, Helen (2011) 'The Impact of Counter-Terrorism Measures on Muslim Communities', *Equality and Human Rights Commission Research Report 72*, Manchester: Equality and Human Rights Commission.

Cohen, Stanley (2002) *Folk Devils and Moral Panics*, London: Routledge.

Commission On British Muslims And Islamophobia (2004) *Islamophobia: Issues,*

Challenges and Action, Stoke on Trent: Trentham Books.

Cowan, Rosie (2004) 'Young Muslims "Made Scapegoats" in Stop and Search', *The Guardian*, July 3.

De Vries, Gijs (2006) *The Fight Against Terrorism: Five Years After 9/11* [online], Presentation given at the 'Annual European Foreign Policy Conference', London School of Economics and King's College London, 30 June 2006, available: http://www.consilium.europa.eu/uedocs/cmsUpload/060630LondonSchoolEc onomics.pdf (accessed 19.12.11).

Dodd, Vikram (2005) 'Asian Men Targeted in Stop and Search', *The Guardian*, August 17.

Eriksen, Thomas (2006) 'Diversity Versus Difference: Neo-Liberalism in the Minority Debate', in Rottenburg, Richard, Schnepel, Burkhard and Shimada, Shingo (eds.), *The Making and Unmaking of Difference*, Bielefeld: Transaction, pp. 13–36.

Foucault, Michel (1977) *Discipline and Punish: The Birth of the Prison*, translated by Sheridan, Alan, London: Allen Lane.

Evans, Rob and LEWIS, Paul (2011) 'Progressive Academic Bob Lambert is Former Police Spy', *The Guardian*, October 16.

Field, Clive (2007) 'Islamophobia in Contemporary Britain: The Evidence of the Opinion Polls, 1988-2006', *Islam and Christian-Muslim Relations*, 18 (4), pp. 447-477.

Frost, Diane (2008) 'Islamophobia: Examining Causal Links between the Media and "Race Hate" from "Below"', *International Journal of Sociology and Social Policy*, 28 (11-12), pp. 564–578.

Garland, David (2001) *The Culture of Control*, Oxford: Oxford University Press.

Giddens, Anthony (1991) Modernity and Self-Identity: Self and Society in Late Modern Age, Stanford: Stanford University Press.

Goffman, Erving (1983) 'The Interaction Order: American Sociological Association, 1982 Presidential Address', *American Sociological Review*, 48 (1), pp. 1-17.

Goffman, Erving (1990a) *The Presentation of Self in Everyday Life*, London: Penguin Books.

Goffman, Erving (1990b) *Stigma: Notes on the Management of Spoiled Identity*, London: Penguin Books.

Goode, Erich and Ben-Yehuda, Nachman (1994) 'Moral Panics: Culture, Politics, and Social Construction', *Annual Review of Sociology*, 20, pp. 149-71.

Gregory, Frank (2009) 'CONTEST (2009): An Evaluation of Revisions to the UK Counter-Terrorism Strategy with a Special Focus on the CBRNE Threat (ARI)', *Real Instituto Elcano de Estudios Internacionales y Estratégicos*, 130, pp. 1-14.

Hallsworth, Simon and LEA, John (2011) 'Reconstructing Leviathan: Emerging Contours of the Security State', *Theoretical Criminology*, 15 (2), pp. 141-157.

Hellyer, Hisham (2007) 'British Muslims: Past, Present and Future', *The Muslim*

World, 97 (2), pp. 225-258.

Hewitt, Steve (2008) *The British War on Terror: Terrorism and Counter-Terrorism on the Home Front Since 9/11*, London: Continuum.

Hickman, Mary, Thomas, Lyn, Silvestri, Sara and Nickels, Henri (2011) '*Suspect Communities'? Counter-Terrorism Policy, the Press, and the Impact on Irish and Muslim Communities in Britain*, London: London Metropolitan University.

Hillyard, Paddy (1993) *Suspect Community: People's Experience of the Prevention of Terrorism Acts in Britain*, London: Pluto Press.

Hobbes, Thomas (1914) *Leviathan*, London: Dent.

Foreign and Commonwealth Office and Home Office (2004) *Draft Report on Young Muslims and Extremism* [online], Unpublished Report, available: http://www.globalsecurity.org/security/library/report/2004/muslimext-uk.htm   (accessed 19.12.11).

Home Office (2009) *The United Kingdom's Strategy for Countering International Terrorism*, London: The Stationery Office.

Home Office (2010) *The United Kingdom's Strategy for Countering International Terrorism. Annual Report*, London: The Stationery Office.

Home Office (2011) *Prevent Strategy*, London: The Stationery Office.

Hopkins, Nick, Greenwood, Ronni and Birchall, Maisha (2007) 'Minority Understandings of the Dynamics to Intergroup Contact Encounters: British Muslims' (Sometimes Ambivalent) Experience of Representing Their Group to Others', *South African Journal of Psychology*, 37 (4), pp. 679-701.

Hopkins, Peter (2004) 'Young Muslim Men in Scotland: Inclusions and Exclusions', *Children's Geographies*, 2 (2), pp. 257-272.

House of Commons (2005) *Terrorism and Community Relations*, vol. 1, London: The Stationery Office.

Huntington, Samuel (1993) 'The Clash of Civilizations?', *Foreign Affairs*, 72 (3), pp. 22-49.

Hussain, Asifa and Miller, William (2006) *Multicultural Nationalism: Islamophobia, Anglophobia, and Devolution*, Oxford: Oxford University Press.

Hutchison, Paul and Rosenthal, Harriet (2011) 'Prejudice Against Muslims: Anxiety as a Mediator Between Intergroup Contact and Attitudes, Perceived Group Variability and Behavioural Intentions', *Ethnic and Racial Studies*, 34 (1), pp. 40-61.

Jackson, Richard (2008) 'Counter-Terrorism and Communities: An Interview with Robert Lambert', *Critical Studies on Terrorism*, 1 (2), pp. 293-308.

Jackson, Richard (2011) 'The Failed Paradigm of Prevent', *Soundings* [online], June 15, available: http://soundings.mcb.org.uk/?p=35 (accessed 19.12.11).

Jarvis, Lee and Lister, Michael (2011) 'Values and Stakeholders in the 2011 Prevent Strategy', *Soundings* [online], 15 June, available http://soundings.mcb.org.uk/?p=31 (accessed 19.12.11).

Jenkins, Richard (2008) *Social Identity*, 3rd ed., London: Routledge.

Joppke, Christian (2009) 'Limits of Integration Policy: Britain and Her Muslims', *Journal of Ethnic and Migration Studies*, 35 (3), pp. 453-472.

Kabir, Nahid (2010) *Young British Muslims: Identity, Culture, Politics and the Media*, Edinburgh: Edinburgh University Press.

Kyriakides, Christopher, Virdee, Satnam and Modood, Tariq (2009) 'Racism, Muslims and the National Imagination', *Journal of Ethnic and Migration Studies*, 35 (2), pp. 289-308.

Innes, Martin (2004) 'Reinventing Tradition? Reassurance, Neighbourhood Security and Policing', Criminal Justice, 4 (2), pp. 151-171.

Lambert, Robert and Githens-Mazer, Jonathan (2011) *Islamophobia and Anti-Muslim Hate Crime: UK Case Studies 2010*, Exeter: European Muslim Research Centre, University of Exeter.

Lambert, Robert (2008) 'Empowering Salafis and Islamists Against Al-Qaeda: A London Counterterrorism Case Study', *Political Science & Politics*, 41 (1), pp. 31-35.

Lambert, Robert (2011) *Countering al-Qaeda in London: Police and Muslims in Partnership*, London: Hurst.

Lewis, Paul (2010) 'Birmingham Stops Camera Surveillance in Muslim Areas', *The Guardian*, June 17.

Lewis, Philip (2007) *Young, British and Muslim*, London: Continuum.

Lowe, Trudy and INNES, Martin (2008) 'Countering Terror: Violent Radicalisation and Situational Intelligence' *Prison Service Journal*, 179, pp. 3-10.

Malik, Kenan (2005) 'The Islamophobia Myth', *Prospect*, 107 (February).

Malik, Shiv (2011) 'Muslim Rioters Say Police Discrimination Motivated Them', *The Guardian*, December 8.

Manningham-Buller, Eliza (2005) *The International Terrorist Threat and the Dilemmas in Countering it* [online], Speech delivered at the Ridderzaal-Binnenhof, The Hague, Netherlands, 1 September 2005, available: http://www.mi5.gov.uk/output/director-generals-speech-to-the-aivd-2005.html (accessed 20.12.11).

McDonald, Zahra (2011) 'Securing Identities, Resisting Terror: Muslim Youth Work in the UK and its Implications for Security', *Religion, State and Society*, 39 (2-3), pp. 177-189.

Meer, Nasar (2010) *Citizenship, Identity and the Politics of Multiculturalism: The Rise of Muslim Consciousness*, Basingstoke: Palgrave Macmillan.

Melossi, Dario (1990) *The State of Social Control: A Sociological Study of Concepts of State and Social Control in the Making of Democracy*, Cambridge: Polity Press.

Modood, Tariq (2003) 'Muslims and the Politics of Difference', *The Political Quarterly*, 74 (s1), pp. 100-115.

Neild, Rachel (2009) *Ethnic Profiling in the European Union: Pervasive, Ineffective, and Discriminatory*, New York: Open Society Institute.

Noble, Greg (2005) 'The Discomfort of Strangers: Racism, Incivility and Ontological Security in a Relaxed and Comfortable Nation', *Journal of Intercultural Studies*, 26 (1), pp. 107-120.

Pantazis, Christina and Simon Pemberton (2009) 'From the "Old" to the "New" Suspect Community: Examining the Impacts of Recent UK Counter-Terrorist Legislation', *British Journal of Criminology*, 49 (5), pp. 646-666.

Peach, Ceri (2005) 'Muslims in the UK', in Abbas, Tahir (ed.), *Muslim Britain: Communities Under Pressure*, London: Zed Books, pp. 18-30.

Rousseau, Jean-Jacques (1968) *The Social Contract*, translated by Cranston, Maurice, London: Penguin Books.

Sartori, Giovanni (2000) *Pluralismo, Multiculturalismo e Estranei: Saggio sulla Società Multietnica*, Milano: Rizzoli.

Savage, Timothy (2004) 'Europe and Islam: Crescent Waxing, Cultures Clashing', *The Washington Quarterly*, 27 (3), pp. 25-50.

Skogan, Wesley (2006) Police and Community in Chicago: A Tale of Three Cities, Oxford: Oxford University Press.

Smith, David (2005) 'Ethnic Differences in Intergenerational Crime Patterns', *Crime and Justice*, 32, pp. 59-129.

Spalek, Basia (2002) 'Hate Crimes Against British Muslims in the Aftermath of September 11th', *Criminal Justice Matters*, 48 (1), pp. 20-21.

Spalek, Basia (2008) 'Muslim Communities Post-9/11 – Citizenship, Security and Social Justice', *International Journal of Law, Crime and Justice*, 36 (4), pp. 211-214.

Spalek, Basia (2011a) 'A Top Down Approach', *Soundings* [online], 15 June, available: http://soundings.mcb.org.uk/?p=29 (accessed 20.12.11).

Spalek, Basia (2011b) '"New Terrorism" and Crime Prevention Initiatives Involving Muslim Young People in the UK: Research and Policy Contexts', *Religion, State and Society*, 39 (2-3), pp. 191-207.

Thiel, Darren (2009) *Policing Terrorism: A Review of the Evidence*, London: The Police Foundation.

Thomas, Paul (2010) 'Failed and Friendless: The UK's "Preventing Violent Extremism" Programme', *The British Journal of Politics and International Relations*, 12 (3), pp. 442-458.

Tonnies, Ferdinand (1974) *Community and Association*, translated by Loomis, Charles, Thetford: Lowe & Brydone.

Uberoi, Varun; Meer, Nasar; Modood, Tariq and Dwyer, Claire (2011) 'Feeling and Being Muslim and British', in Modood, Tariq and Salt, John (eds.), *Global Migration, Ethnicity and Britishness*, Basingstoke: Palgrave Macmillan, pp. 205-224.

Vaughan, Barry (2002) 'The Punitive Consequences of Consumer Culture',

Punishment and Society, 4 (2), pp. 195-211.

Winkler, Beate (2006) *Racism, Xenophobia and the Media: Towards Respect and Understanding of All Religions and Cultures*, [online], Speech delivered at 'Euro-Mediterranean Seminar', Vienna, 22 May 2006, available: http://fra.europa.eu/fraWebsite/material/pub/general/euromed_speech_dir_220506_en.pdf (accessed 21.12.11).

Zedner, Lucia (2008) 'Terrorism, the Ticking Bomb, and Criminal Justice Values', *Criminal Justice Matters*, 73 (1), pp. 18-19

Beyond the 'Crisis of Multiculturalism': Moves in Theory and Practice

Elise Rietveld [70]

The last decade has seen a protracted 'crisis of multiculturalism'. Across Europe, politicians, academics, and public opinion alike have voiced concerns about the continued viability of multiculturalism as a policy solution for dealing with cultural diversity within society. Britain is no exception. Events such as the riots in Oldham, Burnley, Leeds and Bradford in 2001, the terrorist attacks of 9/11 (2001), and the London bombings of 7/7 (2005) have reinforced a feeling that the integration of minorities, especially Muslims, has failed. This failure is blamed on multiculturalism.

Prior to this crisis of confidence, multiculturalism in political theory developed as a response to liberalism. It challenges the liberal dictum of the neutral state, arguing instead that states always represent a particular culture (Kymlicka 1995). This cultural bias becomes a problem because multiculturalists hold that the recognition of cultural identity is crucial for the self-esteem and the relative position in society of cultural groups and their members (Taylor 1994). Cultural minorities thus need to be compensated for it by special measures designed to publicly recognise their distinctive cultural identity. The division between the public and the private sphere characteristic of liberal philosophy is hence collapsed and cultural differences gain political saliency. This means citizenship becomes differentiated, with cultural minorities receiving special rights and exemptions from general laws (Parekh 2000).

Multiculturalism in Britain was built around a combination of strict immigration controls, deemed necessary to facilitate the ensuing integration process, and progressive race relations legislation (Favell 1998). Issues of race hence became the

---

70 Elise Rietveld is a PhD candidate at Cardiff University. Her thesis title is Re-Constructing Multiculturalism, and her research combines a normative theoretical approach to multiculturalism with empirical research on the development of policy discourses on multiculturalism in the Netherlands and the UK. She was awarded the President's Research Scholarship. She completed her MA between the years 2008-2009 at the University of Bath Euromasters (Contemporary European Studies). Her Final dissertation was 'The Europeanisation of Integration Policy', which sets out to investigate the hypothesis of a European influence on recent developments in integration policy in European countries, following a case study approach focused on France and the Netherlands. The taught element of the programme was based in three different cities (Bath, Paris, Seattle) and included courses on 'Transatlantic Relations' and the 'Transformation of Governance in Europe'.

pivotal questions of multiculturalism, with progressive interpretation in case law extending the reach of the legislation to other characteristics of minority groups. Multiculturalism furthermore followed a largely local logic, with policy responding pragmatically to questions that arose (Favell 1998; Modood 2011). Multicultural integration was famously defined early on by then home secretary Jenkins 'not as a flattening process of uniformity, but cultural diversity, coupled with equality of opportunity in an atmosphere of mutual tolerance' (quoted in Favell 1998 p.104). The retention of minority cultural identity thus was not seen to be antithetical to integration, and Britain has provided exemptions and accommodation of cultural difference to a degree rarely found elsewhere in Europe (Joppke 2009).

Recently both theory and policy have changed their engagement with multiculturalism. While policy has 'retreated' from it (Joppke 2004), emphasising national belonging and identity over minority cultural identity, multicultural theory has evolved to overcome past flaws. In this updated version, it is still considered by some to be the best option for providing justice in the diverse societies of today's globalised world. This chapter will examine the moves made in theory and policy practice following the crisis and assess how the new policy of 'community cohesion' compares to 'new multiculturalism'. Where some (e.g. Joppke 2004) have been swift to declare the reversal of multiculturalism, and others (e.g. Kymlicka 2007) claim this is overstated, such assessments typically do not take into account the recent developments in multicultural theory. These theoretical refinements however need to be considered in order to provide a fair appraisal of recent policy changes and develop a better understanding of multiculturalism in 21st century Britain.

The chapter starts by introducing the main arguments against multiculturalism developed as part of the crisis of multiculturalism. It will then explore the two most elaborate defences of multiculturalism following this crisis in political theory, put forward by Anne Phillips (2007) and Tariq Modood (2007). Subsequently, policy developments following the crisis will be discussed. The moves in theory and practice will then be compared and assessed to see whether recent policy really has retreated from multiculturalism.

Multiculturalism in Crisis

The crisis of multiculturalism as it plays out in the media is mainly about failed integration. Multiculturalism, it is said, has not had the desired effect of creating a harmonious and integrated society, but rather has facilitated the self-segregation of minority communities into pockets of disenfranchisement and disadvantage, that may foster radicalisation and terrorism. Multicultural policies aimed at supporting minority identity are said to have fostered separation and division, especially of Muslim communities (Pilkington 2008).

In political theory, this charge is related to essentialism. Multiculturalism is said to rely on an essentialist notion of culture: it sees cultures as clearly delineated, separate entities with a distinctive essence (Mason 2007). This essence, commonly understood as a mix of values, practices and language, is shared by all the members of these cultural groups. Cultural groups thus are conceived of as displaying a high degree of internal homogeneity. Group members are often portrayed as defined by their culture; their actions and identities are explained by reference to their cultural origin (Barry 2001). By supporting minority cultures, multiculturalism is said to reinforce such imagined group boundaries and divisions in society.

This essentialist conception of culture is dismissed as flawed. It overstates differences between cultures, ignores agency in cultural group-members as well as internal divisions within cultures, and reinforces stereotypes. Cultures should be understood instead as dynamic and hybrid (Benhabib 1999). Cultural identity is constructed in a process of interaction with other cultures and within the parameters of the relevant institutional context (Kukathas 1992). Individuals moreover are not simply carriers of their culture but possess several identities that may vary in importance, with culture being only one factor of identification along with for instance gender, class, race, and religion (Phillips 2007).

The essentialist conception of culture moreover is considered dangerous: conceiving of cultures as monolithic blocs risks disregarding the power relations within groups (Okin 1999). Diversity within groups means that some group members will dissent from the standards and norms accepted by the majority. Furthermore, some group members, especially women and children, will be more vulnerable than others. Group elites may abuse their power by stifling dissent and oppressing vulnerable members (Eisenberg and Spinner-Halev 2005). Where multiculturalism relies on an essentialist notion of culture, it too easily defers power to minority group leaders without taking notice of the position of minorities within minorities.

The crisis of multiculturalism in political theory furthermore asserts the threat multiculturalism poses to redistribution. Redistribution is an egalitarian goal linked to equality; through taxation and the welfare state, material inequality can be alleviated. Multiculturalism and its emphasis on the public recognition of difference, it is argued, deflect attention away from this goal (Fraser 1996). It uses up scarce resources that could have been deployed better: it is material, not cultural inequality that matters in the end (Barry 2001). Multiculturalism moreover threatens to erode the shared foundations of citizenship that facilitate the process of redistribution. With its insistence on differentiated rights and minority cultural identity, it is conducive to loyalty at the group level, rather than the national or societal level. The mutual identification and solidarity needed for taxation and redistribution hence may crumble at the hands of such centrifugal forces (Kymlicka and Banting 2006; Miller 1995).

Beyond the Crisis: Phillips and Modood

Both Phillips (2007) and Modood (2007) argue that despite the criticisms outlined above, multiculturalism deserves to be saved from the battle field. In a somewhat more nuanced version, it remains the best way of accommodating and integrating different groups in society. Both versions of 'new multiculturalism' discussed here start with a conscious decision to avoid relying on an essentialist notion of culture. For Phillips (2007), this extends to a concern with power relations within cultural groups. Her aim is to demonstrate that multiculturalism does not have to be antithetical to feminism. Modood (2007) is more trusting of group leaders and allows groups a political role. He seeks to extend the scope of multiculturalism to religious groups. He also takes issue with the notion that multiculturalism erodes shared citizenship.

'New multiculturalism' dismisses the essentialist notion of cultures as bounded and homogeneous and appreciates their diverse, hybrid and dynamic nature. Phillips (2007) argues that previous versions of multiculturalism have not done enough to avoid the use of such an essentialist notion of culture, with the result of providing fuel to unhelpful stereotypical oppositions drawn between Western and non-Western groups. Non-Western minority groups in this discourse are represented as determined by their culture, thereby depriving them of agency. Such a stereotype opposes these groups to Western groups that are portrayed as non-cultural, liberal and whose members are autonomous individuals. Gender inequality has been used to reinforce this opposition: Western groups are equated with respect for gender equality, and non-Western minorities portrayed as violating these norms. Modood (2007) points out how the non-Western minority groups in this discourse tend to be Muslims, portrayed as a monolithic bloc opposed to the secular West. Where culture is understood as enjoyed only by minorities, and determining and restricting the actions of group members, the agency of minority citizens is effectively negated (Phillips 2007).

Relying on an essentialist notion of culture moreover, Modood (2007) argues, risks failing to appreciate the current complexity of diversity. He emphasises how the 'multi' in multiculturalism refers not just to a duality of majority and minority, but to a plurality within that minority. Difference hence is not limited to difference from the mainstream, but also from other minority groups. Groups are groups in different ways; they make different claims, take different socio-economic positions in society, have different levels of organisation, and demand different loyalties from their members. Members moreover relate to these groups in different ways: for some group-membership will be more important (in terms of behaviour and identity) than for others (Modood 2007). Multiculturalism needs to respect this multiplicity and engage with people and groups in ways they themselves feel appropriate; it needs to be 'multilogue' (Modood 2007 p. 127) rather than dialogue.

Despite dismissing the essentialist concept of culture, however, 'new multiculturalism' retains the older multicultural principle that culture matters. The liberal solution of relegating it to the private sphere is deemed insufficient to provide justice and equality. Cosmopolitan or 'multiculture' (Meer and Modood 2009 p. 476) approaches that champion a particular attitude to culture, which is open and detached, fail to capture the strength of cultural attachment felt by many people (Modood 2007; Phillips 2007). Culture remains important in social life as people identify with it, draw on its norms to shape their behaviour, and rely on it to give meaning to reality (Phillips 2008). Cultural membership and identity moreover are considered at least partly inherited – that is, not freely adopted (Modood 2007; Phillips 2007). As such, cultural groups both matter to people and affect life chances; multicultural policy needs to appreciate the former and compensate for the latter.

For Phillips (2007), that means enabling agency. Previous approaches in European countries that aimed at dialogue between different cultures, by relying on an essentialist concept of culture, have too often exaggerated value conflicts. In reality, these are not that significant; the real issue for multiculturalism in Europe is the identification of consent and coercion in practices that involve cultural pressure (Phillips 2007). That means first and foremost the protection of the rights of individuals (often women) at risk of cultural coercion, followed by policy to empower them. She challenges the tendency to portray minority women as dupes and posits that agency is shared across cultures, although it needs to be understood not as absolute but as potentially varying in degree depending on personality and upbringing. Culture and agency hence are not mutually exclusive (Phillips 2007).

Nevertheless, culture does influence (rather than determine) behaviour and identity, much like class and gender do. For the latter two categories, a more nuanced and subtle understanding of this influence exists, which needs to be extended to culture (Phillips 2007). People are more likely to make certain decisions in light of their cultural origins; however they may just as well behave differently. Culture moreover, like gender and class, positions people in society and sustains 'social hierarchies' (Phillips 2007 p. 15). These power and material inequalities cannot be addressed without acknowledging the differences that carry them. Accepting that a state can never be culturally neutral and institutions tend to be culturally biased, multicultural accommodations should be made for minorities to compensate for their marginalised position and challenge indirect discrimination (Phillips 2007). However, in contrast to most older approaches to multiculturalism, Phillips (2007) argues that to avoid the oppression of vulnerable group members states should not delegate any rights or authority to cultural groups. Ethno-cultural organisations may receive funding, but only so as to carry out important functions. Representation needs to proceed not through elites but through more open democratic institutions; this will ensure not the representation of groups as such but a more proportional representation of diversity itself (Phillips 2007). The focus thus lies with the individual.

Modood (2008 p. 550) disagrees with this focus. Groups matter to people and therefore deserve to play a role in politics, he argues. Minority groups may thus be represented by spokespeople to further their claims for recognition and justice. Modood's (2007) understanding of culture hence is more tightly tied up with communities than that of Phillips (2007). For multicultural policy, these communities or groups however are defined by difference, rather than culture. The state reflects majority norms and culture, and minorities stand out because they differ from these norms (as well as from each other). Multiculturalism for Modood (2007) is about turning negative difference (stereotypes, marginalisation) into positive difference, where all groups are recognised and supported publicly following assertive identity statements. The public recognition of group identity here is understood as crucial to equality as well as self-esteem.

Against the general climate, Modood (Meer and Modood 2009; Modood 2007) argues that this of type of multiculturalism has been present in Britain and has generally delivered good results. However, it ran into problems when Muslims started to assert their identity politically. Although their claims for inclusion are similar to those made by other groups, they have been received with much more caution. In a global climate of heightened security sensitivity, Muslims have become targets of fear, racism and exclusion (Modood 2007). The key issue for multiculturalism in Europe therefore is not the identification of coercion, but the integration of Muslims. A more moderate engagement with Muslim claims-making is needed: a multicultural approach that allows Muslims to organise as a group in a way they see fit. This entails developing a more nuanced understanding of secularism as a political reality, different per context, rather than a philosophical axiom of liberal states (Modood 2007). Western democracies have different ways of drawing boundaries between the secular and the sacred, but these are nowhere absolute. Engaging with Muslims thus may mean engaging with religious leaders, where these are chosen as civic leaders by their communities (Modood 2007).

Importantly, however, multiculturalism does not stop at recognising the diversity of difference in society. Modood (2007) here goes further than most older versions of multiculturalism and argues that in order to work, it requires a strong shared national citizenship to counterbalance the emotional pull of cultural groups. Citizenship presents the site of common, shared experiences for all groups in society. It needs to be conceptualised as a process of renegotiation, where minorities and majority enter into constructive dialogue to forge a national identity that is inclusive and reflects the present and future make-up of the population (Modood 2007). Such a national identity thus is not antithetical to minority cultural identity: successful multicultural integration will result in hyphenated identities, where citizens define themselves as for example Black-British or British-Indian (Modood 2007). Multiculturalism in this form hence does not threaten the solidarity required for redistribution, as it was charged by critics, but rather strengthens it.

'New multiculturalism' hence avoids the essentialist concept of culture but acknowledges the importance of culture for people and their position in society. It is about inclusion and equality through recognition and accommodation. The key disagreement between the approaches discussed here is with the focus of such measures: for Phillips (2007) it needs to lie with the individual, whereas for Modood (2007) it should be with the group (Squires 2008). Multiculturalism has thus evolved from its earlier conceptualisations that fuelled the criticisms developed against it. It is this updated and more nuanced version that we should consider when evaluating multiculturalism in policy practice.

Beyond the Crisis: Community Cohesion

To study the development of multiculturalism in policy practice since the eruption of the crisis in 2001, the chapter will now focus on the policy discourse as expressed in key reports and statements. Policy discourse shows a rupture with the previous multicultural period. The riots in Oldham, Burnley, Leeds and Bradford (2001) led a number of figureheads to conclude that multiculturalism had allowed ethnic communities to live 'parallel lives', withdrawing themselves from mainstream society in separate enclaves (Grillo 2007). In line with the final argument presented as part of the crisis of multiculturalism, the notion that Britain had become too diverse gained currency: it was argued that diversity had a negative effect on solidarity (Goodhart 2004). The new strategy that was to replace the old multicultural consensus of restricted immigration and progressive race relations therefore aims at managing diversity and strengthening a common sense of belonging to overcome the divisions exposed by the riots (Worley 2005). This strategy, consisting of managed immigration and 'community cohesion', was expressed in a flurry of reports and strategy initiatives (see Grillo 2007 p. 988).

The rationale of this new strategy is clearly presented in the Cantle report (2001) and the *Secure Borders, Safe Haven: Integration with Diversity* White Paper (Home Office 2002). The Cantle report, introducing the notion of community cohesion into policy, presents it as multifaceted and 'about helping micro-communities to gel or mesh into an integrated whole. These divided communities would need to develop common goals and a shared vision' (Cantle 2001 p. 70). *Secure Borders,*

Safe Haven established the link between immigration and diversity; put forward the strategy of managed migration to attract immigrants in accordance with labour market needs; and called for a strengthening of citizenship and shared values around the concept of community cohesion. It is to citizenship, in other words, that divided communities should look to develop common purpose.

The community cohesion strategy emphasised the need for interaction and dialogue between different groups in society, in order to reduce racial and cultural tensions. Interaction will lead to the development of more open attitudes to difference and the eradication of prejudice and stereotypes that impede cohesion (Cantle 2001; Home Office 2002). Policy was to support initiatives that will build and strengthen ties and trust between different cultural communities, rather than promote separate cultural identities. In order to sustain such dialogue, cultural groups need to overcome their differences and converge around shared values in an open and inclusive civic realm, reflective of a newly invigorated sense of citizenship (Cantle 2001; Home Office 2002). This citizenship was conceptualised as entailing rights and responsibilities, and reflecting the cultural diversity within Britain whilst also embodying certain 'common elements of "nationhood"' (Cantle 2001 p. 19), such as tolerance, the rule of law, and the English language. Citizenship was emphasised not only for new Britons (with a citizenship test upon acquisition) but for all, with citizenship education in schools and efforts to instigate a society-wide debate about the meaning of citizenship and national identity (Home Office 2002).

Although some welcome the new citizenship culture (Alibhai-Brown 2001), the community cohesion strategy has attracted criticism on two fronts. The first challenges the assumptions underlying the strategy, centring on the concept of social capital. The second points out how the emphasis on shared values and citizenship works to target and exclude Muslims. Running through both of these critiques is the charge that recent policy developments have focused too narrowly on cultural factors (Pilkington 2008). Concerns for material inequality and racism have been relegated to the background, despite their importance in explaining high levels of segregation and exclusion (McGhee 2003; Phillips 2006).

Social capital has become an influential concept in policy circles. It refers to social networks and levels of trust. Its dominant understanding comes from the work of Putnam (2007) who draws on Bourdieu (1986) to argue that diversity erodes solidarity, and social capital is the solution to overcoming divisions. Social capital in Putnam's perception comes in two forms: bonding social capital, with strong ties and high levels of trust within communities, and bridging social capital, where levels of interaction and trust are elevated between different communities. It is this latter form of social capital that community cohesion seeks to stimulate (McGhee 2003). What this concept fails to take into account, however, is that interaction between groups does not occur in a vacuum. Different cultural groups employ different socio-economic positions in society and interaction may therefore not be equal. Moreover, reiterated experiences of tension, stigmatisation, and denigration will impact on the interaction between groups (Cheong et al. 2007).

The emphasis on shared values furthermore has a tendency to demarcate Muslims as fundamentally different. Discourse opposes 'liberal' British values and practices to 'illiberal' 'Muslim' practices such as forced marriage (Yuval-Davis et al. 2006). Although Muslims are not explicitly marked out in the policy discourse, it is they who are urged to integrate into the shared values of Britain and make clear their allegiance to the nation (Kalra and Kapoor 2008; Worley 2005). In a context of global security concerns surrounding Muslims, this discourse serves to normalise a new, subtle type of anti-Muslim racism that targets values and beliefs rather than skin colour (Abbas 2004; Kundnani 2007). Despite its apparent openness to diversity, community cohesion thus requires integration of Muslims into the supposedly superior values of Western citizenship (Kundnani 2007) and hence displays assimilationist undertones (Pilkington 2008).

Community cohesion is about interaction, integration, and citizenship and is widely understood as a move away from multiculturalism (Joppke 2004; Pilkington 2008; Worley 2005). This claim will be assessed hereafter by bringing in the updated understanding of multiculturalism developed above.

Comparing Community Cohesion and 'New Multiculturalism'

Multiculturalism for Phillips (2007) should engage not with overstated value conflicts but with questions of coercion, whereas Modood (2007) thinks it needs to address Muslim integration and develop shared citizenship. The community cohesion strategy adopted by the UK government in that respect is clearly closer to the latter. It starts with the assumption that communities are divided and separate, embodying their own value universes. These communities need to integrate into a shared citizenship, reflective of diversity.

Community cohesion moreover shares the multicultural concern with the dangers of essentialism. It avoids essentialism by not naming any communities (Yuval-Davis et al. 2006). The emphasis on interaction and mixing precisely overcomes essentialist limitations, as it relies on the potential for transformation of groups and group identity. Increased contact between groups would serve to build new ties between them and forge new cohesive communities. Such mixing, to be established through for example twinning largely mono-cultural schools and joint events (Cantle 2001 p. 30), consists of individual community members developing new relations with members from other communities. It thereby differs notably from the type of interaction advocated in older versions of multiculturalism, criticised by Phillips (2007), which attempt to develop dialogue between different groups by engaging group leaders. The rationale of interaction is significantly different: where old multicultural dialogue seeks to establish equal relations between groups in society (cf. Parekh 2000), community cohesion attempts to forge new unity and cohesion out of the diverse groups in society.

Although the individual focus is reminiscent of that in Phillips' (2007) multiculturalism, this rationale does set the community cohesion strategy apart from multiculturalism. The emphasis is on integration into a shared civic citizenship linked to an inclusive national identity that will provide a strong sense of belonging. This focus does not contradict multiculturalism per se, as in practice it was always about integration and the importance of citizenship is equally stressed by Modood (2007). However, in his account it is developed as a complement to multicultural policy. The state in his view needs to both promote, or at least accommodate the cultivation of minority cultural identities and develop a sense of shared national citizenship. The result of this policy-tandem would be hyphenated identities. The community cohesion strategy however does not develop measures to strengthen minority cultural identities and thus develops only the national side of the hyphen. This should not be taken as a full-out rejection of minority cultural identity however, as the national identity that is being developed is characterised as civic, diverse and inclusive. The development of this national identity, through interaction, community cohesion and citizenship, can thus be seen to subsume multicultural recognition. Rather than deploy special policies affirming difference, then, the community cohesion strategy includes the recognition of difference in the elaboration of citizenship and national belonging.

Multiculturalism, both old and new, holds that the recognition of minority cultural identity is a requirement for equality. The community cohesion strategy with its goal of cohesion and integration pays significantly less attention to cultural membership and identity than both Phillips (2007) and Modood (2007) do. That is not to say community cohesion does not appreciate the importance of cultural identity for individuals, as it promotes 'integration with diversity' (Home Office 2002 p. 1). The strategy however seems less concerned with inequality than it is with interaction; it does not take into account the inequalities that exist between different cultural groups, especially where these inequalities combine economic with cultural exclusion. Rather, it treats all groups as similar and equal. It hence fails to differentiate between groups and fully acknowledge the intense diversity characterising contemporary Britain (cf. Vertovec 2007), and falls into the trap of treating all groups simply as 'minorities' that Modood (2007) warns against.

This lack of concern with the present context of inequality extends to the depiction of agency in minority communities. By avoiding the use of the essentialist notion of culture, the community cohesion discourse manages to circumvent the portrayal of minorities as restricted and directed by their culture that Phillips (2007) denounces. Minorities are represented as equally capable and autonomous as the majority. There is a risk, however, that the current discourse has moved too far in the other direction: where minorities were previously presented as devoid of agency, they are now portrayed as completely in charge of their own destiny. Segregation thereby becomes explained as the result of free choice ('self-segregation'), ignoring the realities of racism, poverty and exclusion that surround such processes.

By failing to consider culture as a significant factor in the life chances of the individual and therefore requiring compensation, the community cohesion strategy decisively deviates from multiculturalism. Although some elements of the strategy are compatible with new understandings of multiculturalism, the overall rationale centres on the creation of national unity, albeit reflective of diversity, rather than the pursuit of equality through cultural recognition. With its emphasis on mixing rather than recognition, the strategy thus comes closer to the concept of interculturalism (James 2008) that aims for the elimination of stereotypes and the fostering of social harmony through interaction.

Conclusion

The crisis of multiculturalism that has been asserted in the past decade has evoked re-evaluations in both theory and policy practice. Multicultural theory saw a refinement of its principles during this period. It avoids the use of a bounded notion of culture, but retains its emphasis on cultural membership and equality: minority cultural identity deserves public recognition in a state that reflects the majority's culture to ensure equality of esteem. Moreover, it requires intervention in the form of accommodations and exemptions in order to compensate for cultural disadvantage, counter indirect discrimination and ensure equal opportunities. Policy practice saw the adoption of the community cohesion strategy, emphasising interaction between cultural groups, integration, and citizenship in the quest for a national sense of belonging.

There are some similarities between these developments, most notably the rejection of essentialism. However, since the crisis, and despite overlaps in its interpretation, theory and practice have diverged in focus. Policy practice has modified the principles of multiculturalism that were in place to an extent beyond the reformulations of multiculturalism in theory. Although it still demonstrates a concern for cultural diversity, it no longer aims for its public recognition, but rather for integration with diversity. Where multiculturalism stresses the need to recognise difference in order to combat inequality, community cohesion emphasises interaction and mixing between cultural groups in order to forge social and community cohesion.

Despite this move towards interculturalism, however, many old structures, institutions and policies of the multicultural approach that preceded it remain in place. Multiculturalism in Britain thus retains a foothold. Moreover, the ideas and concepts expressed as part of the multicultural tradition may still find their way into new policy solutions. The community cohesion strategy already shows similarities with new versions of multiculturalism; a restatement of the strategy that would place greater concern on issues of equality relating to cultural difference would firmly reinvest multiculturalism in practice. However, given the continuing climate of anti-multiculturalism (with the heads of state of Germany (Weaver 2010), Britain (Doward 2011) and France (Telegraph 2011) declaring its failure only recently), it is unlikely that such a restatement would explicitly avow this allegiance.

Bibliography

Abbas, Tahir (2004) 'After 9/11: British South Asian Muslims, Islamophobia, multiculturalism, and the state' in *The American Journal of Islamic Social Sciences* 21, 3, pp. 26-38

Alibhai-Brown, Yasmin (2001) 'After multiculturalism' in *The Political Quarterly* 72, S1, pp. 47-56

Barry, Brian (2001) *Culture & equality: an egalitarian critique of multiculturalism*, Cambridge: Polity Press.

Benhabib, Seyla (1999) '"Nous" et "les Autres": the politics of complex cultural dialogue in a global civilization' in JOPPKE, Christian & Lukes, Steven (eds.) *Multicultural Questions*, Oxford: Oxford University Press, pp. 44-62

Bourdieu, Pierre (1986) 'The forms of capital' in Richardson, John (ed.) *Handbook of Theory and Research for the Sociology of Education*, New York: Greenwood, pp. 241-258

Cantle, Ted (2001) *Community Cohesion: a report of the independent review team*, London: Home Office.

Cheong, Pauline, Edwards, Rosalind, Goulbourne, Harry & Solomos, John (2007) 'Immigration, social cohesion and social capital: a critical review' in *Critical Social Policy* 27, 1, pp. 24-49

Doward, Jamie (2011) 'David Cameron's attack on multiculturalism divides coalition' in *The Guardian*, 6 February

Eisenberg, Avigail & Spinner-Halev, Jeff (eds.) (2005) *Minorities within Minorities: Equality, Rights and Diversity*, Cambridge: Cambridge University Press.

Favell, Adrian (1998) *Philosophies of Integration*, Houndmills: Macmillan Press Ltd.

Fraser, Nancy (1996) 'Social justice in the age of identity politics: redistribution, recognition, and participation', *The Tanner Lectures on Human Values*, Stanford University.

Goodhart, David (2004) 'Too diverse?' in *Prospect* 95, February [www.prospect-magazine.co.uk]

Grillo, Ralph (2007) 'An excess of alterity? Debating difference in a multicultural society' in *Ethnic and Racial Studies* 30, 6, pp. 979-998

Home Office (2002) *Secure borders, safe haven: integration with diversity in modern Britain*, London: Home Office.

James, Malcolm (2008) *Interculturalism: theory and policy*, London: The Baring Foundation [www.baringfoundation.org.uk]

Joppke, Christian (2004) 'The retreat of multiculturalism in the liberal state: theory and policy in *The British Journal of Sociology* 55, 2, pp. 237-257

Joppke, Christian (2009) 'Limits of integration policy: Britain and her Muslims' in *Journal of Ethnic and Migration Studies* 35, 3, pp. 453-472

Kalra, Virinder & Kapoor, Nisha (2008) *Interrogation segregation, integration and the community cohesion agenda*, CCSR Working Paper 2008-16, Manchester: Cathie Marsh Centre for Census and Survey Research.

Kukathas, Chandran (1992) 'Are there any cultural rights?' in *Political Theory* 20, 1, pp. 105-139

Kundnani, Arun (2007) 'Integrationism: the politics of anti-Muslim racism' in *Race & Class* 48, 4, pp. 24-44

Kymlicka, Will (1995) *Multicultural Citizenship: a liberal theory of minority rights*, Oxford: Oxford University Press.

Kymlicka, Will (2007) 'The new debate on minority rights (and postscript)' in Laden, Anthony & Owen, David (eds.) *Multiculturalism and Political Theory*, Cambridge: Cambridge University Press, pp. 25-59

Kymlicka, Will & Banting, Keith (2006) 'Immigration, multiculturalism, and the welfare state' in *Ethics & International Affairs* 20, 3, pp. 281-304

Mason, Andrew (2007) 'Multiculturalism and the critique of essentialism' in Laden, Anthony & Owen, David (eds.) *Multiculturalism and Political Theory*, Cambridge: Cambridge University Press, pp. 221-243

Mcghee, Derek (2003) 'Moving to 'our' common ground – a critical examination of community cohesion discourse in twenty-first century Britain' in *The Sociological Review* 51, 3, pp. 376-404

Meer, Nasar & Modood, Tariq (2009) 'The multicultural state we're in: Muslims, 'multiculture' and the 'civic re-balancing' of British multiculturalism' in *Political Studies* 57, 3, pp. 473-497

Miller, David (1995) *On nationality*, Oxford: Clarendon Press.

Modood, Tariq (2007) *Multiculturalism: a civic idea*, Cambridge: Polity.

Modood, Tariq (2008) 'Multiculturalism and groups' in *Social & Legal Studies* 17, 4, pp. 549-553

Modood, Tariq (2011) 'Multiculturalism, Britishness and Muslims' in *Open Democracy*, 27 January [www.opendemocracy.net]

Okin, Susan (1999) 'Is multiculturalism bad for women?' in Cohen, Joshua, Howard, Matthew & Nussbaum, Martha (eds.) *Is multiculturalism bad for women?*, Princeton: Princeton University Press, pp. 7-24

Parekh, Bikhu (2000) *Rethinking multiculturalism*, Basingstoke: Palgrave Macmillan.

Phillips, Anne (2007) *Multiculturalism without culture*, Princeton: Princeton University Press.

Phillips, Anne (2008) 'More on culture and representation' in *Social & Legal Studies* 17, 4, pp. 555-558

Phillips, Deborah (2006) 'Parallel lives? Challenging discourses of British Muslim self-segregation' in *Environment and Planning D: Society and Space* 24, 1, pp. 25-40

Pilkington, Andrew (2008) 'From institutional racism to community cohesion: the changing nature of racial discourse in Britain' in *Sociological Research Online* 13,

3, p. 6

Putnam, Robert (2007) 'E pluribus unum: diversity and community in the twenty-first century. The 2006 Johan Skytte Prize lecture' in *Scandinavian Political Studies* 30, 2, pp. 137-174

Squires, Judith (2008) 'Multiculturalism, multiple groups and inequalities', in *Social & Legal Studies* 17, 4, pp. 535-542

Taylor, Charles (1994) 'The politics of recognition' in Gutmann, Amy (ed.) *Multiculturalism: examining the politics of recognition*, Princeton: Princeton University Press, pp. 25-73

Telegraph (2011) 'Nicolas Sarkozy declares multiculturalism had failed' in *The Telegraph*, 11 February

Vertovec, Steven (2007) 'Super-diversity and its implications' in *Ethnic and Racial Studies* 30, 6, pp. 1024-1054

Weaver, Matthew (2010) 'Angela Merkel: German multiculturalism has "utterly failed"' in *The Guardian*, 17 October

Worley, Claire (2005) '"It's not about race. It's about the community": New Labour and "community cohesion"' in *Critical Social Policy* 25, 4, pp. 483-496

Yuval-Davis, Nira, Anthias, Floya & Kofman, Eleonore (2006) 'Secure borders and safe haven and the gendered politics of belonging: beyond social cohesion' in *Ethnic and Racial Studies* 28, 3, pp. 513-535

Has Multiculturalism Failed? With Reference Primarily to the UK, Outline and Assessment of Both Sides of the Debate

Sevgi Basman [71]

At the start of the 60s we invited the guest-workers to Germany. We kidded ourselves for a while that they wouldn't stay, that one day they'd go home. That isn't what happened. And of course the tendency was to say: let's be 'multikulti' and live next to each other and enjoy being together, [but] this concept has failed, failed utterly (Angela Merkel 2010).

This speech by the German chancellor is still buzzing in my ears. Being home for millions of people from many different cultures, nations and beliefs for decades Europe is now zooming into a backlash against multiculturalism and trying to produce an answer to the question of whether multiculturalism is a 'failed experiment' or not. This essay will analyse this important question especially from the UK perspective first by defining multicultural society and the policy of multiculturalism. Secondly it will briefly have a look at the history of multiculturalism by pointing out the changing state policies ranging from assimilation, integration and multiculturalism to community cohesion. Later on it will explore the factors leading backlash against multiculturalism and then draw out the opposing positions and arguments. In the conclusion, I will state my opinions supporting multiculturalism and come up with the view that multiculturalism is not a failed experiment.

There are two aspects of multiculturalism. We should make it clear that a multicultural society and multiculturalism as a policy are different things. Multicultural society stands for a society which is composed of people from various ethnicities. The UK is a good example of a multicultural society where there are shops, restaurants, clothes, music, sportsmen, religious institutions, festivals and etc from all over the world (Bourne 2007 p. 2). However, as Bourne states, 'multiculturalism as a policy emanated from both central and local government as a conscious attempt to answer racial inequality (and especially the resistance to it after the 'riots' of 1981 and 1985) with cultural solutions' (Bourne 2007 p 2). So, it can be claimed that

---

71 Sevgi is currently completing a 10 week internship at the Dialogue Society as part of her Dialogue Studies MA at Keele University. She is a graduate of Istanbul University, holds a BA in English Language Teaching and has had experience in teaching English, Humanities, Turkish and Religious Education in the UK for three years. Her areas of interest include literature, cultures, languages and intercultural dialogue.

a multicultural policy aids to all citizens equally and with economic and social justice by being blind to colour and ethnic differences. It is based on the concept of cultural pluralism and necessitates respect and recognition for every culture as argued by Modood (2007).

According to Solomos (2003) the politics of race and immigration in the UK goes back to 1940s after the Second World War when black settlement began and brought the concerns about immigration to the agenda. The UK has had various strategies for managing diversity. The black population was thought to be posing a threat to English way of life and the state strategy was formerly assimilation between 1950s and mid 1960s (Solomos 2003). Assimilation is the dominance of only one culture or religion and requires other and new ethnic groups to leave their own cultures and values behind and accept the dominant one (Bourne 2007 p. 2). After assimilation the state strategy turned into integration in 1960s and 1970s. Compared to assimilation integration was, in my view, better as it was recognising the other cultures, customs, values and religions, but still wanted people to accept the dominant culture. Integration was considered as a starting point for a multicultural society as it put forward the idea that everyone had the right to express his/her culture (Bourne 2007 p. 3). Integration policy gave way to multiculturalism in 1970s, and multiculturalism was institutionalised in 1980s when the Thatcher government encouraged cultural policies in order to prevent division within minority ethnic groups (Bourne 2007 p. 3). Multiculturalism is the acceptance of a plurality of cultures and promotes these cultures existing together at the same time happily by giving equal chances, opportunities and respect. Crick (2004) describes multiculturalism as '... made up of a diverse range of cultures and identities, and one that emphasises the need for a continuous process of mutual engagement and learning about each other with respect, understanding and tolerance'. When it gained dominance multiculturalism enabled people to obtain better education, health and social services (Cheong et al. 2007 p. 26), for instance people could send their children whichever school they want and they could practise their religion in their own churches, mosques or temples.

However, the 2001 inner-city disturbances and arguments in the northern towns have changed the attitudes and brought a critical approach towards multiculturalism (Cheong et al. 2007 p. 26). Afterwards it was the Cantle Report – the official report about the inner city disturbances – in 2001 shifting the way of multiculturalism into Community Cohesion and suggested strategies for possible threats to help manage diversities in the UK (Cantle 2001). 'Community cohesion is about ensuring different groups of people share a common vision and sense of belonging, where similar life opportunities are available to all' (National College). The UK has always been a charming place for immigrants, asylum seekers and refugees mainly as it has offered education and employment opportunities. However, the increasing number of these new comers has caused new concerns to be raised (Lupton and Power 2004, Census). Multiculturalism was more challenged with 9/11, the war on terror (Gilroy 2004) and the 7/7 London underground bombing and Paris banlieues' riots protest in 2005 (Cheong et al. 2007). These incidents were followed by arguments about radicalisation and triggered a lack of tolerance, targeting the Muslims across the Europe and in the UK. All these as factors led to the backlash against multiculturalism and brought the new term community cohesion to the public agenda.

There are arguments going on about multiculturalism which take us to the hot debate if multiculturalism has failed or not. We have people who are against multiculturalism on the one hand and who are in defence of it on the other. Those who are against mainly argue that multiculturalism promotes separatism and ethnicism, undermines solidarity, can lead to segregation and alienation from processes of democracy, and to religious radicalisation. First of all we see that many politicians are now taking a side against multiculturalism. As stated above, the German Chancellor, Angela Merkel revealed her position by saying 'this concept (multiculturalism) has failed, failed utterly' (2010). In 2011 David Cameron made a parallel speech on radicalisation and Islamic extremism at the Munich Security Conference. He stated that the doctrine of state multiculturalism has failed, pointing to the policy 'under the doctrine of state multiculturalism, we have encouraged different cultures to live separate lives, apart from each other and the mainstream' and he called for a stronger national identity to prevent extremism. He made a direct link between security and multiculturalism and this speech reminded us of a 40-50 years back policy of integration even assimilation. As well as triggering an anti-Islamist demonstration in Luton this speech has generated quite a lot tension and resentment among Muslim people across the UK. Prior to this Tony Blair (2006) made a speech where he precisely spotlighted on common, shared British values and the necessity of integration. He underlined that everyone has the right to be different, but they also have a duty to integrate; he called for Britishness to be adopted by all UK citizens. Considering these political speeches it can easily be claimed that multiculturalism is not universally favoured anymore as it once used to be and the state policy is shifting from multiculturalism on the grounds that multiculturalism fosters alienation and segregation which in return poses a danger for all society.

In addition to politicians there are also some other people opposing multiculturalism both from academic world and media. For instance after London bombings Trevor Phillips (2004), then Chair of Commission for Racial Equality, said 'We should kill off the word multiculturalism. Multiculturalism suggests separateness'. Moreover, he claimed 'Britain is sleepwalking to segregation' and called for measures to prevent racial and religious divisions (cited in Guardian, 19 November 2005). Kenan Malik also argues that arguments for multiculturalism are flawed and he proposes that cultures are not equal. That`s why he rejects arguments about respect for different cultures and beliefs claiming that it undermines solidarity (2002).

If we shed light on the arguments in defence of multiculturalism we can mention quite a lot from that perspective, too. The ones who are defending multiculturalism believe that multiculturalism unites people; for instance: unite people in order to fight against poverty, fights racism, fights for civil rights like wearing a particular clothing (Bourne 2007 p. 6-7) and it is argued that a developed view of multiculturalism can complement democratic citizenship and nation-building (Modood 2007). A multicultural society can aid the socio-economic, welfare and cohesion of a whole country in Ouseley`s defence:

> When diverse communities all stay together, are all engaged in making the decisions and, however poor they are relatively, are contributing to making decisions that benefit everyone, resentment, hostility and intolerance will be reduced and eliminated. That is contributing to building cohesion (Lord Ouseley cited in IRR 2007 p. 6).

Multiculturalism is claimed to be the way of forming certain human rights. According to Lerman (2010) the balance between respect for diversity and a sense of national belonging is still something to be achieved in the UK and it was once multiculturalism securing this balance. Modood (2007) is pointing to multiculturalisms being multi not mono which is more pluralistic and democratic. He also places emphasis on equality which is better provided for by multiculturalism and besides, he suggests that it is possible to maintain difference and have integration. These can all be achieved in multiculturalism according to him. In addition to these rather than a problem itself, Moodod (2007) evaluates multiculturalism as a solution to present displeasure if kept alive in the context of democratic citizenship. The debate on multiculturalism is also tried to be linked to Islam and Muslims by some people. Allen criticises the idea by saying 'because Muslims fail to integrate and assimilate, it is they that are seen to be undoing and ultimately killing multiculturalism' (Allen 2007 p.113). Muslims are seen as scapegoats and they are placed in the centre of the main problem as Allen (2007) argues in *The death of multiculturalism: blaming and shaming British Muslims* that the criticism of multiculturalism is a coded attack on Muslims and Islam.

Exemplified above, the arguments for and against multiculturalism can be summarised: those who are against multiculturalism mainly argue that multiculturalism creates segregation, division, ethnicism, alienation, radicalisation, cultural clashes, etc. On the contrary, those who are in defence of it argue that multiculturalism supports solidarity, anti-racism, civil/human rights, multi not mono cultures, equality, justice, unity and integration.

In my view, considering the meaning, historical shifting policies and the opposing arguments over multiculturalism, I would like to place my position in defence of multiculturalism on the grounds that first of all 'Multiculturalism means cultures influencing one another, interacting' (Bourne 2007 p. 4) which creates a rich and fruitful society with contributions of differences. This is a quite clear and positive phenomenon which does not include any distracting points. To me multiculturalism is something that can be shaped either in positive or negative way depending on how we and the State manage it. Thus, if it is well managed with justice, equality and respect, a multicultural society may turn into a treasure which can build a society with one heart beating at the same rhythm at all times either in good or bad times. It can also erode all prejudices between different cultures and beliefs by sharing and interacting more. Moreover, empathy can be developed more in a multicultural society where people can form an objective viewpoint towards each other and learn new and interesting things as a product of their harmony and cohesion. Multiculturalism as a state policy is not a danger or threat. On the contrary, that kind of a policy erodes prejudices and gives trust in the State to its citizens. Of course there may appear some problems or some people whom you cannot make pleased whatever strategy you suggest. However, a whole picture should not be sacrificed for few negative incidents. So, multiculturalism cannot be blamed because of some extremist people. One religion also should not be chosen as a victim, it is not the religion making people extremist or isolated from society. Looking at the urban riots in 2011 especially in London, Manchester and Liverpool for instance, no one can claim that it was extremist religious ideology oriented. What 'difference' will be the victim now? – Religion? Race? Or colour? Actually none of them.

Another example proving that any religion either Islam or other beliefs are not the roots of terrorist activities and cannot be related to multiculturalism is the 2011 Norway attacks which was carried out by a non-Muslim person who was the own citizen of Norway. This sad event once again proved that it is not right to address a specific community, belief or race to be the reason of a decline or failure. Instead government policies should be the address where the failures and declines should be looked for (Bourne 2007).

It is significant to touch on the relation between economic decline and multiculturalism as well. Since the economic crisis started across Europe for a few years now, multiculturalism has filled the politicians' agenda more than before. Blaming immigrants and ethnic communities for not integrating has been intensified which in return has caused public tension towards these addressed people holding them responsible for unemployment and getting the jobs. Choosing a scapegoat may be an easy but nasty way of getting out of problems for a while, but a real sincere approach would deeply investigate where in reality the problems are lying. To this end, I claim that multiculturalism has not failed but chosen as a scapegoat to shelve the real problems for a while.

Bibliography

Allen, Chris (2007) 'The death of multiculturalism: blaming and shaming British Muslims', 14 January http://www.dur.ac.uk/anthropology.journal/vol14/iss1/allen.html (accessed 15.11.11).

Blair, Tony (2006) 'The duty to integrate: shared British values', http://ukingermany.fco.gov.uk/en/news/?view=Speech&id=4616073 (accessed 14.11.11).

Bourne, Jenny (2007) In Defence of Multiculturalism, IRR Briefing Paper

Cameron, David (2011) 'Munich speech on Multiculturalism', *New Statesman,* http://www.newstatesman.com/blogs/the-staggers/2011/02/terrorism-islam-ideology (accessed 14.11.11).

Cantle, Ted (2001) Community Cohesion: A report of the Independent Review Team. London, Home Office.

Cheong, Pauline Hope, EDWARDS, Rosalind, GOULBOURNE, Harry and SOLOMOS, John (2007) 'Immigration, social cohesion and social capital:A critical review' in *Critical Social Policy* 27 (1), pp 24-4.

Crick, Bernard (2004) 'So what exactly is multiculturalism?', BBC News, 5 April http://news.bbc.co.uk/1/hi/uk/3600791.stm# (accessed 22.11.11).

Gilroy, Paul (2004) 'Melancholia and Multiculture', *Open Democracy*, 2 August. http://www.opendemocracy.net/arts-multiculturalism/article_2035.jsp (accessed 14.11.11).

Lerman, Antony. (2010) 'In Defence of Multiculturalism', *The Guardian*, 22 March. http://www.guardian.co.uk/commentisfree/2010/mar/22/multiculturalism-blame-culture-segregation (accessed 14.11.11).

Lupton, Ruth, POWER, Anne (2004) Minority Ethnic Groups in Britian, Census Brief

http://sticerd.lse.ac.uk/dps/case/CBCB/census2_part1.pdf (accessed 14.11.11).

Malik, Kenan (2002) ' Against Multiculturalism', New Humanist http://www.kenanmalik.com/essays/against_mc.html Accessed (accessed 14.11.11).

Merkel, Angela. (2010) 'Multiculturalism has utterly failed', http://www.youtube.com/watch?v=UKG76HF24_k&feature=related (accessed 14.11.11).

Modood, Tariq (2007) 'Multiculturalism, citizenship and national identity', *Open Democracy*, 16 May http://www.opendemocracy.net/faith-europe_islam/multiculturalism_4627.jsp (accessed 14.11.11).

National College, Community Cohesion http://www.nationalcollege.org.uk/index/leadershiplibrary/leadingschools/ecm/school-families-communities/community-cohesion.htm (accessed 22.11.11).

Solomos, John (2003) pp 48-75 *Race and Racism in Britain*, (Chap 3 'The politics of race and immigration since 1945') Basingstoke, Palgrave Macmillan.

The Guardian (2005) ' Britain 'sleepwalking to segregation' ', 19 September http://www.guardian.co.uk/world/2005/sep/19/race.socialexclusion (accessed 14.11.11).